ENTRANCE OF THE ARMY INTO THE GRAND PLAZA AT MEXICO.

THE MEXICAN WAR:

A

HISTORY OF ITS ORIGIN,

AND

A DETAILED ACCOUNT OF THE VICTORIES WHICH TERMINATED IN THE SURRENDER OF THE CAPITAL; WITH THE OFFICIAL DESPATCHES OF THE GENERALS.

TO WHICH IS ADDED

THE TREATY OF PEACE,

AND VALUABLE TABLES OF THE STRENGTH AND LOSSES OF THE UNITED STATES ARMY.

BY EDWARD D. MANSFIELD,

GRADUATE OF THE UNITED STATES MILITARY ACADEMY.

TENTH EDITION.

NEW YORK:
PUBLISHED BY A. S. BARNES & BURR
51 & 53 JOHN STREET.
SOLD BY BOOKSELLERS, GENERALLY, THROUGHOUT THE UNITED STATES.
1860.

Stereotyped by
RICHARD C. VALENTINE.
New York.

PREFACE.

It has been wisely remarked by a distinguished American statesman, that "the commencement of the Mexican War was the opening of a new volume of American history."

Nations, like individuals, are often borne along in their progress, without pausing to consider the particular acts which are to shape and control their future destiny; and perhaps there is no subject on which the public mind is less likely to act with caution and deliberation than on the momentous question of peace or war.

The present Mexican war is a striking illustration of this principle. It would appear, from the public documents, that neither the President nor Congress anticipated it until hostilities had actually commenced, and it may well be doubted if either can see the consequences which yet may flow from it.

To pause, therefore, and review the past, to examine into all the causes which have led to the unhappy estrangement of two sister Republics, has seemed a fitting introduction to the narration of those military achievements which now form a part of the history of the country.

We have felt no pleasure in tracing the causes which led to this war, and certainly none in contemplating its progress and looking forward to its final consequences. But when we pass to the army, and behold the brilliant results obtained with such small means, against such immense superiority of force, and see the high military skill of the commanding officers sustained by the courage and heroism of the troops, we feel a just pride in describing their actions and recording their deeds.

In the preparation of this work great care has been taken to select the most reliable sources of information.

Those who have taken part in the stirring scenes which are described must have viewed them from different positions, and an honest difference of opinion in regard even to facts will sometimes be found to exist. But the description of the great movements and battles is based on public documents, despatches, and orders, which must ever be the material of a reliable history of a war.

CONTENTS.

CHAPTER I.

Origin of the War with Mexico.—Settlement of Texas.—Declaration of Independence.—Santa Anna's Treaty.—Movement towards Annexation.—Correspondence of Boconegra.—Declaration of Almonte.—Mr. Calhoun's Reasons.—Lord Aberdeen's Declaration.—The Tyler Treaty.—The Joint Resolution.—Departure of Almonte.—General Taylor ordered to Texas.—Strength of the Army at Corpus Christi . . Page 9

CHAPTER II.

War inevitable.—General Scott at Washington.—Recommends an Increase of the Army.—Mission of Mr. Slidell.—Downfall of Herrera.—Departure of Slidell.—General Taylor marches from Corpus Christi.—Arrives at Point Isabel—In front of Matamoras.—Capture of Captain Thornton's Party.—March of General Taylor to Point Isabel.—Battles of Palo Alto and Resaca de la Palma.—Taylor's Official Reports . 22

CHAPTER III.

Action of Congress.—Declaration of the President.—Legislation.—General Scott's Views of the War.—His Comments on the Plan of Campaign.—His Correspondence with Secretary Marcy.—The Grounds for his Opinions.—Is ordered to remain at Washington 44

CHAPTER IV.

Campaign of the Rio Grande continued.—Movement of the Army.—March to Monterey.—Battle of Monterey.—Armistice.—March to Saltillo.—Wool's Corps.—Tampico.—Occupation of Victoria.—Conclusion of the Campaign.—General Taylor's Despatches.—Results 56

CHAPTER V.

Government Plan to invade Northern Mexico.—Assemblage of Troops at Fort Leavenworth.—Kearney's March to Santa Fé.—Nature of the Country.—Retreat of the Mexicans.—Arrival at Santa Fé.—Kearney's Proclamation.—Kearney departs for California.—Wool's Expedition.—Assembling of the Troops at San Antonio.—The Object of the Expedition.—March to Monclova ; to Pedas.—Wool joins Worth at Saltillo.—Taylor's March to Victoria 76

CHAPTER VI.

Expedition of Captain Fremont.—Arrival at Monterey, California.—Suspicions of Governor de Castro.—Fremont takes position.—Returns by Oregon.—Returns again to Monterey.—Is threatened by De Castro.—Declares War.—Capture of Mexicans.—Sails from Monterey to Diego. —Capture of the City of Angels.—Conquest of California.—Object of the Government.—Marcy's Letter to Stevenson.—Marcy's Orders to Kearney.—Scott's Orders.—Insurrection in New Mexico.—Murder of Bent. —Battle of Covoda.—Battle of Pueblo de Taos.—Insurrection in California.—March of Doniphan.—Battle of Brozitos.—Capture of El Paso —Battle of Sacramento.—Capture of Chihuahua.—March to Saltillo.—Arrival at New Orleans.—March of Gilpin to the Rocky Mountains . . . . Page 91

CHAPTER VII.

General Scott ordered to Mexico.—Letter of the Secretary of War to General Taylor.—Letter of the Secretary of War to General Scott.—General Scott leaves Washington.—His Letter to General Taylor.—Plan of appointing a Lieutenant-General.—Scott reaches the Rio Grande.—Condition of things there.—Withdraws a part of Taylor's Troops in compliance with the Orders of the War Department . 110

CHAPTER VIII.

General Taylor's Movements.—Taylor's Position.—Santa Anna's Advance.—Importance of the event.—Battle of Buena Vista.—Retreat of the Mexicans.—Taylor's Official Account.—Santa Anna's Report, 119

CHAPTER IX.

Advance of the Army to Lobos; thence to Antonio Lizardo.—Siege and Capture of Vera Cruz.—Official Despatches.—March to the Interior.—Battle of Cerro Gordo.—Official Despatches.—Capture of Puebla, 163

CHAPTER X.

Entrance of the American Army into Puebla.—Mexican Account.—American Officers.—Conduct of the Army.—Situation of Puebla.—Character of the Country.—The Ancient Cholula.—Strength of the Army.—Scott's Proclamation.—Humanity of the Army.—Mission of Trist.—Reasons for remaining in Puebla.—Drilling of the Army.—Raising new Regiments.—New Volunteers.—Attack on the Train of M'Intosh.—Advance of Pierce.—Concentration of the Army . 202

CHAPTER XI.

Strength of the Army.—Reinforcements.—Divisions of the Army.—March from Puebla.—Hospitals of Puebla.—Volcano of Popocatapetl.—

Pass of Rio Frio.—View of Mexico.—Valley of Mexico.—Lakes.—Inundations.—Topography of the Valley.—Position of the Army on the 13th of August.—Reconnoissance of the Rifles.—El Penon.—Mexicalcingo.—Turning of Lake Chalco.—March to San Augustine.—Skirmish at Buena Vista.—Concentration.—Position of the Army on the 18th . . . . Page 221

CHAPTER XII.

Mexican Line of Defence.—Position of the American and Mexican Armies.—Action of the 19th.—Position in the Hamlet of Contreras.—Position of General Scott.—Arrangements for the Battle.—Distribution of the American and Mexican Forces.—Battle of Contreras.—Rout of the Mexicans.—Surrender of Mexican Generals.—Recapture of the Buena Vista Guns.—Scott's Arrangements.—Evacuation of San Antonia.—Storm of the Tête du Pont.—Battle of Churubusco.—Defeat of the Mexicans.—Loss.—Truce 241

CHAPTER XIII.

Peace Negotiations.—President Polk's Commission.—Mexican Conditions.—American Ultimatum.—Failure of Negotiations.—Scott's Notice to Santa Anna.—Trial and Execution of the Deserters.—Description of Chapultepec.—Of Molino del Rey.—Mexican Defences.—March of Worth.—Strength of his Corps.—Battle of Molino del Rey.—Mexican Loss.—Evacuation of Molino del Rey.—Preparations for the Attack of Chapultepec.—Erection of Batteries.—Storm of Chapultepec.—Action of the 13th.—Capture of Mexico.—Entrance into the City.—Scott's Address to the Soldiers.—Insurrection of the Leperos.—Appearance of the City.—Reflections 273

CHAPTER XIV.

Siege of Puebla.—March of Santa Anna.—Desertion of his troops.—March of Rea.—Battle of Haumantla.—Santa Anna's resignation.—Peña y Peña President.—Negotiations for peace.—Treaty signed.—Ratifications.—The treaty.—Territory acquired.—Losses of the army.—Names of officers killed.—Conclusion 324

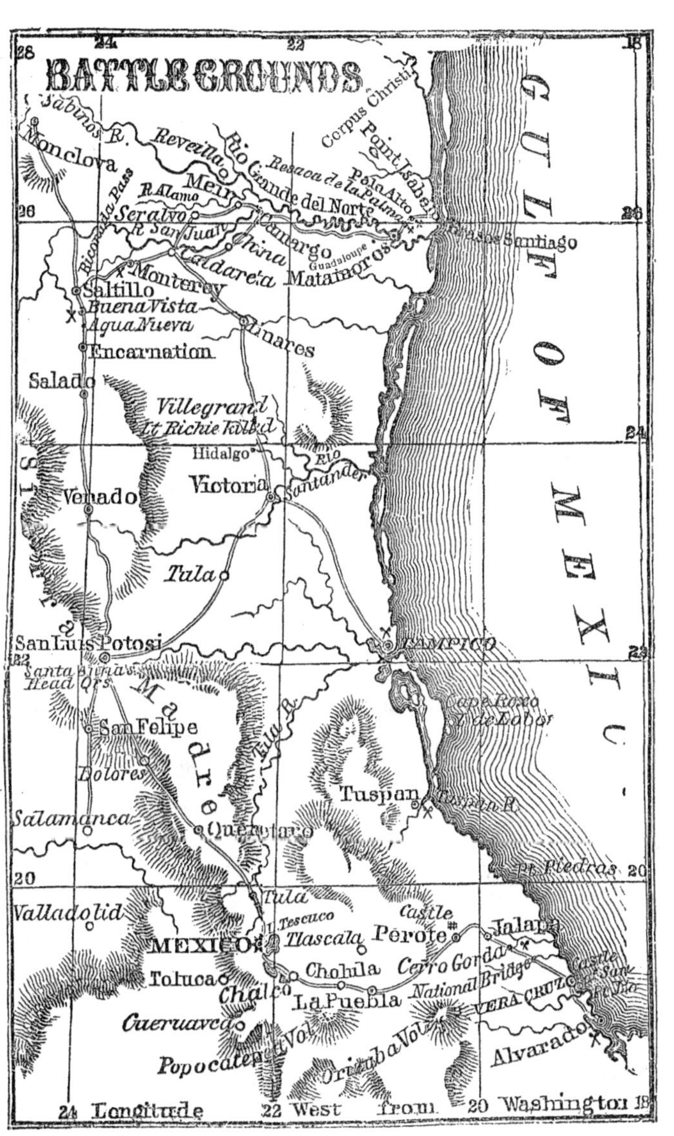
BATTLE GROUNDS
GULF OF MEXICO
Sabinos R.
Monclova
Reveilla
Rio Grande del Norte
Corpus Christi
Point Isabel
Resaca de la Palma
Palo Alto
Mier
R. Alamo
Seralvo
R. San Juan
Camargo
China
Guadaloupe
Brasos Santiago
Matamoros
Caldareta
Monterey
Saltillo
Buena Vista
Agua Nueva
Linares
Encarnation
Salado
Villegrand
Lt. Richie Killed
Hidalgo
Rio
Santander
Victoria
Venado
Tula
Tampico
San Luis Potosi
Santa Anna's Head Qrs.
Madre
San Felipe
Cape Roxo
Dolores
Tuspan
Tuspan R.
Salamanca
Queretaro
Pt. Piedras
Tula
Valladolid
L. Tescuco
Castle
Perote
Jalapa
MEXICO
Tlascala
Cholula
Cerro Gorda
Toluca
National Bridge
Chalco
La Puebla
Vera Cruz
Cuernavca
Alvarado
Popocatepetl Vol.
Orizaba Vol.
24 Longitude 22 West from 20 Washington 18

MEXICAN WAR.

CHAPTER I.

Origin of the War with Mexico.—Settlement of Texas.—Declaration of Independence.—Santa Anna's Treaty.—Movement towards Annexation. —Correspondence of Bocanegra.—Declaration of Almonte.—Mr. Calhoun's reasons.—Lord Aberdeen's Declaration.—The Tyler Treaty.—The Joint Resolution.—Departure of Almonte.—General Taylor ordered to Texas.—Strength of the Army at Corpus Christi.

TILL quite recently, the immense territory extending from the Sabine to the Rio Grande was comparatively uninhabited. Comprehending a space large enough for an empire, and within the mildest part of the temperate zone, it was yet too remote from the inhabitants of ancient Mexico on one hand, or from those of the northern Atlantic States on the other, to be reached and cultivated at an earlier period by the adventurous and advancing settlers of America. The country belonged to Mexico, but was hardly possessed by her people. A few towns immediately east of the Rio Grande, and an occasional village or settlement in the interior—such as Antonio de Bexar, Goliad, and Nacogdoches—were the only marks of improvement which indicated the civilization of the white man, or the dominion of Mexico. Nor did the aboriginal inhabitants appear much more numerous. The Camanches of the northern districts, and a few scattered and fleeting tribes, wandered over the vast territories of uninhabited Texas, but offered no very formidable obstacle to the progress of civilization.

Texas was in this almost desolate condition when it attracted the roving eye of land speculation. Certain persons in the United States foresaw the rapid and inevitable movement of the United States of the North towards the Western Ocean, and sought to enhance their fortunes by obtaining grants of Texan lands from the Mexican government. Among these was Stephen Austin, who obtained a large tract, and whose name has since been attached both to a county and a town. With him, and with others to whom Mexico had made grants, came numerous parties of colonists and adventurers, who sought, like their leaders, to pursue their fortunes and avoid their adversities, by successful enterprise in a new country, and by sharing in the distribution of vast bodies of unoccupied land. The number of these adventurers rapidly increased, till they became more numerous than the Mexicans who previously inhabited the country. The difference of race, religion, and laws, was soon apparent in diversities of sentiment and objects between the old and new inhabitants. The Texan of the United States brought with him, not only greater energy and industry, but a wild and restless ambition—a more intense and speculative pursuit of future objects.

Where differences so deep and original as these exist among different classes of people, they will soon become manifested in external action. The new inhabitants soon seized the direction of all public affairs, and Texas became, in fact, the possession of these adventurers from a foreign land, rather than of those ancient citizens to whose government it professed allegiance. The power thus obtained was soon manifested in other acts. It is not in the nature of things, that a country should change its inhabitants and not also change its government. The new possessors will assume the laws and institutions to which their habits have been used and their sentiments assimilated. It was so with Texas. No sooner did the settlers from the United States possess the power, than they looked round for the means of establishing their own forms of government.

In the revolutions of Mexico, so rapid and often so disastrous, the opportunities for change could never be long wanting. In the case of Texas, such an occasion was offered in the overthrow, by Santa Anna, of the Mexican Federal Government. This powerful chief being invested with the supreme magistracy, in a short time after assumed absolute power. About this time, the people of Texas having increased largely in population and resources, petitioned the Mexican Congress for admission into the confederation, as a separate State. The bearer of this petition, and a commissioner to represent their claims, was Stephen Austin. The Congress of Mexico paid no attention to the petition; but Austin imprudently wrote back to the Texan authorities, advising them to organize a State, without waiting for the consent of the government. The letter was intercepted, and Austin, on his return, arrested, carried back to the capital, and placed during a year in solitary confinement. The people of the United States who had become citizens of Texas, were naturally indignant at what they considered an outrage on the right of petition, and an insult to the dignity of their commissioner.

Such was the feeling in Texas, when Santa Anna, having completed his usurpation of the supreme power and defeated the Zacatecans, who opposed him, sent General Cos into Texas to enforce certain requisitions of the government. One of these was the execution of the Act of 1830, prohibiting the emigration of Americans into Texas. Another was the surrender of Lorenzo de Zavala, who had become a refugee in Texas, in consequence of moving a law, in the Mexican Congress, directed against church property. To enforce these demands, General Cos took possession of Antonio de Bexar. On the other hand, the Texans prepared for an armed resistance, and on the 28th of September, 1835, they attacked and defeated a party of Mexicans at the town of Gonzales, on the Rio Guadalupe.

Thus was commenced the war and revolution of Texas: a war which arose, on the part of Mexico, from an attempt to enforce the authority of the government *de facto* (without reference to the Constitution) over the province of Texas; and on the side of Texas, in an obvious attempt to make that province virtually independent of Mexico.

On the 3d of November, 1835, the delegates of Texas assembled at San Felipe de Austin, and issued a solemn declaration against Santa Anna and other military chieftains, "who had by force of arms overthrown the Federal Institutions of Mexico, and dissolved the social compact which existed between Texas and the other members of the Mexican confederacy."

The war thus commenced between Texas and the mother country continued, with various fortune, till the 21st of April, 1836, when General Santa Anna was captured at the battle of San Jacinto, and the Mexican authority over the Texans really destroyed.

On the 2d of March previously, the Texan delegates assembled at Washington on the Brazos, made a formal declaration of independence, signed a constitution, and organized a government. This independence Santa Anna, a captive in the hands of the Texan army, afterwards bound himself to "solemnly acknowledge, sanction, and ratify;" and to use his personal and official powers to procure without delay the ratification and confirmation of that treaty by the legitimate government of Mexico.

The boundaries of Texas, as then defined, are of importance as constituting one of the grounds of claim on the part of the government of the United States against Mexico. They were declared to be as follows:—

"Beginning at the mouth of the Rio Grande; thence up the principal stream of said river to its source; thence due north to the 42° of north latitude; thence along the boundary line, as defined in the treaty between the United States and Spain, (February, 1819,) to the beginning."

To any claim of boundary, however, resting upon this concession of Santa Anna, it is well replied, that it was made when he was under constraint, and was in its very terms of no effect till ratified by the legitimate government of Mexico. Accordingly when, a little while afterwards, Bustamente became president of Mexico, he repudiated this treaty, and recommenced the war with Texas. This war was continued, in desultory and predatory excursions, on both sides, till Texas was finally annexed to the United States.

While things were in this state—the mother country contending for its continued dominion, and the young province for absolute independence—the QUESTION OF ANNEXATION (as it is politically called) arose both in the United States and Texas. The inhabitants of the latter, we have said, were chiefly citizens of the United States—persons whom past adversities or future hopes had impelled to this new region in pursuit of fortune or adventure. If it was natural for them thus to pursue these new objects, it was equally natural that they should desire to remain politically and socially connected with the land of their birth and the home of their associations. Accordingly, as early as the 4th of August, 1837, soon after she declared her independence, Texas proposed to annex herself to the United States.[1] The then president of this country, Mr. Van Buren, declined the terms, for reasons which were alike honorable to his sagacity as a man, and his principles as a statesman. He declared, that so long as we were bound by a treaty of amity and commerce with Mexico, to annex Texas would necessarily involve the question of war; and that a disposition to espouse the quarrel with Mexico was at variance with the spirit of the treaty, and with the policy and welfare of the United States.[2]

Texas continued negotiations with the United States, with Great Britain, France, and Mexico—the object of which was to procure the acknowledgment of her independence by Mexico, or her protection by some more powerful government. Thus matters continued—a partial war at one time, and a series of negotiations at another—till the administration of President Tyler revived the plan of annexation. On the 6th of October, 1843, the Hon. A. P. Upshur, Secretary of State, proposed to the Texan envoy the renewal of negotiations for the annexation of

---

[1] Vide State Papers. [2] Idem.

Texas to the United States; which was accepted by the Texan executive.

In the mean while, the subject had been discussed in the newspapers, and the Mexican government availed itself of this information to make a formal declaration of its views on this important point. Mr. Bocanegra, the Mexican Minister of Foreign Relations, addressed a note[1] (August 23, 1843) to Waddy Thompson, our minister in Mexico, of which the following is a passage:—

"And if a party in Texas is now endeavoring to effect its incorporation with the United States, it is from a consciousness of their notorious incapability to form and constitute an independent nation, without their having changed their situation, or acquired any right to separate themselves from their mother country. His Excellency the Provisional President, resting on this deep conviction, is obliged to prevent an aggression, unprecedented in the annals of the world, from being consummated; and *if it be indispensable for the Mexican nation to seek security for its rights at the expense of the disasters of war, it will call upon God, and rely on its own efforts for the defence of its just cause.*"

This declaration was a notice to the American government of *the effects to be anticipated* from the annexation, and fully justified the sagacity and firmness of Mr. Van Buren. It was replied to, by Mr. Waddy Thompson, in a haughty note, affirming that the notice of the Mexican minister was a threat, or a warning; but silent as to the attitude really assumed by the United States.

A short time subsequent to this correspondence, and

---

[1] State Papers—Letter of Bocanegra.

as if to prevent any misunderstanding of the meaning of Mexico, General Almonte, Mexican minister at Washington, addressed a note to Mr. Upshur, Secretary of State, of which the following passage is a part:—

"But if, contrary to the hopes and wishes entertained by the government of the undersigned for the preservation of the good understanding and harmony which should reign between the two neighboring and friendly republics, the United States should, in defiance of good faith, and the principles of justice which they have constantly proclaimed, commit the unheard-of act of violence of appropriating to themselves an integrant part of the Mexican territory, the undersigned, in the name of his nation, and now for them, protests in the most solemn manner against such an aggression; and he moreover declares, by express order of his government, that on sanction being given by the Executive of the Union to the incorporation of Texas into the United States, he will consider his mission ended, seeing that, as the Secretary of State will have learned, *the Mexican government is resolved to declare war as soon as it receives intimation of such an act.*"[1]

Long previous to actual annexation, it will be observed, the Mexican government had officially informed the Executive of the United States, that war must inevitably result from that act. It cannot, therefore, be said, with any regard to truth, that the government of the United States, in annexing Texas, did not have reason to anticipate that result, and did not neglect that preparation which such anticipations required of a prudent administration.[2]

---

[1] General Almonte's Letter, dated November 3d, 1843.

[2] In fact they made none till the war was commenced.

The plan of annexation, notwithstanding these explicit declarations of the Mexican government, was anxiously and sedulously pursued by the Executive of the United States. Mr. J. C. Calhoun, who had succeeded Mr. Upshur[1] as Secretary of State, signed with the Ministers Plenipotentiary of Texas (Messrs. Van Zandt and Henderson) a Treaty of Annexation, on the 12th of April, 1844. In the same month, the Secretary of State (Mr. Calhoun) advised the Chargé d'Affaires in Mexico, "that the step had been forced on the government of the United States in self-defence, in consequence of the policy adopted by Great Britain in reference to the abolition of slavery in Texas."[2] At the same moment, there had been presented by Mr. Pakenham, (British minister,) and was on file in the Department of State, a solemn declaration of the British government, by Lord Aberdeen, that this idea of British interference was a gross mistake.[3] In this declaration, Lord Aberdeen says,—

"With regard to Texas, we avow that we wish to see slavery abolished there, or elsewhere; and we should rejoice, if the recognition of that country by the Mexican government, should be accompanied by an engagement on the part of Texas to abolish slavery, and under proper conditions throughout the republic. But although we earnestly desire and feel it to be our duty to promote such a consummation, *we shall not interfere unduly, or with an improper assumption of authority with either*

[1] Mr. Upshur was killed on board the Princeton.

[2] State Correspondence, April, 1844.

[3] Lord Aberdeen's Letter was dated December 26th, 1843; and presented by Mr. Pakenham, February 26th, 1844.

party, in order to insure the adoption of such a course. We shall counsel, but we shall not seek to compel or unduly control either party."

Did the President and Secretary of State disbelieve this declaration? In any case, upon what *evidence* did the Secretary declare, that the government of the United States was forced into this step, in consequence of the interference of Great Britain with slavery in Texas? Upon what principle of the Constitution did the American government interfere with Texas for such a cause?—The plan of annexation, however, was strenuously pushed by its projectors.

On the 22d of April, 1844, Mr. Tyler submitted to the Senate a Treaty of Annexation, which was soon after rejected, and the question left open for public discussion.[1]

In consequence of the election of President Polk in November, 1844, and the apparent approval of annexation by the people of the United States, Congress on the 1st of March, 1845, passed what is called the JOINT RESOLUTION, giving its consent that the territory "rightfully belonging to the Republic of Texas" might be erected into a new State called the State of Texas; subject, however, to the adjustment by this government of "all questions of boundary that may arise with other governments."

The terms of this Resolution admit that Texas might have claimed boundaries which were not *rightfully* belonging to her, and that these "questions of boundary" had *yet to be settled.*

To the terms of the Joint Resolution, Texas assented

---

[1] See the Public Documents of 1844

by her ordinance of July 4th, 1845, and having formed her Constitution, became virtually a State in the American Union.[1] Two days after this (July 7th) the same Convention requested the President of the United States to occupy the ports of Texas, and send an army to their defence. This desire the President of the United States immediately complied with.

General Zachary Taylor, then in command at Camp Jessup, was ordered to move his forces into Texas, weeks before the War Department had received information of the Texan ordinance. On the 28th of June, Mr. Donelson, then minister to Texas, and to whom General Taylor was referred for advice upon his movements, wrote him that he had best move his forces "without delay to the western frontier of Texas," and also informing him that Corpus Christi, on Aranzas Bay, was the best point for the assembling of his troops. The same letter also admitted that the country between the Nueces and the Rio Grande *was in dispute, the Texans holding Corpus Christi and the Mexicans Santiago, at the mouth of the Rio Grande.*[2]

General Taylor proceeded immediately with the forces under his command to Aranzas Bay, and in the beginning of August, 1845, had taken the position assigned him by the government. All the troops in the west, the northwest, and the Atlantic which could be spared, were ordered to join him. In November, 1845, by the report of the Adjutant-General, his army was composed as follows:—[3]

---

[1] Documents of 1845.

[2] Mr. Donelson's Letter 28th of June 1845.—Public Documents.

[3] Adjutant-General's Report, November 26th, 1845.

General Staff - - - - -	24
2d Regiment of Dragoons - - -	596
1st " of Artillery - - -	236
2d " " " - - -	233
3d " " " - - -	219
4th " " " - - -	235
3d Regiment of Infantry - - -	533
4th " " " - - -	511
5th " " " - - -	573
7th " " " - - -	442
8th " " " - - -	447
Aggregate - - -	4,049

This was General Taylor's army in November, 1845, when, by the confession of the government, the territory between his position and Santiago, or rather, between the Nueces and the Rio Grande, was *in dispute*, and the subject of negotiation for boundaries.

What, however, was at this moment the real position of affairs in regard to the question of war? Was there any room to doubt that war was the necessary consequence of annexation? Was there any thing to justify the total neglect of all preparation for so serious a conflict, as war with a nation, however inferior, of seven millions of people? The facts, as we have reviewed them, are simple and brief.

Mexico, hearing from the United States the distant rumors of an intended annexation of Texas, announces by Mr. Bocanegra to the American minister, that she will resent such an act at the expense of the disasters of war.

In the same year, (1843,) and a few months later, the Mexican minister, General Almonte, reaffirms the same fixed determination of his government in a letter to the American Secretary of State.

When the act for annexation is passed, Almonte declares in his final note to the Secretary of State, that it is the most unjust act recorded in the annals of history; protests against it; declares that his government will resist it by all the means in its power; and demands his passports.

The diplomatic correspondence of our government shows, that it apprehended war—that it knew well the sole cause by which war would come—and that in the minds of the President and his cabinet, the annexation of Texas, and its disputed boundaries, was the sole foundation for any rupture with Mexico.

The march of General Taylor's army was evidently and declaredly[1] intended to meet the contingencies of such a rupture.

The most remarkable fact in this transaction, is that, with this apprehension of war vividly impressed upon the mind of the government, the President should never have asked Congress for one dollar of money, or one company of soldiers in addition to the provisions of the peace establishment! Upon what principle was it assumed, that an entire province could be wrested from one empire and give no cause for war? Upon what idea of prudence or sagacity was all preparation for that war neglected, till battles were already fought, and the opposing nation excited by all the worst feelings of national and martial controversy?

The effect of this neglect we shall see in the series of subsequent events.

---

[1] See Donelson's Correspondence.

CHAPTER II.

War inevitable—General Scott at Washington—Recommends an increase of the Army—Mission of Mr. Slidell—Downfall of Herrera—Departure of Slidell—General Taylor marches from Corpus Christi—Arrives at Point Isabel—In front of Metamoras—Capture of Captain Thornton's party—March of General Taylor to Point Isabel—Battles of Palo Alto and Resaca de la Palma—Taylor's Official Report.

We have traced in the preceding chapter the negotiations of the United States with Mexico and Texas to that point, in which the Mexican Secretary for Foreign Affairs, and the Mexican minister at Washington, officially announced that the annexation of Texas to the United States would be considered just cause of war, and the latter had departed from Washington with hostile declarations. That this declaration was believed, and that war would result from that act, the American *Chargé d'Affaires* in Texas (Mr. Donelson) shows in his entire correspondence. In his letter of June 4th, 1845, to the Secretary of State, he declares his full belief that war will occur, although he chose to attribute it to the instigation of the British minister, Mr. Elliott.

Mr. Donelson makes this remarkable announcement:—

"I look upon war with Mexico as inevitable—a war dictated by the British minister here for the purpose of defeating annexation, and intended at all events to deprive both Texas and the United States of all claim to the country between the Nueces and the Rio Grande, at the time the right of Texas to the protection of the United States arises under the contingency anticipated by you at the date of your last despatch to me."

The "contingency" here spoken of by the Chargé, was stated in Mr. Buchanan's letter of May 23d, 1845, and was simply the acceptance, by Texas, of the conditions of annexation stated in the joint resolution of Congress.

The question of "boundaries" was by that resolution and by all prior negotiations, left open for future discussion. Mr. Buchanan, therefore, cautiously uses the term "state," in reference to the annexation of Texas, and tells Mr. Donelson (23d of May, 1845) that, in the event of annexation, the President will deem it his duty to "employ the army in defending *that state* against the attacks of any foreign power." It was *the state* of Texas, whatever that might be, which, in May, 1845, the President undertook to defend, and not any imaginary boundary, or supposed claim of Texas beyond the Nueces, the Rio Grande, or any other stream.

Under the idea, however, as expressed in his letter of the 4th of June, that war was inevitable, Mr. Donelson asks the government for an army to defend the supposed frontier of Texas, and it is under this requisition that the corps of General Taylor was ordered to Corpus Christi, and became, in another year, the invading army of Mexico! The cause of the war—the manner in which it was to arise and to be carried on, are projected and shadowed out so minutely in the diplomatic correspondence of Messrs. Buchanan and Donelson, as to leave the historian of these events no doubtful points to discuss. If they are not certain and fixed on the map of Time, in vain shall we look for any faithful volume of human transactions.

What was in prospect for the army when arrived in Texas, and its purpose there, is thus stated by Mr. Donelson :—

"Under such circumstances, the officer intended for the command of the United States troops on the Texan frontier may expect to find a large force of the enemy there; and it is suggested whether that officer ought not at once to be selected, and ordered to some near and convenient point for the purpose of communicating with me, and providing the most prompt means of action the moment he is advised of the decision of the Convention of Texas on the terms of union proposed in our joint resolution."

The requisition of Mr. Donelson was complied with. An express was sent to General Taylor, at Fort Jessup; his troops were ordered into Texas; and Captain Stockton was ordered with a squadron into the Gulf of Mexico; both with the avowed object of repelling the attacks of Mexico,—an anticipated consequence of annexation.[1]

During this period General Scott was at Washington, in the diligent performance of his military duties as the commander of the army, without taking any public part in the political discussions of the day.

The commander of the army, even on the peace establishment of the United States, must necessarily carry on an extensive correspondence, and have the oversight of many and various departments of the public service. General Scott found ample scope for his official talents and time, in both the superintendence and the anticipation of the wants and means of the army. At the time General Taylor was despatched to the frontier of Texas, the American army

[1] Mr. Bucnanan's letter to Mr. Donelson, dated June 15th, 1845.

was actually of less numerical strength than it had been in any year since 1808! And yet the official documents prove that at that very moment of time the government was in daily expectation of war; and yet the Executive did not ask from Congress an additional regiment, nor did Congress anticipate the need of additional means![1]

General Scott, however, in his annual report upon the state of the army, recommended, what the other departments of the government seem strangely to have overlooked,—a small increase of the army. He pointed out a very easy method of doing this, without raising additional regiments, or even requiring additional officers. During the presidency of Mr. Monroe, and while Mr. Calhoun was Secretary at War, (and, indeed, upon his recommendation,) the plan had been adopted of having *skeleton regiments*, in which all the officers were retained, but the number of privates reduced one-half. The reason for this was very strong. It was that, having all the officers ready, and a skeleton of the regiment, the number of the army might be doubled, in time of emergency, by new enlistments, without the expense of permanent maintenance. Accordingly, the regiments of artillery and infantry had but *forty-two privates* in each company, when the number should have been eighty-four. The Military Academy had furnished a large number of valuable officers, many of whom were attached to the regiments by *brevet*.

General Scott proposed to increase the army, simply by filling up these skeleton companies, and giving em-

[1] The President twice in his Message (December, 1845) alluded to the danger of a war with Mexico; but recommended nothing for the army.

ployment to these brevet officers. In his report (November 20th, 1845) he says:

"By adding ten privates to each company of dragoons, now fifty privates each, and twenty privates to each company of artillery and infantry, now forty-two privates each, of the present establishment, we should have a total increase (by this plan) for twenty companies of dragoons, forty of artillery, and eighty of infantry, of twenty-six hundred privates—without the addition of a regiment, or of one non-commissioned officer, musician, or artificer. See *organization* (table) *of the regular army of the United States*, Army Register. But, in this case, an additional subaltern (second lieutenant) to each company of dragoons and infantry (one hundred) would be necessary. There are, at present, about ninety-five *brevet* second lieutenants (graduates of the Military Academy—strangely called *supernumerary* by act of April 29, 1812, sec. 4) attached to companies, and doing duty with them. These officers would be absorbed, by promotion, should this second plan of augmentation be carried out, and the future supernumerary or brevet second lieutenants (graduates of the Academy) be kept down, for a series of years, to a small number—not more than sufficient to supply three officers constantly on duty with each company, and to give others for staff and detached duties which the progress of the service will, in five or seven years, cer tainly demand."

This was General Scott's recommendation without looking at the question of war with Mexico; although it now appears from official documents, that the war was then in the contemplation of the cabinet. Had the President recommended, and Congress acceded to even this small increase of the military force, it may be doubted whether the invasion of Mexico, and the sanguinary battles which followed, would ever have occurred. General Taylor's army would have been increased early in the spring, and the Mexican general would, not improbably, have refrained from an attack, to which he was tempted and invited by the weakness of the American force.

In the autumn previous to this report, but after General Taylor's army were assembled at Corpus Christi, and while war was apparently inevitable, the President again resorted to negotiation by means of an indirect correspondence with Mr. Black, American consul at Mexico. The Mexican government was inquired of,[1] whether they would receive an envoy, "intrusted with full powers to adjust all the questions in dispute between the two governments." The Mexican Minister for Foreign Affairs (Manuel De La Peña Y. Peña) acceded to this proposition, provided the mission was frank and free, without the appearance of coercion—and that the American squadron, then off Vera Cruz, was recalled.[2] In saying this, and making other statements to the American agents, the Mexican cabinet alleged, that they wished to avoid irritation in the people of Mexico; and in fact, intimated that the existing administration was, as to this point, weak—and feared the appearance of yielding too readily to the wishes of the United States. The Mexican government desired peace; but feared the popular excitement.

The cabinet at Washington immediately appointed Mr.

---

[1] Mr. Buchanan's Letter to Mr. Black, September 17th, 1845.

[2] Mr. Peña Y. Peña, (October 18th, 1845,) to Mr. Black.

John Slidell envoy to Mexico. He arrived at Sacrificios on the 29th of November,[1] and hastened to the city of Mexico. At Puebla, he was met by our consul, (Mr. Black,) who informed him that the Mexican government were surprised that the United States had sent an envoy so suddenly—that they were not prepared to receive him—that he was not expected till January—and in fine, that they were afraid his appearance would prove destructive to the government, and thus defeat the intentions of peace.[2] Mr. Slidell seems not to have understood the obvious position of the Mexican minister, nor to have subjected his impatience, in any degree, to the dictates of prudence. He hurried on, and from the 6th to the 20th of December, but two weeks, addressed three imperative notes to Mr. Peña Y. Peña, demanding the consideration of his credentials, and an answer to his demand. The Mexican administration was in instant danger of dissolution, and desired delay, that they might better secure peace. The effect of Mr. Slidell's imperative haste was, to defeat the peaceful intentions of the Mexican government, and hurry it to an abrupt denial of the American minister. On the 20th of December, twelve days from the date of his first note, Mr. Slidell was officially informed, that the Mexican government could not admit him "to the exercise of the functions of the mission conferred on him by the United States government."[3] The ground of the re-

---

[1] Mr. Black to Mr. Buchanan, December 18th, 1845.

[2] Mr. Black's Letter to Buchanan, December 18th, 1845. Slidell's Letter to Buchanan, December 17th, 1845.

[3] M. Peña Y Peña's Letter to Slidell, December 20th, 1845

fusal was, that the American envoy was appointed as a general and ordinary minister—when, in consequence of the interrupted and broken relations between the two nations, he should have been appointed a commissioner to settle the specific differences which were in dispute between the countries. The diplomatic correspondence, however, proves conclusively, that a fear of impending revolution, as a consequence of negotiating with the United States, was hurried to a premature crisis by the untimely importunities of Mr. Slidell. The dreaded revolution took place, and in nine days after, (the 29th of December,) the administration of President Herrera was overthrown. His successor, PAREDES, was a military chief—who, on the 2d January, (1846,) was ushered by the troops into the capital of Mexico. A temporary government was soon formed, of which General Almonte, late minister to the United States, was a leading member.[1]

Mr. Slidell retired to Jalapa, where he remained till March, when under instructions from the Department of State, he again made overtures to the Mexican government.[2] To this new proposition, the Mexican minister for Foreign Affairs (Mr. Costillo Y. Lanzas) again returned an unequivocal denial.[3] He informed the American envoy, that it was the firm intention of the Mexican government to admit only a plenipotentiary from the United States, clothed "with special powers to treat

[1] Slidell to Buchanan, January 14th, 1846.

[2] Slidell to Costillo Y. Lanzas, March 1st, 1846.

[3] Costillo Y. Lanzas to Slidell, March 12th, 1846.

upon the question of Texas, and upon this alone;" and that upon this point its resolve was immutable. When this answer was returned, the reader of history will observe, that General Taylor's troops had already taken position on the Rio Grande, and that their presence there was deemed, in Mexico, a new wrong and injury[1] to that republic.

This letter closed, on the part of Mexico, its diplomatic correspondence with the United States. On the 21st of March, Mr. Costillo Y. Lanzas enclosed to Mr. Slidell his passports from the Mexican territories.

Long before this final refusal of the Mexican government to receive Mr. Slidell, the President of the United States had determined to take the *initial*, and advance his troops to the Rio Grande. On the 20th of January, Mr. Buchanan informed Mr. Slidell, that the President had already ordered the army of Texas to advance and take position on the left bank of the Rio Grande, and a strong fleet to assemble in the Gulf of Mexico.[2] This was done before the answer of Mr. Peña Y. Peña was known at Washington; and when the Mexican government had earnestly desired that no appearance of coercion should be allowed.

The order, by which the army was moved from Corpus Christi to the Rio Grande, was dated January 13th, 1846, before the government had received the correspondence of Slidell with Peña Y. Peña, and before it knew of the overthrow of Herrera, and the accession

---

[1] General Taylor's Report, March 8th, 1846.

[2] Buchanan to Slidell, January 20th, 1846.

of Paredes.[1] It suggested to General Taylor the "points opposite Metamoras and Mier, and the vicinity of Laredo," as stations for the American army.[2]

On the 8th of March, the advance column of the army under Colonel Twiggs commenced its march from Corpus Christi,[3] and on the 18th, the whole was concentrated near the banks of the Arroyo Colorado, about thirty miles from Metamoras. Here a party of irregular Mexican cavalry (rancheros) appeared on the opposite banks, and signified to the officer making a reconnaissance, that an attempt to pass the river would be an act of hostility.[4] Notwithstanding this notice, the army crossed the river on the 20th, and on the 25th, established its position at Point Isabel; the buildings of which the Mexican prefect attempted to burn, as he left the place.[5] On the 28th of March, General Taylor took his position within cannon range of Metamoras.[6] The Mexican forces in the town commenced preparing batteries to bear on the American camp; and General Taylor also erected batteries to command Metamoras. Such was the position of the parties, when a conference was held between Generals Worth and La Vega as to the objects

---

[1] Public Documents. Secretary Marcy's Letter to General Taylor, January 13th, 1846.

[2] These were Mexican towns, in sight of which, and on territory claimed by Mexico, the army was directed to take post.

[3] General Taylor's Report, March 8th, 1846.

[4] General Taylor's Letter, 21st of March, 1846

[5] General Taylor's Report, March 25th.

[6] General Taylor's Report, March 29th. In this letter he states, that a battery of four pieces had been so mounted, as to command the public square of Metamoras

in advancing the army. The conference was fruitless of any results.

At this time, it was obvious to all intelligent minds that war was unavoidable. The crisis—to which the annexation of Texas clearly pointed—had come. Mr. Slidell had received his final rejection from Mr. Costillo Y. Lanzas, on the 12th of March. On the 8th, (four days before,) the army had marched from Corpus Christi to the Rio Grande. It had now arrived in front of Metamoras, where the forces of Mexico were arrayed, and where the declarations of officers, the armament of batteries, and all the paraphernalia of martial display, indicated an instant conflict. Notwithstanding all these plain indications of war, the movements of the administration at home exhibited no symptoms of any thing but unbroken and continued peace. The recommendations of General Scott for an increase of the army were disregarded. The President and Congress moved placidly on, as if neither arms or money, strength or blood were required to secure its easy victory over a weak and effeminate foe. Some preparations had heretofore been deemed necessary by statesmen to meet the exigencies of war, even with very inferior powers. In this instance, there was none. The official returns show that one-half the entire army of the United States was in the corps of General Taylor, while various military posts and forts in the northwest and on the Atlantic, were entirely deprived of their garrisons to make up the forces on the Rio Grande.[1] Even this army was almost totally without the wagons, animals, and drivers necessary for common field transportation. They had to be

[1] Report of General Scott. Public Documents of 1845.

procured in the heart of the country, at places near two thousand miles from the scene of operations.[1] The march of the American army to the Rio Grande—the erection of batteries within gunshot of Metamoras—the appearance of Mexican parties on the Arroyo Colorado—the notice by them that the passage of that stream by the American troops would be considered an act of war—and the concentration of large bodies of Mexican troops, known to have been marched to that vicinity—all announced, by no uncertain indications, that the conflict of war was about to commence, and the annexation of Texas to be followed by its natural and necessary consequences.

On the 24th of April, General Arista assumed the chief command of the army of Mexico. On the same day General Taylor detached a party of 63 dragoons to watch the course of the river above Metamoras. This party, under the command of Captain Thornton, were watched by the Mexicans, and at a point about thirty miles from the American camp, were surprised and attacked. After the loss of sixteen men killed and wounded, they were compelled to surrender to the superior forces of the Mexicans, who in large numbers had surrounded them in a fenced plantation field.[2] This was the first actual fight of the war, and was received by the Mexicans as an augury favorable, but fallacious in the events which followed, to their success. General Arista, desirous of making a favorable impression, treated his prisoners with distinguished respect and kindness.

---

[1] See the Letter of Colonel Cross, dated November 23d, 1845, detailing the fact, that the army had no means of field transportation whatever.—Public Doc. 119, 29th Congress.

[2] Captain Hardee's Report, April 26th, 1846.—Pub. Doc. 119.

Three days after this affair, the camp of Captain Walker's Texan Rangers was surprised, and several killed and wounded.[1] This was between Point Isabel and Metamoras. In the mean while, it was ascertained that a large body of the Mexican army had crossed the river (Rio Grande) above,[2] and that another corps was about to cross below. General Taylor was convinced that the object of attack was Point Isabel, which had been left in care of a small detachment, and where a large depot of provisions invited the enemy. Leaving an unfinished field-work, under the command of Major Brown, and garrisoned by the 7th infantry, with Lowd's and Bragg's companies of artillery, he marched for Point Isabel on the 1st of May, with his main force, and arrived on the next day.

The departure of General Taylor with his army, furnished the enemy in Metamoras with the opportunity for a safe attack on Fort Brown. At five in the morning of the 3d of May, a heavy bombardment was commenced from the batteries in Metamoras, and continued at intervals till the 10th, when the gallant defenders of the fort were relieved. In this defence, Major Brown, Captain Hawkins, and Captain Mansfield were greatly distinguished, both for skill and gallantry. The former was killed by a shell, and the defence was vigorously continued by Captain Hawkins. Captain Mansfield was an engineer officer, under whose direction the fort was built, and by whose skilful conduct the defences were increased and strengthened during the siege.[3]

The siege of Fort Brown was raised by the arrival of

---

[1] General Taylor's Report, May 3d, 1846. Captain Walker was not present. [2] Same.—Pub. Doc. 119.

[3] Reports of Major Brown, Captain Hawkins, and General Taylor.

the victorious army of Taylor, which had just fought the battles of Palo Alto and Resaca de la Palma. It appears that General Arista, who was now in command of the Mexican army, had assembled in all about eight thousand men at Metamoras, and being well advised of the strength of the American forces, thought the time had arrived for a decisive blow. The capture of Captain Thornton's party had also emboldened the Mexican troops. Arista saw that Point Isabel, the depot of large quantities of provisions and military munitions, was comparatively defenceless. To take this place would, therefore, both cut off the supplies of Taylor's army, and leave it isolated in the heart of the enemy's country. The plan of Arista was to cross the Rio Grande, get in the rear of General Taylor's army, capture Point Isabel, and then fall on the American army.[1] The plan was judicious, and was only prevented from being carried out, by the accidental information brought to General Taylor by one of Thornton's party—sent in by the Mexican commander![2] The rapid return of the army to Point Isabel was a consequence of this information, and the additional fact that the enemy was preparing to cross below. Either the Mexican army was dilatory in its movement, or the body detailed to cross below was unable to form a junction, for the forces of Taylor reached the depot at Isabel without encountering the enemy.

Having obtained the object of his expedition, and garrisoned the depot with new troops, the American general

---

[1] This is an inference from the facts stated by General Taylor.

[2] General Taylor states in his letter of May 3d, that in consequence of the deficiency in light troops, he was "kept ignorant" of the enemy's movements.

commenced his return to Fort Brown on the 7th of May, a week after his departure. The army was accompanied by a train of wagons, and encamped at night about seven miles from Isabel. The next day (the 8th) the march was resumed, and at noon the enemy was discovered drawn up in battle array upon a prairie three miles from the Palo Alto. The army was halted, and the men refreshed at a pool. The line was formed in two wings The right, commanded by Colonel Twiggs, was composed of the 5th Infantry, Colonel McIntosh ; 3d Infantry, Captain Morris ; 4th Infantry, Major Allen ; Ringgold's Light Artillery ; two eighteen-pounders under Lt. Churchill ; and two squadrons of Dragoons under Captains Ker and May. The left wing, under the command of Lt. Colonel Belknap, was formed by a battalion of Artillery, Colonel Childs, Captain Duncan's Light Artillery, and the 8th Infantry, under Captain Montgomery. The train was left in the rear, protected by a guard.

At two P. M., the army advanced by heads of columns, till the Mexican cannon opened upon them, when they were deployed into line, and Ringgold's Light Artillery on the right, poured forth its rapid and deadly fire on the enemy. The Mexican cavalry, mostly Lancers, were on their left, and were forced back by the destructive discharges of artillery. To remedy this, General Arista ordered Torrejon, general of cavalry, to charge the American right. This he did, but was met by the Flying Artillery, under Lt. Ridgely, and by the 5th Infantry. The Lancers were again driven back. At this period the prairie grass was set on fire, and under cover of its smoke the Americans advanced to the position just occupied by the Mexican cavalry. Again a Mexican division of Lancers

GENERAL TAYLOR AT THE BATTLE OF PALO ALTO.
May 8th, 1846.

charged, under the command of Col. Montero,[1] but with as little success. The continuous fire of artillery disordered and drove back the enemy's columns. On the left wing of our army, attacks of the Mexicans were met by Duncan's battery, and by other troops of that division. The combat on our side was chiefly carried on by artillery; and never was there a more complete demonstration of the superior skill and energy of that Arm of service, as conducted by the accomplished graduates of West-Point. He who was the life and leader of the Light Artillery, —MAJOR RINGGOLD—was in this engagement mortally wounded, and died in a few days.

The battle terminated with the possession, by the Americans, of the field, and the retreat during the night of the Mexicans. Arista, dating his despatch, says, "*in sight of the enemy, at night.*" This might be true; but he was in retreat, and took a new position several miles off, at Resaca de la Palma. A ravine here crossed the road, and on either side it was skirted with dense thickets. This ravine was occupied by the Mexican artillery. The position was well chosen; and with troops better skilled in the use of artillery, and with greater energy of body, might have easily been defended.

General Taylor had encamped on the field of battle, from which he did not depart till two P. M. the next day. In two hours, the American army came in sight of the Mexican array. The dispositions of our troops were soon made. A battery of artillery, under Lt. Ridgely, moved up the main road, while the 3d, 4th, and 5th Regiments of Infantry deployed on either flank to support it and act

---

[1] Arista's Despatch.

as skirmishers. The action commenced by the fire of the Mexican artillery, which was returned by Ridgely's battery and by the infantry on the wings. In this firing, the Mexican cannon were well managed by Generals La Vega and Requena, and the effect began to be severely felt on the American lines. It was necessary to dislodge them; and this duty was assigned to Captain May of the Dragoons. It was here that this officer became so distinguished. The charge was gallantly made. The Dragoons cut through the enemy. The artillerymen were dispersed, and General La Vega taken prisoner. The Dragoons, however, had advanced beyond support, and in turn fell back on the main body. The regiments of infantry now charged the Mexican line, and the battle was soon ended. Their columns, now broken by successive charges, were unable to bear the continued and well-directed fire poured upon them by both infantry and artillery. They fled precipitately from the field, and were rapidly pursued by the American rearguard. The Mexicans lost many prisoners, and ceased not their flight till they either crossed or were overwhelmed in the waters of the Rio Grande. In these engagements neither cowardice nor feebleness was attributed to them. They fought gallantly, behaved well, and were only conquered by that union of physical strength and superior skill, with which some nations are fortunately gifted, by the natural influence of climate and the artificial developments of science.

In these engagements the commander of the American forces, General Zachary Taylor, displayed the utmost coolness and bravery—exposing himself in the most dangerous positions, and encouraging the troops by his heroic example. After the battles were ended, his attention to

GENERAL TAYLOR AT THE BATTLE OF RESACA DE LA PALMA.
May 9th, 1846

the wounded and the dying, whether friend or foe, evinced that sympathy with suffering humanity which is ever inseparable from true courage.

We here insert the official report:

HEADQUARTERS ARMY OF OCCUPATION,
Camp at Palo Alto, Texas, May 9, 1846.

SIR:—I have the honor to report that I was met near this place yesterday, on my march from Point Isabel, by the Mexican forces, and after an action of about five hours, dislodged them from their position, and encamped upon the field. Our artillery, consisting of two 18-pounders and two light batteries, was the arm chiefly engaged, and to the excellent manner in which it was manoeuvred and served is our success mainly due.

The strength of the enemy is believed to have been about six thousand men, with seven pieces of artillery, and eight hundred cavalry. His loss is probably at least one hundred killed. Our strength did not exceed, all told, twenty-three hundred, while our loss was comparatively trifling—four men killed, three officers and thirty-seven men wounded, several of the latter mortally. I regret to say that Major Ringgold, 3d artillery, and Captain Paige, 4th infantry, are severely wounded. Lieut. Luther, 2d artillery, slightly so.

The enemy has fallen back, and it is believed has repassed the river. I have advanced parties now thrown forward in his direction, and shall move the main body immediately.

In the haste of this first report, I can only say that the officers and men behaved in the most admirable manner throughout the action. I shall have the pleasure of making a more detailed report when those of the different commanders shall be received.

I am, sir, very respectfully, your obedient servant,

Z. TAYLOR,
Brevet Brigadier-general, U. S. A. Commanding.

HEADQUARTERS ARMY OF OCCUPATION,
Camp at Resaca de la Palma, 3 miles from Matamoras,
10 o'clock, P. M.—May 9, 1846.

SIR:—I have the honor to report that I marched with the main body of the army at 2 o'clock to-day, having previously thrown forward a body of light infantry into the forest, which covers the Matamoras road. When near the spot where I am now encamped, my advance discovered that a ravine crossing the road had been occupied by the enemy with artillery. I immediately ordered a battery of field artillery to sweep the position, flanking and sustaining it by the 3d, 4th, and 5th regiments, deployed as skirmishers to the right and left. A heavy fire of artillery and of musketry was kept up for some time, until finally the enemy's batteries were carried in succession by a squadron of dragoons and the regiments of infantry that were on the ground. He was soon driven from his position, and pursued by a squadron of dragoons, battalion of artillery, 3d infantry, and a light battery, to the river. Our victory has been complete. Eight pieces of artillery, with a great quantity of ammunition, three standards, and some one hundred prisoners have been taken; among the latter, Gen. La Vega, and several other officers. One general is understood to have been killed. The enemy has recrossed the river, and I am sure will not again molest us on this bank.

The loss of the enemy in killed has been most severe. Our own has been very heavy, and I deeply regret to report that Lieut. Inge, 2d dragoons, Lieut. Cochrane, 4th infantry, and Lieut. Chadbourne, 8th infantry, were killed on the field. Lieut. Col. Payne, 4th artillery, Lieut. Col. McIntosh, Lieut. Dobbins, 3d infantry, Capt. Hooe, and Lieut. Fowler, 5th infantry, and Capt. Montgomery, Lieuts. Gates, Selden, McClay, Burbank and Jordan, 8th infantry, were wounded. The extent of our loss in killed and wounded is not yet ascertained, and is reserved for a more detailed report.

The affair of to-day may be regarded as a proper supplement to the cannonade of yesterday; and the two taken together, exhibit the coolness and gallantry of our officers and men in the most favorable light. All have done their duty, and done it nobly. It will be my pride in a more circumstantial report of both actions, to dwell upon particular instances of individual distinction.

It affords me peculiar pleasure to report that the field-work opposite Matamoras has sustained itself handsomely during a cannonade and bombardment of 168 hours. But the pleasure is alloyed with profound regret at the loss of its heroic and indomitable commander, Major Brown, who died to-day from the effect of a shell. His loss would be a severe one to the service at any time, but to the army under my orders, it is indeed irreparable. One officer and one non-commissioned officer killed, and ten men wounded, comprise all the casualties incident to this severe bombardment.

I inadvertently omitted to mention the capture of a large number of pack mules left in the Mexican camp.

I am, sir, very respectfully, your obedient servant,

Z. TAYLOR,

Brevet Brigadier-general, U. S. Army Commanding.

[ORDERS No. 59.]

1. The commanding general congratulates the army under his command upon the signal success which has crowned its recent operations against the enemy. The coolness and steadiness of the troops during the action of the 8th, and the brilliant impetuosity with which the enemy's position and artillery were carried on the 9th, have displayed the best qualities of the American soldier. To every officer and soldier of his command the general publicly returns his thanks for the noble manner in which they have sustained the honor of the service and of the country. While the main body of the army has been thus actively employed, the gar-

rison left opposite Matamoras has rendered no less distinguished service by sustaining a severe cannonade and bombardment of many successive days. The army and the country, while justly rejoicing in this triumph of our arms, will deplore the loss of many brave officers and men who fell gallantly in the hour of combat.

2. It being necessary for the commanding general to visit Point Isabel on public business, Colonel Twiggs will assume command of the corps of the army near Matamoras, including the garrison of the field-work. He will occupy the former lines of the army, making such dispositions for defence and for the comfort of his command as he may deem advisable. He will hold himself strictly on the defensive until the return of the commanding general.

By order of Brigadier-general Taylor.

W. W. J. Bliss, Act. Adjutant General.

Headquarters Army of Occupation,
Point Isabel, Texas, May 12, 1846.

Sir:—I am making a hasty visit to this place, for the purpose of having an interview with Commodore Connor, whose squadron is now at anchor off the harbor, and arranging with him a combined movement up the river. I avail myself of the brief time at my command to report that the main body of the army is now occupying its former position opposite Matamoras. The Mexican forces are almost disorganized, and I shall lose no time in investing Matamoras, and opening the navigation of the river.

I regret to report that Major Ringgold died the morning of the 11th inst., of the severe wounds received in the action of Palo Alto. With the exception of Capt. Paige, whose wound is dangerous, the other wounded officers are doing well. In my report of the second engagement, I accidentally omitted the name of Lieut. Dobbins, 3d infantry, among the officers slightly wounded, and desire that the omission may be supplied in the despatch itself. I am under the painful necessity of reporting that Lieut. Blake, topographical engineers, after rendering distinguished service in my staff during the affair of the 8th inst., accidentally shot himself with a pistol on the following day, and expired before night.

It has been quite impossible as yet to furnish detailed reports of our engagements with the enemy, or even accurate returns of the killed and wounded. Our loss is not far from 3 officers and 40 men killed, and 13 officers and 100 men wounded; while that of the enemy has in all probability exceeded 300 killed; more than 200 have been buried by us on the two fields of battle.

I have exchanged a sufficient number of prisoners to recover the command of Captain Thornton. The wounded prisoners have been sent to Matamoras—the wounded officers on their parole. General La Vega and a few other officers have been sent to New Orleans, having declined a parole, and will be reported to Maj. Gen. Gaines. I am not conversant with the usages of war in such cases, and beg that such provision may be made for these prisoners as may be authorized by law. Our own prisoners have been treated with great kindness by the Mexican officers.

I am, sir, very respectfully, your obedient servant,

Z. TAYLOR,
Brevet Brigadier-general, U. S. A. Commanding.

The RESULT of these battles, however, was fatal. The Mexican republic lost all power, either present or future, of retaining one foot of that vast territorial empire which they once held east of the Rio Grande. The conquerors were tempted, in the flush of victory, to carry their arms beyond that melancholy river;—to seek for glory in conquests;—to find the gratification of dominion in foreign lands;——to indulge the rapacious lust of power;—to leave fields fertile in blessings for others fertile only in blood;—and finally, to make it uncertain whether even the best of Republics can resist the universal tendency of man to build up Empires—by the destruction of Justice.

CHAPTER III.

Action of Congress.—Declaration of the President.—Legislation.—General Scott's Views of the War.—His Comments on the Plan of Campaign.—His Correspondence with Secretary Marcy.—The Grounds for his Opinions.—Is ordered to remain at Washington.

THE news of the capture of Captain Thornton's party was received with great surprise by the nation, and the government. Notwithstanding all the acts of the United States and Mexico, both diplomatic and legislative, during the previous four years, had tended to this and no other result; and notwithstanding General Taylor had been ordered to the Rio Grande with four thousand regular troops, yet neither people nor President seem to have realized that war was actually near at hand. They appear to have relied upon some invisible Providence to prevent a catastrophe, which to a reasonable mind, and especially to one imbued with the spirit of a statesman, seemed inevitable.[1]

The intelligence of hostilities on the Rio Grande, was therefore received with astonishment, and for a time occasioned a powerful excitement. Congress was then in session, and the President immediately sent in an extraordinary Message.[2] In this, he declared that the

[1] Mr. Clay declared in the canvass of 1844, that the annexation of Texas was equivalent to a war with Mexico, and that war must follow

President's Message, dated the 11th of May, 1846.

Mexican government had "at last invaded *our territory, and shed the blood of our fellow-citizens on our own soil.*" In the same Message, and in the paragraph immediately following, he stated that Mr. Slidell was sent to Mexico with full powers to adjust all the questions in dispute between the two governments, "*both the questions of the Texas boundary*, and of indemnification to our citizens." The *boundary* in dispute was the *western boundary of Texas* only, and hence this was a clear admission, that the territory adjacent was in dispute, and was *not our soil*, till the question of boundary was settled.

Congress, however, with less than two days' deliberation, adopted the declaration of the President, and declared that, "by the act of the Republic of Mexico, a state of war exists between that government and the United States." At the same time, that body authorized the President to accept the services of fifty thousand volunteers, and placed ten millions of dollars at his disposal. The intention was to put an end to the war, by a vigorous effort and decisive victories. The President declared that in his opinion, "the immediate appearance in arms of a large and overpowering force," would be the best means of producing peace.[1]

Just two days before this declaration, the decisive battle of Resaca de la Palma had been fought, and the army of Arista pursued beyond the Rio Grande. We are now to see what plans the government had formed for the further prosecution of the war.

---

[1] The term most commonly used to express this idea was "to conquer a peace." The original authorship of this phrase appears to belong to the poet Coleridge.—See Cottle's Reminiscences.

At this time, General Scott, as commander of the army, was stationed at Washington, engaged in arranging and superintending the various staff duties of the army. He would be naturally consulted on the plans to be formed, and the means to execute them. This was the case. Immediately after the act of Congress of the 13th of May was passed, he was invited to call upon the President, who in that interview informed him that it was his determination to assign him the command of the army in Mexco.[1] From that moment, he was busily engaged in the necessary arrangements to carry into effect the views and instructions of the President. He was employed fourteen hours a day in all those various duties which pertain to the movements, supplies, equipage, direction, and objects of the army. No one can imagine the magnitude of these labors, their responsibility or importance, who does not reflect, that the geography, climate, military armament, means of supply, in fine, the whole detail of the physical and social condition of Mexico, were almost utterly unknown in the United States, and that information on these topics had to be obtained by inquiry and study, before even a general of the army could make prudent military arrangements. The Rio Grande was assumed by the government, as the *base line* of military operations from the beginning. Yet this river was itself not less than seven hundred miles from the Mississippi river, separated by lands so unproductive, and so sparsely populated, as to be incapable of supporting either man or beast on the extended scale required by the operations of war. The

---

[1] Marcy's Letter to the President, published in the Public Documents of 1846.

Mississippi then became the true and real base of supply and movement, and New Orleans the great depot for provisions and armament. From this point, General Scott had to calculate the march and support of an army whose field embraced Texas and California, the Rocky Mountains and the Sierra Madre; the cold regions of eternal snow, and those sunburnt climes where snow was never known! To prepare the clothing and guard the health of troops who were to visit regions on the one side swept over by the frosty air of health, and on the other filled with the pestilence which walketh in darkness! To make these plans and arrangements required skill, sagacity, labor, and experience. The duties, services, and knowledge acquired in his previous life, amply qualified General Scott for this duty; and that he performed it well, is now universally acknowledged by the people and the government.

Congress had declared that "war existed" on the 13th of May. The armies were then in conflict on the Rio Grande, and it was known that the American force was much inferior in number, while their base of supply was seven hundred miles distant. Not a moment was to be lost. The plan of the campaign must be instantly formed; the volunteers must be hurried into the field; and what was another and yet greater difficulty, an army larger than the American Republic had yet raised at one time, must be supplied in the course of a few weeks, with the armament, equipment, provisions, and means of transportation necessary to maintain that army actively in the field. This was the task which now devolved on the executive officers of the government, and especially upon those of the military department.

The plan of the campaign in Mexico for the year 1846,

seems to have been arranged jointly, by consultations between the President, Secretary at War, and General Scott. What share either had in any particular plan, we have now no means of knowing. The fact of such consultations is disclosed in the correspondence of the War Department.[1]

Two days only after the declaration of Congress, the plan of the campaign had been completed—the requisitions on the governors of states determined upon—and General Scott issued to the chief of the General Staff at Washington, his memoranda relative to transportation. On his order, the immediate movements of the army depended. The following extracts are taken from the "Memoranda."[2]

"An army of some twenty odd thousand men, regulars and volunteers, including the troops already in Texas, is about to be directed against Mexico, in several columns.

"For the numbers of troops, yet to be sent into Texas, the rendezvous or points of departure, and the routes of march thither, each chief of the General Staff will obtain the information needful to his particular department, from the Secretary of War, calls upon the governors of the several states, and from the Adjutant-General.

"Arms, accoutrements, ammunition, and camp equipage, must be thrown in advance upon the several rendezvous or points of departure, unless depots or arsenals

---

[1] Appendix to the Congressional Globe, 1845–6, pages 649–51, Message of the President, Letters of Scott and Marcy.

[2] Public Documents, 29th Congress, 2d Session, number 119.

should be in the routes which may be given to volunteers.

"Subsistence will also be thrown in advance upon the several rendezvous given, and as far as practicable, on the several routes thence to be given to both regulars and volunteers. Hard bread and bacon, (side-pieces or middlings,) are suggested and recommended for marches, both on account of health and comparative lightness of transportation. On many of the routes, it is supposed that beef cattle may be obtained in tolerable abundance.

"With the means of transportation by water and land, according to the several routes to be given to the troops, and on land, whether wagons or pack-mules, or both wheels and packs, the Quartermaster-General will charge himself at once, and as fast as the necessary data can be settled or known.

"For marches by land, a *projet* for the means of transportation, by company, battalion, or regiment, according to route, is requested, as a general plan. The means of transportation on and beyond the Rio Grande—using for the latter purpose those which may accompany the troops—will require a particular study; but boats for transporting supplies on that river, should be early provided—assuming the depth of water to a certain height (up the river) at three or three and a half feet, and to another distance, higher up, at two and a half feet."

This "Memoranda" immediately set the Staff officers and the subordinates in motion, and notwithstanding the government had provided nothing previously for the extraordinary emergencies of war,—yet so well skilled and judicious were the officers of the Staff of the army, that it may be regarded as one of the remarkable features of the war—that twenty thousand men could be put in motion, fed, equipped, and marched with so much rapidity and effect over thousands of miles, for the most part of barren territory.[1] These "Memoranda" of Scott were dated the 15th of May, and on the 1st of August, all the foot regiments of the volunteer army had been mustered into service, marched several thousand miles, and assembled on the Rio Grande.[2]

The views of General Scott at this time, as to the number of the army, and the service it was required to perform, in order to conquer a peace, were fully expressed in his letter to Secretary Marcy, dated the 21st of May.[3] In that document he says, and it was admitted by the President, that a "special army of some thirty thousand regulars and twelve months' volunteers," would be necessary to march against Mexico;[4] and that such an army (especially the *horse regiments*) could not be assembled and ready for service much before the 1st of September; that in the mean time, (from June to September,) the rainy season occurred, and would unfit the horses in that country for active service; and that finally, to pro-

---

[1] The extensive correspondence of the Quartermaster-General's department proves, that much was due to the energies of General Jesup, Colonels Hunt and Cross, Majors Whiting and Tompkins, and other officers of the service.

[2] Public Document 119, 2d Session of 29th Congress; Tavlor's Letter of the 30th July, 1846.

[3] Appendix to Congressional Globe, 1845–6, page 650.

[4] It will be observed here, that the *thirty thousand effective men* required by Scott, were never in service at one time during the campaign of 1846. The regulars were less than 7000, and the twenty-four regiments of volunteers made but 18,000—in all 25,000.

duce a peace by the operations of war,—*regular*, *incessant*, *forward movements* were necessary. Subsequent events proved, that each and all these positions were strictly correct. The army was not ready for a march against Mexico till the first of September; and because it was not kept up to the *full amount of effective men* required, (for it was rapidly diminished by sickness,) it could not make *incessant*, *forward movements*, and thus it failed of obtaining those ends, of which its energy and victories were fully worthy. In no part of the war with Mexico, was more sagacity, correct information, and sound judgment exhibited, than in the correspondence of General Scott with the War Department, and the chiefs of the army, in May and June, 1846.

In the mean time, an unpleasant controversy, or rather misunderstanding occurred between General Scott, Secretary Marcy, and President Polk. The effect of this misunderstanding, was to deprive the army for a time, of the experience and services of General Scott in the field, and throw a most undeserved ridicule on his name, —as disgraceful to those who, for political purposes, were engaged in its dissemination, as it was entirely foreign to any part of the public business, or any conduct of its distinguished subject.

On the 20th of May, Mr. Dix, a senator from the state of New York, and an active friend of the President, had advocated a bill before the Senate, which proposed to authorize the appointment of two additional major-generals, giving the President power also to assign them their command and relative rank. The effect of this measure, if adopted, would give the President the power of appointing, by law, some new or junior, or merely political general, over the head of Scott. That this proposition, coming from the political friends of the President, should excite the sensibilities of Scott, with the idea that he was to be supplanted in the command of the army, was most natural. That such an idea was not unjust to the President or his friends in Congress, was sufficiently shown by subsequent events, when the attempt was openly made and nearly succeeded,[1] to appoint a lieutenant-general to the command of the American army.

About the same time—although but *one week* after Congress had declared that "war existed,"—Scott was informed by the Secretary of War, that *much impatience was already felt*, that he had not placed himself on the route to the Rio Grande.[2] It was under these circumstances, which candor will admit, were well calculated to irritate a sensitive mind—that Scott, in one of his communications to the Secretary of War, wrote the following passage:

"Not an advantageous step can be taken in a forward march, without the confidence that all is well behind. If insecure in that quarter, no general can put his whole heart and mind into the work to be done in front. I am therefore not a little alarmed, nay, crippled in my energies, by the knowledge of the impatience in question, and I beg to say I fear no other danger.

"My intentions have been, after making all preliminary arrangements here, to pass down the Ohio and the Mississippi, to see, or to assure myself by correspondence,

---

[1] Proceedings of the 2d Session of the 29th Congress.
[2] Scott's Letter to Marcy, May 21st, 1846.

that the volunteers, on whom we are mostly to rely in the prosecution of the existing war, are rapidly assembling for the service; to learn the probable time of their readiness to advance upon Mexico; to ascertain if their supplies of every kind are in place, or are likely to be in place in sufficient time; to hasten one and the other; to harmonize the movements of volunteers, and to modify their routes, (if necessary,) so that all, or at least a sufficient number, shall arrive at the indicated points on the Mexican frontier at the best periods, and as far as practicable about the same time. All that I have but *sketched*, I deem to be not only useful to success, but indispensable. As a soldier I make this assertion, without the fear of contradiction from any *honest* and *candid* soldier.

"Against the *ad captandum* condemnation of all other persons, whoever may be designated for the high command in question, there can be no reliance, in his absence, other than the active, candid, and steady support of his government. If I cannot have that sure basis to rest upon, it will be infinitely better for the country, (not to speak of my personal security,) that some other commander of the new army against Mexico should be selected. No matter who he may be, he shall at least be judged and supported by me, in this office and everywhere else, as I would desire, if personally in that command, to be judged myself and supported.

"My explicit meaning is, that I do not desire to place myself in the most perilous of all positions—*a fire upon my rear from Washington, and a fire in front from the Mexicans*."[1]

[1] Scott's Letter, 21st of May, 1846.—Appendix to the Congressional Globe, p. 650.

In a reply to this communication, Mr. Marcy, Secretary of War, in a letter of the 25th of May,[1] assumed that this passage referred to the President only, said that the country would feel impatient if the volunteers were to remain inactive on the Rio Grande till the 1st of September, and finally concluded by informing Scott that his services would be confined to the city of Washington, and to the preparations for the vigorous prosecution of hostilities against Mexico.[2]

The letter of Marcy, dated May 25th, General Scott did not receive till the close of the day, and it was immediately replied to. In his answer, Scott denied that he intended to charge either the President or Secretary with any unworthy motives or indirect designs. He acknowledged the courtesy and kindness of both, but explained that he meant other persons in high quarters, who might be willing enough either to misrepresent him to the President, or impair his public influence. He also asked to be ordered to the army on "the following, or any other day the President might designate."

In the commencement of his reply to Mr. Marcy, Scott had used an expression which is now memorable as an example of the ease with which the public mind may be abused, of the malignity with which partisans pursue

---

[1] Appendix to the Congressional Globe, 651.

[2] The sufficient answer to this *impatience*, and the crude ideas of war formed by Mr. Secretary Marcy, is contained in the fact—that the advance of the army, under General Worth, did not leave the valley of the Rio Grande till the 20th of August, and General Taylor could not leave Camargo till the 5th of September. From May till September nothing was done, as Scott had anticipated, but *prepare* for the coming campaign.

their objects, and of the final triumph of true greatness over all the malice and the intrigues of jealous or hostile politicians.

The expression was caught up, and repeated, and returned, in squibs and witticisms, by hostile newspapers and by doubtful friends, till, for a time, the fame of the Hero of Niagara, alike dear to his country and to martial renown, seemed obscured in the mists of folly and of prejudice. Even the justice of the country seemed about to depart, and leave to a ribald ridicule the pen of history and the decrees of government.

But such an ingratitude and so gross a malice could not endure. The same administration, which had thus coolly confined Scott to Washington, was compelled, in its necessities, to demand his services. He hurried to the Gulf of Mexico, and, in the splendid siege of Vera Cruz—the storm of Cerro Gordo—and the well-ordered and successful march to the city of the Montezumas—brushed away and obliterated forever the memory of the recent past, and silenced the voice of ridicule in the shouts of applause. The once celebrated phrase now remains only as a monument to the folly of those who used it to pervert the sense and abuse the justice of the people. It points a moral, if it does not adorn a tale.

CHAPTER IV.

Campaign on the Rio Grande continued.—Movement of the Army.—March to Monterey.—Battle of Monterey.—Armistice.—March to Saltillo.—Wool's Corps.—Tampico.—Occupation of Victoria.—Conclusion of the Campaign.—General Tayior's Despatches.—Results.

From the period at which the American army occupied Metamoras, after the battle of Resaca de la Palma, both the general government at home, and the officers of the army on the Rio Grande, were busied with preparations for an advance into the interior of Mexico. The Rio Grande was assumed as the military base-line of operations, although the real base was necessarily the Mississippi. Quartermasters and Commissariat Departments became at once very active:[1] wagons, horses, provisions, and supplies of all sorts were to be found and purchased chiefly in the valley of the Ohio; while military equipments were to be furnished from the Atlantic arsenals. More than three months were consumed in these preparations. In the mean time, the Mexican villages of Reinosa, Comargo, Mier, and Revilla surrendered, and were occupied. Comargo, a town about one hundred and eighty miles above the mouth of the Rio Grande, was the point selected as the depot of supplies. Here the various

---

[1] It is due to General Jessup—Quartermaster-general—to say, that the official correspondence proves that he was most assiduous, industrious, and successful in the performance of the very responsible duties of his office.

divisions which were to compose the particular army of General Taylor were gradually concentrated. The entire army of General Taylor consisted of about nine thousand men. A small portion was assigned to garrisons, while the main body, numbering six thousand six hundred, were destined for the march to Monterey.[1] On the 20th of August General Worth began his march for Monterey, the capital of New Leon; and on the 5th of September, the general-in-chief left Comargo, leaving that town garrisoned by about two thousand men. Worth reached Ceralvo—about

---

[1] The army was divided into three divisions, whose component parts were as follows,—as determined by General Taylor's order of September 3d, 1846, and variations subsequently made.

1st Division—Brigadier-general Twiggs.

2d Dragoons, (Captain May,) 4 companies . . .	250 men.
Ridgeley's and Webster's Batteries	110 "
1st, 3d, and 4th Regiments of Infantry, and Bragg's Battery	1,320 "
Baltimore Battalion . .	400 "
Total . .	2,080

2d Division—Brigadier-general Worth.

Duncan's and Taylor's Batteries	100 men.
5th, 7th, and 8th Regiments of Infantry	1,500 "
Blanchard's Louisiana Volunteers	80 "
Texas Rangers—2 companies	100 "
Total . .	1,780

3d Division, (Volunteers,) Major-general Butler.

1st Ohio Regiment, (Col. Mitchell)	540 men
1st Kentucky, (Col. Ormsby)	540 "
1st Tennessee, (Col. Campbell)	540 "
Mississippi Regiment, (Col. Davis)	690 "
Texas Regiment, (Col. Hays)	500 "
Total . .	2,810

Total of the army (in all) 6,670 effectives.

seventy miles—on the 25th of August, and at that point sent out reconnoitring parties, who discovered strong bodies of the enemy in front. Being reinforced, he advanced to the village of Marin, where the entire army was in a few days concentrated under the command of General Taylor.

The city of Monterey is situated in the valley of the San Juan; and in the rear, and around it, rise the mountain-ridges of the Sierra Madre. In the rear of the city, and under the ridges of hills, runs the river San Juan. On the east, or on the left of the road approaching from Marin, the river makes a turn, so as nearly to cover that flank. The road to Cardereita thence crosses the river. On the opposite side—the right, as the army approached—lay the road to Saltillo, up the valley of San Juan. In front, the road from Ceralvo and Marin entered the town. On the heights, in rear of the town and beyond the river, works were erected which commanded the valley and the approaches from the north. Above the Saltillo road was a height upon which was the Bishop's Palace, and near it other heights, all fortified. In front of the city was the Cathedral Fort, or citadel, which was regularly fortified, and about two thousand yards in front and below the Bishop's Palace. The opposite side of the city, to the left, as the Americans approached, were forts also erected, and there were barricades in the streets of the city.

Both the natural and the artificial defences of Monterey seem to have been very strong. Notwithstanding this neither the extant of the defences nor the garrison within them seem to have been known to the American army previous to its arrival in front of the city.

On the 25th of August, General Taylor writes to the

War Department[1] that he had intelligence from Monterey, by a confidential messenger, who said that there were "at Monterey not more than 2000 or 2500 regular troops, the remnant of those who fled from Metamoras, and a considerable number of the militia of the country gathered together, many of them forcibly. Some attempts had been made to fortify the city by the erection of batteries which command the approaches. He heard of no reinforcements in rear." On the 17th of September, from the camp near Morin, General Taylor writes to the War Department—"It is even doubtful whether Ampudia will attempt to hold Monterey. A few days will now determine. His regular force is small—say 3000—eked out perhaps to 6000 by volunteers, many of them forced."[2]

These statements show that the military *information* of the army, as derived from scouts, spies, out-parties, and correspondents, was very scant. The army, however, pressed forward, and on the 19th of September arrived at Walnut Springs, three miles from Monterey, having met with no more serious resistance than that of skirmishing parties of Mexican cavalry.

Monterey was then under the command of General Pedro Ampudia, and the garrison under his command consisted of about seven thousand regular troops, and two or three thousand irregulars. Notwithstanding this strong garrison, superior in numbers to the American army, General Taylor thought it possible to carry the place by storm, with the bayonet and the artillery. On the evening of the 19th a *reconnaissance* of the works in the direc-

---

[1] Document 119 of the 29th Congress, 2d Session, page 130.

[2] Document 119, page 139, 29th Congress, 2d Session

tion of the Saltillo road was ordered, and this important enterprise was ably executed by Major Mansfield of the engineer corps. A reconnaissance was also made on the east side of the town.

In the afternoon of the 20th of September, General Worth, with his division, was ordered to make a detour to the right—turn the hill of the Bishop's Palace—take a position on the Saltillo road—and, if practicable, carry the enemy's works in that quarter. This movement was executed during the evening, and the troops remained upon their arms, just beyond the range of the enemy's shot. During the night two 24-pounder howitzers and a ten-inch mortar were placed in battery against the citadel. In rear of this battery was General Butler's Division.

On the morning of the 21st the main battle came on. Twiggs' and Butler's Divisions, supported by the Light Artillery, were both ordered forward; May's Dragoons, and Wood's Texan Cavalry, were detached to the right, to the support of General Worth. A column of six hundred and fifty men, with Bragg's Artillery, was ordered to the left, to attack the lower part of the town. The point of attack was designated by Major Mansfield, who accompanied the party in its advance. The front defence here was a redoubt, into the rear of which, in spite of its fire, the column rapidly moved, and commenced its assault on the town. Here it was opposed by intrenched streets and barricaded houses. On one of these the company of Captain Backus succeeded in getting, and fired upon the redoubt. Garland's force, however, were withdrawn. It was then that General Taylor ordered up the 4th Infantry, and the Volunteer regiments from Ohio, Tennessee, and Mississippi, commanded by Colonels

BATTLE OF MONTEREY

The Americans forcing their way to the Main Plaza, Sept. 23d, 1846.

Mitchell, Campbell, and Davis. The two last regiments, with three companies of the 4th regiment, advanced against the redoubt. The last companies being in front were received with a deadly fire, which killed or disabled one-third of the men, and they were compelled to retire. The brigade of General Quitman (Tennessee and Mississippi) pushed on, and with the aid of Captain Backus's company (on the roof of a house) captured the fort, with its cannon and ammunition.

In the mean while the Ohio regiment, with General Butler and Colonel Mitchell, entered the town to the right, and advanced against the second battery, but the fire was so severe that the regiment was withdrawn; General Butler, who had advanced with it, being wounded. The guns of the first battery were turned upon the second, and Colonel Garland was again ordered forward with another column. They were compelled to pass several streets trenched and barricaded, and after another severe contest retired in good order. Up to this time, it is obvious, no important success had been obtained against the lower town. The Mexican cavalry had also made several charges, but always unsuccessfully. On the same day (the 21st) Worth's Division had advanced to the right, defeated the enemy, and carried several fortified heights. At night General Taylor ordered a large part of Twiggs' and Butler's Divisions back to Walnut Springs—a portion remaining to guard the battery in the ravine, while Garland's command held the captured redoubt on the enemy's extreme right.

At dawn of the 22d, Worth and his Division, which had bivouacked on the Saltillo road, recommenced the advance. The height above the Bishop's Palace was stormed and taken; when the Palace and the guns of both were turned upon the enemy below.

The guns of the Citadel continued, during this day, to fire upon the American positions; but General Taylor made no important movement in front. The turning of the enemy's position by Worth, and the capture of the Bishop's Palace, gave a new face to affairs. This was the key to Monterey, and General Ampudia concentrated his troops in the heart of the city. General Taylor, on the morning of the 23d, found nearly all the works in the lower part of the city abandoned. He immediately ordered General Quitman to enter the place; but here a new resistance was made. The houses were fortified, and our troops actually dug through from house to house! On the upper side of the city, Worth's Division had also gained a lodgment. The firing continued during the 23d—the Americans having possession of the greater part of the city, and the Mexicans confined, in their defence, chiefly to the Citadel and Plaza. That evening (at 9 P. M.) General Ampudia sent in propositions to General Taylor which, after some negotiation, resulted in the surrender and evacuation of Monterey. The main part of the capitulation was, that the Mexican troops should retire beyond a line formed by the Pass of Rinconada, the city of Linares, and San Fernando de Prezas; and that the forces of the United States would not advance beyond that line before the expiration of eight weeks, or until the orders or instructions of the respective governments should be received.

As this armistice has been the subject of much comment, we have thought best to insert it in full.

The following are the articles of capitulation:

ARTICLE I. As the legitimate result of the operations before this place, and the present position of the contending armies, it is agreed that the city, the fortifications, cannon, the munitions of war, and all other public property, with the undermentioned exceptions, be surrendered to the commanding general of the United States forces now at Monterey.

ART. II. That the Mexican forces be allowed to retain the following arms, to wit: the commissioned officers their side-arms, the infantry their arms and accoutrements, the cavalry their arms and accoutrements, the artillery one field battery, not to exceed six pieces, with twenty-one rounds of ammunition.

ART. III. That the Mexican armed forces retire, within seven days from this date, beyond the line formed by the pass of the Rinconada, the city of Linares, and San Fernando de Presas.

ART. IV. That the citadel of Monterey be evacuated by the Mexican, and occupied by the American forces, to-morrow morning at ten o'clock.

ART. V. To avoid collisions, and for mutual convenience, that the troops of the United States will not occupy the city until the Mexican forces have withdrawn, except for hospital and storage purposes.

ART. VI. That the forces of the United States will not advance beyond the line specified in the 2d [3d] article before the expiration of eight weeks, or until the orders or instructions of the respective governments can be received.

ART. VII. That the public property to be delivered shall be turned over and received by officers appointed by the commanding generals of the two armies.

ART. VIII. That all doubts as to the meaning of any of the preceding articles shall be solved by an equitable construction, and on principles of liberality to the retiring army.

Art. IX. That the Mexican flag, when struck at the citadel, may be saluted by its own battery.

Done at Monterey, Sept. 24, 1846.

W. J. Worth,
Brigadier-general U. S. A.

S. Pinkney Henderson,
Major-general commanding the Texan volunteers.

Jefferson Davis,
Col. Mississippi riflemen.

Manuel M. Llano,

Ortega,

T. Requena,

Pedro Ampudia.

Approved:

Z. TAYLOR,
Major-general, U. S. A. Commanding.

The Mexicans marched out with their arms, and the terms were unusually favorable to them. For this concession there were strong reasons. A change of government had just taken place in Mexico, believed to be favorable to peace, and to have reduced the citadel of Monterey would have cost the lives of many men. Besides all this, the American army had but a short supply of provisions, and were one hundred and eighty miles distant from their depot. The American loss in this battle was (killed and wounded) four hundred and eighty-eight,[1] a large portion of whom fell in the attacks of the 21st on the lower town.

The War Department did not choose to continue the armistice; but, on the 13th of October, directed General

[1] One hundred and twenty killed, and three hundred and sixty-eight wounded.

Taylor to give notice that the armistice should cease, and that each party should be at liberty to resume hostilities. In communicating this notice to General Santa Anna, then in command of the Mexican army, General Taylor took occasion to suggest the idea of an honorable peace. To this the Mexican chief replied,—"You should banish every idea of peace while a single North American, in *arms*, treads upon the territory of this republic."[1]

The following are General Taylor's reasons for the armistice, given in a letter to the Secretary of War:

"In reply to so much of the communication of the Secretary of War, dated October 13th, as relates to the reasons which induced the convention resulting in the capitulation of Monterey, I have the honor to submit the following remarks:

"The convention presents two distinct points. *First*, the permission granted the Mexican army to retire with their arms, &c. *Secondly*, the temporary cessation of hostilities for the term of eight weeks. I shall remark on these in order.

"The force with which I marched on Monterey was limited by causes beyond my control to about six thousand men. With this force, as every military man must admit, who has seen the ground, it was entirely impossible to invest Monterey so closely as to prevent the escape of the garrison. Although the main communication with the interior was in our possession, yet one route was open to the Mexicans throughout the operations, and could not be closed, as were also other minor tracks and passes through the mountains. Had we, therefore, insisted on more

---

[1] Santa Anna's letter to General Taylor, November, 1846.

rigorous terms than those granted, the result would have been the escape of the body of the Mexican force, with the destruction of its artillery and magazines, our only advantage being the capture of a few prisoners of war, at the expense of valuable lives and much damage to the city. The consideration of humanity was present to my mind during the conference which led to the convention, and outweighed in my judgment the doubtful advantages to be gained by a resumption of the attack upon the town. This conclusion has been fully confirmed by an inspection of the enemy's position and means since the surrender. It was discovered that his principal magazine, containing an immense amount of powder, was in the cathedral, completely exposed to our shells from two directions. The explosion of this mass of powder, which must have ultimately resulted from a continuance of the bombardment, would have been infinitely disastrous, involving the destruction not only of Mexican troops, but of non-com batants and even our own people, had we pressed the attack.

"In regard to the temporary cessation of hostilities, the fact that we are not at this moment, within eleven days of the termination of the period fixed by the convention, prepared to move forward in force, is a sufficient explanation of the military reasons which dictated this suspension of arms. It paralyzed the enemy during a period when, from the want of necessary means, we could not possibly move. I desire distinctly to state, and to call the attention of the authorities to the fact, that, with all diligence in breaking mules and setting up wagons, the first wagons in addition to our original train from Corpus Christi, (and but one hundred and twenty-five in number,) reached my headquarters on the same day with the secretary's communication of October 13th, viz. the 2d inst. At the date of the surrender of Monterey, our force had not more than ten days' rations, and even now, with all our endeavors, we have not more than twenty-five. THE TASK OF FIGHTING AND BEATING THE ENEMY IS AMONG THE LEAST DIFFICULT THAT WE ENCOUNTER—the great question of supplies necessarily controls all the operations in a country like this. At the date of the convention, I could not of course have foreseen that the Department would direct an important detachment from my command without consulting me, or without waiting the result of the main operation under my orders.

"I have touched the prominent military points involved in the convention of Monterey. There were other considerations which weighed with the commissioners in framing and with myself in approving the articles of the convention. In the conference with General Ampudia, I was distinctly told by him that he had invited it to spare the further effusion of blood, and because General Santa Anna had declared himself favorable to peace. I knew that our government had made propositions to that of Mexico to negotiate, and I deemed that the change of government in that country since my last instructions, fully warranted me in entertaining considerations of policy. My grand motive in moving forward with very limited supplies had been to increase the inducements of the Mexican government to negotiate for peace. Whatever may be the actual views or disposition of the Mexican rulers or of General Santa Anna, it is not unknown to the government that I had the very best reason for believing the statement of General Ampudia to be true. It was my opinion at the time of the convention, and it has not been changed, that the liberal treatment of the Mexican army and the suspension of arms, would exert none but a favor able influence in our behalf.

"The result of the entire operation has been to throw the Mexican army back more than three hundred miles to the city of San Luis Potosi, and to open the country to us as far as we choose to penetrate it up to the same point.

"It has been my purpose in this communication, not so much to defend the convention from the censure which I deeply regret to find implied in the secretary's letter, as to show that it was not adopted without cogent reasons, most of which occur of themselves to the minds of all who are acquainted with the condition of things here. To that end I beg that it may be laid before the General-in-chief and Secretary of War."

We subjoin the official report of General Taylor:

HEADQUARTERS, ARMY OF OCCUPATION,
Camp before Monterey, Sept. 22, 1846.

SIR:—I have the honor to report that the troops under my command, including the mounted volunteers from Texas, marched from Marin on the 18th, and encamped before Monterey on the 19th inst. It was immediately discovered that the enemy occupied the town in force, and had added greatly to its strength by fortifying the approaches and commanding heights. A close reconnoissance was made the same evening by the officers of engineers and topographical engineers on both flanks of the town, and it was determined, from the information procured, to occupy the Saltillo road in the rear of the town, carrying, if practicable, the several fortified eminences in that direction. The 2d division of regular troops and a portion of Col. Hays' regiment of mounted volunteers was accordingly detached under Brig. General Worth on this service, at noon on the 20th. A 10-inch mortar and two 24-pounder howitzers were placed in battery during the night, to play upon the citadel and town. At 7 o'clock these guns opened and continued a deliberate fire, which was returned. To create a still farther diversion in favor of Gen. Worth's movement, the remainder of the force, except a camp guard, was displayed around the centre and left of the town. The infantry and one battery of the 1st division made a strong demonstration on the left, and soon became so closely engaged that I moved forward the volunteer division under Major-general Butler to its support, leaving one battalion (1st Kentucky) to cover the mortar battery. A close contest then ensued, which resulted in the capture of one strong battery of four guns, which with some adjacent defences our troops now occupy. A garrison was left to hold this position, and the remainder of the force returned to camp.

In the mean time General Worth had engaged the enemy early in the morning, and defeated him with considerable loss. In the course of the day two of the batteries in rear of the town were carried by storming parties of the 2d division, and a third was carried this morning at dawn of day.—The Bishop's Palace occupied the only remaining height in rear of the town, and is completely commanded by the works already carried. Gen. Worth's division occupies the Saltillo road, and cuts off all succor or support from the interior. I must reserve a more minute report of the important operations of yesterday, until those of the different commanders are rendered, and also until a topographical sketch of the country can be prepared.

I regret to report that our successes have not been obtained without severe loss, to be attributed in a good measure to the ardor of the troops in pressing forward. No returns of killed and wounded have yet been received, nor is it known what corps of Gen. Worth's division have suffered most. In the other portion of the army, the 1st, 3d, and 4th regiments of infantry, and regiment of Tennessee volunteers, have sustained the greatest loss. The following is believed to be an accurate list of the officers killed and wounded:

KILLED.—2d infantry—Brevet 1st Lieutenant J. S. Woods, (serving with 1st infantry.) 3d infantry—Capt. L. N. Morris; Capt. G. P. Field; Brevet Major P. F. Barbour; 1st Lieut. and Adjutant D. S. Irwin; 2d Lieut. R. Hazlitt. 4th infantry—1st Lieut. and Adjutant C. Hoskins. 8th infantry—Captain McKavett. Maryland and Washington battalion volunteers—Lieut. Col. W. H. Watson.

VOLUNTEER DIVISION.—Ohio regiment—1st Lieut. M. Hett. Tennessee regiment—Captain W. B. Allen; S. M. Putnam.

WOUNDED.—Corps of Engineers—Brevet Major J. K. T. Mansfield, slightly. Corps of Topographical Engineers—Capt. W. G. Williams, (in hands of the enemy.) 1st infantry—Brevet Major J. L. Abercrombie, slightly; Capt. J. H. Lamotte, severely; 1st Lieut. J. C. Terrett, (in hands of the enemy;) 2d Lieut. R. Dilworth, severely. 3d infantry—Major W. W. Lear, severely; Capt. H. Bainbridge, slightly. 5th infantry—1st Lieut. R. H. Graham, severely. 5th infantry—1st Lieut. N. B. Rossell, slightly. 7th infantry—2d Lieut. J. H. Potter, severely. 8th infantry—2d Lieut. George Wainwright, severely.

VOLUNTEER DIVISION.—General Staff—Major-general W. O. Butler, slightly. Ohio regiment—Colonel A. M. Mitchell, slightly; Captain James George, slightly; 1st Lieut. and Adjutant A. W. Armstrong, very severely; 1st Lieut. N. Niles, severely; 1st Lieut. L. Motter, slightly. Mississippi regiment—Lieut. Col. A. M. McClung, severely; Captain R. N. Downing, slightly; 1st Lieut. H. F. Cook, slightly; 2d Lieutenant R. K. Arthur, do.

DIVISION OF TEXAS MOUNTED VOLUNTEERS.—1st regiment —Capt. R. A. Gillespie, mortally.

I need hardly add, that the conduct of our troops, both regulars and volunteers, throughout the operations, has been every thing that could be desired. The part which each corps contributed to the successes of the day will appear more fully in future reports. To Major-generals Butler and Henderson, and Brigadier-generals Twiggs and Worth, commanding divisions, I must express my obligations for the efficient support which they have rendered—particularly so to Brigadier-general Worth, whose services, from his detached position, have been most conspicuous.

I am, sir, very respectfully, your obedient servant,

Z. TAYLOR,
Major-general, U. S. A. Commanding

HEADQUARTERS, ARMY OF OCCUPATION,
Camp before Monterey, Sept. 23, 1846.

SIR:—I have the gratification to report that the Bishop's Palace was gallantly carried yesterday by the troops of the 2d division. In the course of the night the batteries below the town were, with one exception, abandoned by the enemy, and this morning were occupied by our troops. To-day the 3d infantry with the field artillery of the 1st division, the Mississippi and Tennessee regiments, and the 2d regiment of Texas riflemen, (dismounted), have been warmly engaged with the enemy in the town, and have driven him with considerable loss to the plaza and its vicinity, which is yet strongly occupied. A portion of the 2d division has also advanced into the town on the right, and holds a position there. The enemy still maintains himself in the plaza and citadel, and seems determined to make a stubborn resistance.

I am particularly gratified to report that our successes of yesterday and to-day, though disastrous to the enemy, have been achieved without material loss.

I cannot speak in too high terms of the gallantry and perseverance of our troops throughout the arduous operations of the last three days.

I am, sir, very respectfully, your obedient servant,

Z. TAYLOR,
Major-general, U. S. A. Commanding

HEADQUARTERS, ARMY OF OCCUPATION,
Camp before Monterey, Sept. 25, 1846.

SIR:—At noon on the 23d inst., while our troops were closely engaged in the lower part of the city, as reported in my last despatch, I received by a flag a communication from the governor of the state of New Leon, which is herewith enclosed, (No 1.) To this communication, I deemed it my duty to return an answer declining to allow the inhabitants to leave the city. By eleven o'clock, P. M. the 2d division, which had entered the town from the direction of the Bishop's Palace, had advanced within one square of the principal plaza, and occupied the city up to that point. The mortar had, in the mean time, been placed in battery in the cemetery, within good range of the heart of the town, and was served throughout the night with good effect.

Early in the morning of the 24th I received a flag from the town, bearing a communication from Gen. Ampudia, which I enclose, (No. 2,) and to which I returned the answer, (No. 3.) I also arranged with the bearer of the flag a cessation of fire until 12 o'clock, which hour I appointed to receive the final answer of Gen. Ampudia at Gen. Worth's headquarters. Before the appointed time, however, Gen. Ampudia had signified to Gen. Worth his desire for a personal interview with me, for the purpose of making some definite arrangement. An interview was accordingly appointed for one o'clock, and resulted in the naming of a commission to draw up articles of agreement regulating the withdrawal of the Mexican forces and a temporary cessation of hostilities.

The commissioners named by the Mexican general-in-chief were Generals Ortega and Requena, and Don Manuel M. Llano, Governor of New Leon. Those named on the American side were Gen. Worth, Gen. Henderson, governor of Texas, and Colonel Davis, of the Mississippi volunteers. The commission finally settled upon the articles, of which I enclose a copy, (No 4,) the duplicates of which (in Spanish and English) have been duly signed. Agreeably to the provisions of the 4th article, our troops have this morning occupied the citadel.

It will be seen that the terms granted the Mexican garrison are less rigorous than those first imposed. The gallant defence of the town, and the fact of a recent change of government in Mexico, believed to be favorable to the interests of peace, induced me to concur with the commission in these terms, which will, I trust, receive the approval of the government. The latter consideration also prompted the convention for a temporary cessation of hostilities. Though scarcely warranted by my instructions, yet the change of affairs since those instructions were issued seemed to warrant this course. I beg to be advised, as early as practicable, whether I have met the views of the government in these particulars.

I regret to report that Capt. Williams, Topographical Engineers, and Lieut. Terrett, 1st infantry, have died of the wounds received in the engagement of the 21st.—Capt. Gatlin, 7th infantry, was wounded (not badly) on the 23d.

I am, sir, very respectfully, your obedient servant.

Z. TAYLOR,
Major-general, U. S. A. Commanding.

In the mean time, the army had been transporting its supplies, opening its communications, and enjoying the fine fruits and climate of Monterey. November had arrived, and yet General Taylor had not received a single wagon in addition to those with which he had left Corpus Christi.[1] On the 2d of November a number arrived, and on the 8th a general order announced that Saltillo, the capital of the State of Coahuila, would be occupied by the United States troops. On the 12th, the division under General Worth took up the line of march for that point, and in a few days Saltillo was garrisoned by Worth's corps. In the mean time, a column under General Wool, which had been originally intended to occupy Chihuahua, changed its direction, by order of General Taylor, and advanced to the town of Parras; thence it soon after proceeded to join General Worth at Saltillo. At this time, the government having determined to occupy Victoria, the capital of the Province of Tamaulipas, a division of volunteers under General Patterson was moved from the lower Rio Grande in that direction; and the brigade of General Quitman, with a field battery from General Taylor's army, marched on the same place, and occupied it (Victoria) on the 29th of December without much opposition. Tampico was captured by Commodore Perry, and garrisoned by the land forces.

The campaign of the Rio Grande was now brought substantially to a close. It commenced in March, 1846, by the march of General Taylor from Corpus Christi over the *disputed territory*, (between the Nueces and the Rio Grande;) and terminated in December with the military occupation of the Provinces of New Mexico, New Leon, Coahuila, and Tamaulipas, in the Mexican republic. In this march of our armies, and in the battles they fought, the officers and soldiers of the United

[1] General Taylor's letter of November 8th, 1846.

States had signalized themselves for courage, energy, and good conduct. They shrank from no duty or danger. They failed in no enterprise or conflict. They endured, without complaint, the perils of a climate in which one-fifth of their number sank to the grave; and they bore with equal firmness the fatigues of marches without the proper means of transportation. This martial energy—this firm endurance—this unconquerable courage—this enterprise in war—and this sagacity in the perception and use of means, thus exhibited on an extensive scale and in a foreign country, developed new features in the American character—the vast *capacity* of the country for war, and the restless thirst of adventure which impelled so many to volunteer in an invasive war. This development of national energy was the only apparent advantage, which was, so far, gained by this invasion. The plan of the campaign, as determined by the War Department, though executed with great military skill by General Taylor, was necessarily *inconsequential;* for it merely caused the conquest of barren territories, at the distance of seven hundred miles from the enemy's capital, and the movement of troops from a base-line nearly as far from our country. It led to no results, nor to any valuable purpose, except that of maintaining garrisons in a barren and useless country.

INVASION OF NORTHERN MEXICO.

CHAPTER V.

Government Plan to invade Northern Mexico.—Assemblage of Troops at Fort Leavenworth.—Kearney's March to Santa Fé.—Nature of the Country.—Retreat of the Mexicans.—Arrival at Santa Fé.—Kearney's Proclamation.—Kearney departs for California.—Wool's Expedition.—Assemblage of the Troops at San Antonia.—The Object of the Expedition.—March to Monclova; to Penas.—Wool joins Worth at Saltillo. Taylor's March to Victoria.

WHILE General Taylor was crossing the Rio Grande, and directing his columns towards Central Mexico, the cabinet at Washington sent two other columns against the northern provinces, under the command, respectively, of Generals Kearney and Wool. The movements of these corps, if less important in a military point of view, were vastly more extensive in their geographical scope and relations. It was their fortune to traverse magnificent plains, perform rapid and, in modern history, unprecedented marches, and conquer to the dominion of the United States lands unmeasured and almost uninhabited.

The origin of these expeditions seems to have been an idea entertained by the administration, that the States of New Mexico,—Chihuahua, Durango, and others in the upper portion of Mexico,—stood ready to declare themselves independent, and that, by this movement, they would be at once detached from the central government. It was stated by some letter-writers, who professed acquaintance with that country, that those States were ready to form a separate and independent republic. One writer even went so far as to declare that the Mexicans themselves, in these provinces, would form an army to march against the central government! With such views, the war department organized a corps, called the Army of the West,[1] which was intended to conquer New Mexico by marching into Santa Fé. This place, though very unimportant as a town, was a point of concentration for the extensive trade which flowed through it from Chihuahua on the southwest and St. Louis on the northeast. Vast as were the plains and uninhabited regions through which this trade was carried on, it had grown, within a few years, to be one of great importance in magnitude and value. On the 16th of May, 1846, at the very time Congress recognised the existence of the war, a company of Mexican traders arrived at St. Louis, through Santa Fé, from Chihuahua, with no less than three hundred and fifty thousand dollars in specie, to expend for wares and merchandise in the United States. The annual trade from Santa Fé with St. Louis, Pittsburg, and Philadelphia, was supposed to be, in amount, from one to two millions of dollars. That trade has been cut off by the events of the war.

The forces which were to compose the Army of the West,—almost wholly of Volunteers,—commenced assembling at Fort Leavenworth early in June, 1846. Col. Kearney received his orders in May,[2] and the Missouri Volunteers were mustered into service before the end of June, and on the 30th of June the entire force had departed. The corps of Kearney was composed thus:—

[1] Lieut. Emory's Journal.

[2] Niles's Register, 70, p. 228

Colonel Price's Regiment,	-	-	800	men.
" Doniphan's "	-	-	800	"
Major Clarke's Battalion,	-	-	400	"
Sumner's Dragoons,	-	-	200	"
Mormon Battalion,	-	-	500	"
Total force,	-	-	2,700	"

A large part of this force were mounted men, accompanied, however, by a regiment of infantry, a body of artillery, and a train of wagons. The point of departure was Fort Leavenworth, on the Missouri river, and the point to be reached (Santa Fé) was one thousand miles distant. For a greater part of that distance, from the Missouri to Bent's Fort on the Arkansas, the road lay over vast plains, which had for ages been the pasturage of the buffalo, or the hunting-ground of the Indian. Short dry grass, or sometimes barren ground, with skirts of trees in the valleys of the streams, made nearly the whole landscape; while occasionally a buffalo in the distance, a prairie-wolf in the trail, or the carcass of some unfortunate horse given to the wild birds or wilder beasts, gave variety to this desolate scene. Bent's Fort, the lonely plantation of Mr. Bonny, and the meeting of a party of traders, were the only signs of civilization. Beyond the Arkansas, and on the head-waters of the Cimarou and Canadian rivers, the country grows mountainous, and the pine, spruce, and other evergreens begin to give verdure to the summits. In passing a dividing ridge of these streams, the army was charmed with one of those splendid mountain-scenes which frequently occur in extraordinary sublimity on the spurs of the Cordilleras. It was the passage of the Raton, a branch of the great Aztec mountains, which made the eastern ridge of the Rio Grande. By barometrical observations, the summit was 7000 feet in height. Towards the northwest, the lofty top of Pike's peak was visible, and around it other peaks whose white limestone cliffs looked like snow-banks in the sunbeams. Above, the rocky tops of the Raton rose in perpendicular ledges, and assumed the form of castles in the air, while all around nature exhibited a wide landscape of wild, various, and beautiful appearances.[1]

Such scenery in this desolate region was, however, uncommon. The weary soldier had to pass many a day's journey without water for his thirst, or grass for his beast. For twenty miles, in some cases, no spring was to be found. An eye-witness relates, that in going from the valley of the Canadian, a traveller might pass a good day's journey without meeting with either wood, water, or grass. Such was the unfruitful and uninviting country through which it was deemed necessary to march an army of the United States for the conquest of Mexico!

On the 3d of August Kearney left Bent's Fort on the Arkansas, and in ten days approached the Mexican settlements. Governor Armijo had previously received intimations of his approach, and, according to the accounts of traders, had gathered from the adjacent provinces a formidable force. On the 16th of August he marched out of Santa Fé, and took post at a remarkably strong position. It was an eminence commanding a defile of not more than forty feet in width, through which lay the road to Santa Fé. Such a position, with good troops, might be deemed almost impregnable. Such was not the result.

---

[1] Lt. Emory's Journal.—Niles's Register, 71, p. 136

Governor Armijo held a council of war. His second in command, and other officers, advised him against defence. The advice was followed. The Mexican army retreated, and Armijo left the province for Chihuahua with a hundred dragoons. In the mean while Kearney had arrived at San Miguel, and assured the alarmed alcaldes, padres, and other influential persons, that he should protect them in their persons, property, religion, and liberty. On the 18th of August he passed through the same defile the Mexicans had just left undefended, and in a few hours entered Santa Fé. Marching with his troops to the palace, or governor's house, Kearney hoisted the standard of the Union, and firing a salute of cannon said, "There, my guns proclaim that the flag of the United States floats over the capital."[1] On the next day (Aug. 19th) the general addressed the people, proclaimed that the American army came to establish free government, offered the people protection, *and absolved them from their allegiance to their former government!*

Thus in about fifty days an army (which had been collected in less than a month) had traversed nearly a thousand miles of uninhabited wastes, and proclaimed the conquest of New Mexico, containing a surface of eighty thousand square miles, though inhabited by only eighty thousand people. Considered as a march for both infantry and artillery, this was a remarkable achievement. The result was, however, as unsatisfactory to the performers as it was fruitless of military results. Santa Fé offered neither the splendor nor pleasures of a rich and voluptuous city. It was a poor town, badly built, inhabited by a half-

[1] Journal of an officer.—Niles, 71, p. 83.

civilized people, in the midst of a barren and uninhabited country. One of the travellers in this expedition thus writes :—" This is the most miserable country I have ever seen. The houses the people live in are built of mud, one story high, and have no flooring. They sleep on the ground, and have neither beds, tables, nor chairs."[1]

This account probably refers to the mass of the people, and not the richer class. The mud spoken of is unburnt brick. When the American officers visited the church, they found it without seats, except one long bench for the chief men.[2]

A few villages and well-cultivated fields lay within a few miles of Santa Fé, and the banks of the Rio Grande below occasionally presented a town. But, for the most part, a country without resources, and a people without civilization, were the tempting prospect which New Mexico offered to her Anglo-Saxon invaders.

On the 31st of August, two weeks after his arrival at Santa Fé, Kearney organized an expedition of nine hundred men to scour the banks of the Rio Grande below. This work was done without a combat, and without any other result than the march.

In the mean while General Kearney, acting, as he declared, by authority and under the instructions of the executive administration of the United States, assumed to direct the civil affairs of New Mexico, and even to declare the assent of the American nation to the incorporation of New Mexico with the United States, and to absolve its citizens from all allegiance to the Mexican government ![3]

---

[1] Niles, 71, p. 80. [2] Diary of an officer, pp. 91, 92 ;—of Niles 71.

[3] Kearney's Proclamation may be found in the appendix to Young's History of Mexico.

These occurrences are so remarkable in American constitutional history, that they have attracted no small attention from the gravest and most intelligent minds. The first in this series of novel proceedings in military history took place at the town of San Miguel, a few miles from Santa Fé, on the 16th of August. Summoning the alcalde and the people of the village into his presence, the commander of the American army informed them that they were absolved from all allegiance to the Mexican government, and that the alcalde must swear allegiance to the United States! After some demur, that officer complied, on condition that his religion was protected. The oath was then administered in this form:—"You swear that you will bear true allegiance to the government of the United States of America, and that you will defend her against all her enemies and opposers, in the name of the Father, Son, and Holy Ghost. Amen."

On the 22d of August, in Santa Fé, General Kearney issued a proclamation, entitled, "From the Army of the West to the Inhabitants of New Mexico."[1] This proclamation was so extraordinary, that some paragraphs may be noted for the very novel ideas they brought before the minds of the American people. In this he first announces his intention to hold the department, with its "original boundaries, (on both sides the Del Norte,) as a part of the United States, and under the name of the Territory of New Mexico."

He next informs the people that "it is the wish and intention of the United States to provide for New Mexico a free government, with the least possible delay, similar

---

[1] Idem.

to those in the United States; and the people of New Mexico will then be called upon to exercise the rights of freemen in electing their own representatives to the territorial legislature."

The most extraordinary passage of this proclamation is the following:—

"The undersigned hereby absolves all persons residing within the boundary of New Mexico from further allegiance to the republic of Mexico, and hereby claims them as citizens of the United States. Those who remain quiet and peaceable will be considered as good citizens, and receive protection; those who are found in arms, or instigating others against the United States, will be considered as traitors, and treated accordingly."

Neither the Constitution of the United States nor the people by act of Congress, or by vote, had provided any means or expressed any wish for the annexation of New Mexico. The laws of nations were equally silent as to any mode by which the allegiance of a citizen can be absolved by any act of a military commander. Nor had the laws of the United States provided any way by which a foreign citizen could become a citizen of the United States, except by naturalization. The conquest of New Mexico has opened, therefore, a new field for legal investigation, as well as a new chapter in constitutional history.

One month after these proceedings, (on the 25th of September,) when the sparse population of that country seemed quiet, and the army found no other motives for activity than such as the amusements of Santa Fé afforded, General Kearney left that place, and with four hundred dragoons departed for California. He took the old Coppermine route, down the Rio Grande to Sorotto, and thence to the Pacific. On the 20th of October, three hundred miles west of Santa Fé, he was informed by a returning party that Fremont had already taken possession of California. He then sent Major Sumner back with the largest part of the dragoons, and taking only one hundred with himself, pursued, with this small force, the daring enterprise of crossing the deserts and mountains of Western America in the cold season.

Thus was effected the conquest of the province of New Mexico by the troops of the United States: bloodless in its achievement, and fruitless of any immediate results, but illustrating the energy of the American people in the collection and movement of troops, and the celerity with which the great western plains may be traversed by military forces.

At the same time that the cabinet at Washington formed the plan of moving a column on Santa Fé, they also organized another against the Central States of Mexico. This was called the "Army of the Centre," and was directed to march on Chihuahua, the capital of the province of that name, and supposed to be the centre of much of the Mexican strength and wealth. The object of this expedition, like that of Kearney, was to detach the northern and northwestern from the central government of Mexico, and thus induce that government to make peace by cutting off its resources.

The "Army of the Centre" was placed under the command of Brigadier-general John E. Wool, one of the small but gallant band who, by their heroic stand upon the heights of Queenstown, had, even in defeat, shed lustre upon the American arms, and acquired a lasting distinction for themselves. This army was thus composed :—

OFFICERS OF THE STAFF.

General John E. Wool—Commander.
Colonel Churchill—Inspector-general.
Captain Cross—Quartermaster.
Captain W. D. Fraser—Engineer.

REGULAR TROOPS.

5 companies U. S. Dragoons—Col. Harney,	300	men.
1 company Artillery—Captain Washington, -	100	"
2 companies U. S. 6th Infantry—Capt. Bonneville, - - - - - -	100	"

VOLUNTEERS.

1 regiment of Arkansas Cavalry—Col. Yell, -	750	"
2 regiments of Illinois Infantry—Col. Hardin,	1,600	"
1 company Kentucky Cavalry—Capt. Williams, - - - - - - -	90	"
Total forces - -	2,940	"

These troops were directed by the War Department to assemble at Antonio de Bexar, on the river Antonio, and thence proceed to Chihuahua by Presidio Rio Grande. At the time the orders for their assembling were given, these troops were in different parts of the United States, remote from each other and remote from the point of rendezvous. Their marches, and the celerity and exactness of their movement and assembling, are among the remarkable incidents of the war with Mexico. The Illinois regiments proceeded by water, in steamboats, down the Mississippi, and by the Gulf of Mexico to Lavaca on Matagorda Bay. Here they commenced their march to San Antonio.

The Illinois regiments arrived at Pallida Creek, twelve miles from Lavaca, on the 7th of August, and on the 11th commenced their march to Antonio de Bexar. The route to Antonio was through a dry prairie, crossing the head-streams of the Antonio and the river Guadaloupe, along whose banks alone the thirsty and tired soldier might expect to find water and shade. A writer, who was a member of the Illinois troops, thus speaks of this tedious march: "Heat—heat—heat; rain—rain—rain; mud—mud—mud, intermingled with spots of sand and gravel, form the principal features of the route from Levacca to San Antonio. Loaded wagons of course move slowly over the roads, and our troops were moreover scourged on the route by the mumps and the measles."[1]

These regiments arrived at Antonio de Bexar (the place of rendezvous) before the 1st of September: so did all the corps who were to assemble there. The movement of these bodies was quite remarkable. Captain Washington with the regular artillery had gone from Carlisle Barracks, Pennsylvania, two thousand miles, and arrived on the 31st of August. Major Bonneville made eight hundred miles in six weeks with the infantry, and arrived on the 27th of August. Colonel Yell, with the Arkansas cavalry, arrived from Washington, Arkansas, on the 28th. Thus, after these immense marches, did the troops of Wool's army concentrate, with remarkable precision, at the place of rendezvous, prepared to march into the territories of Mexico.

The extent of these marches and the extreme barrenness of the country through which the route lay, after

---

[1] "Rondenac" to the National Intelligencer.—Niles's Register, 71, p. 90.

leaving the Mississippi, made this expedition one of great expense and difficulty in its transportation. The real *base-line* upon which an army operates, is that which contains the *depots of subsistence.* In this instance, as throughout the war with Mexico, those depots were on the Mississippi river and the cities of the Atlantic coast. The same writer whom we have quoted says, "Forage and subsistence for the entire army are derived from New York, Baltimore, and New Orleans. The transportation by water, therefore, exceeds thousands of miles, while the total of land transportation may be found among the hundreds. The bare cost of bringing a bushel of corn from Lavaca to this place (Antonio) is $1.20, and other supplies in proportion." This fact at once illustrates the expense which invariably attends the march of an army through barren countries.

Assembled at Antonio, the army was now ready to commence its march against Chihuahua. But with what *object?* The declared object was to aid in establishing the independence of the northern States, and thus act against the central government of Mexico. But was this a probable result? The same writer already quoted pertinently asks, "Are the people of the United States pursuing a war of conquest, of propagandism, or of necessity? Do they hope to convert provinces to their political faith by sending forth among them an armed soldiery to quicken their conclusions, and give energy to their admiration? Are they desirous, by a grand military display, to exhibit to the Mexicans the vast superiority of their free institutions over their more humble neighbors? Do they hope, by a series of marches and counter-marches, by glittering bayonets and flashing sabres, by waving banners and the clangor of martial music, to intimidate a people too proud to work and almost too poor to be pitied? Do they wish, by a lavish expenditure of public funds, to bribe a whole nation to throw off its allegiance? Are we to plant our flags at Presidio Rio Grande,—beat our drums at San Fernando, Santa Rosa, and Monclova,—carry the tramp of our war-steeds through Baria, Saledo, San Carlos, and Chericotti, and let the thunders of our artillery roll within the walls of Chihuahua merely to demonstrate the military prowess of a great nation, and the inherent energies of a free people? So far as can be seen or known at present, these are the sole objects of the expedition, conceived in folly, and which has already cost millions of the national treasury, although it has not yet passed the threshold."[1]

The language of this writer, although strong, was prophetic. The expedition pursued the route, and was attended with no other results than those which these questions indicate. Early in September, the division of Wool took up its line of march from San Antonio for the Presidio Rio Grande, passing, in most of the distance, over the same dry and uninviting plains as those which the Illinois Regiments had passed from Lavaca to San Antonio. Crossing the Rio Grande at the Presidio, General Wool and his corps pushed on by long and wearisome marches to the village of Santa Rosa. Here it was discovered that the geographical knowledge of the War Department was by no means equal to its martial energies Looking to the west for the road to Chihuahua the army beheld in front the lofty mountain-range of the Sierra

[1] Letter of "Rondenac" to the National Intelligencer.

Gorda, lifting their summits four thousand feet above the level of the plains! The officer of Topographical Engineers in vain looks for a single defile through which the army may pass to the west.[1] It is compelled to turn south towards Saltillo. On the 29th of October, six weeks after leaving the Rio Grande, it reaches Monclova, one of the principal towns of Coahuila. Here the troops were received in a friendly manner, the Prefect contenting himself simply with a protest against the occupation of the Mexican country. For a month the army continued to enjoy the Mexican hospitalities as if no hostilities interrupted the harmony of the respective nations. The soldiers of Wool's corps acted as the armed watchmen of Coahuila. The robber and the savage alike fled from the drum-beat of the guard and the echoes of the bugle. The discipline of the army was equal to its energy; and the inhabitants around slept peacefully while the conquering invader unfurled his flag along the base of the Sierra Gorda.

At length General Wool, writing to General Taylor, inquired—"What is to be gained by going to Chihuahua?" General Taylor, then about to occupy the state of Tamaulipas by marching to Victoria, replied, that he (Wool) should abandon the expedition to Chihuahua, and advance with his column to Parras, a place still further to the south, and not very distant from Saltillo. Here the army remained for a short time, till, in the month of December, it joined the division of Worth, in the town of Saltillo. The object of the enterprise,—the conquest of Chihuahua,

---

[1] Report of Captain Hughes, of the Topographical Corps, February 1847.

—had previously been abandoned ; but this division, which had so far been employed only in marches, was soon to appear, under the able Wool and the veteran Taylor, victorious on the bloody and memorable field of Buena Vista.[1]

The march of Wool, like that of Kearney, was remarkable for the steadiness and celerity with which new troops, of all the different arms, traversed vast deserts uninhabited, and unsupplied, except by provisions brought from the interior of the United States. By the route pursued it was seven hundred miles from San Antonio de Bexar to Saltillo, and this distance, deducting the period at Monclova and Parras, was performed in about six weeks.

General Wool arrived just in time at Saltillo to meet the intentions of General Taylor, and prepare for the events which followed.

The commander on the Rio Grande had proceeded with a large body of troops to meet another corps, under General Patterson, marching from Matamoras to occupy Victoria, the capital of the state of Tamaulipas. At Montemorlos, sixty-eight miles from Monterey, Taylor was informed that Santa Anna was about to move on Saltillo, with a view to attack Worth. This recalled him, with the regulars, to Monterey. Generals Patterson and Quit man proceeded to Victoria, and ultimately to Tampico, where they made a portion of the army of Scott, and took part in the brilliant and successful siege and capture of Vera Cruz.

---

[1] The Illinois Regiments, the Arkansas Regiment, and Washington's Artillery, were in the battle of Buena Vista, and constituted one-third of Taylor's army.

CHAPTER VI.

Expedition of Captain Fremont.—Arrives at Monterey, California.—Suspicions of Governor de Castro.—Fremont takes position.—Returns by Oregon.—Returns again to Monterey.—Is threatened by De Castro.—Declares War.—Capture of Mexicans.—Sails from Monterey to Diego.—Capture of the City of Angels.—Conquest of California.—Object of the Government.—Marcy's Letter to Stevenson.—Marcy's Orders to Kearney.—Scott's Orders.—Insurrection in New Mexico.—Murder of Bent.—Battle of Canada.—Battle of Pueblo de Taos.—Insurrection in California.—March of Doniphan.—Battle of Brozitos.—Capture of El Paso.—Battle of Sacramento.—Capture of Chihuahua.—March to Saltillo.—Arrival at New Orleans.—March of Gilpin to the Rocky Mountains.

In the autumn of 1845, Captain Fremont, of the Topographical Corps of Engineers, set out with an armed party of men, prepared for hunting and Indian warfare, to cross the mountains and penetrate the interior of California. This officer had been greatly distinguished in a previous expedition for bold enterprise, scientific attainments, and interesting researches amidst the wilderness of Rocky Mountains. The ostensible object of his present journey was to seek a new route to Oregon, further south than the one heretofore travelled by emigrants, and to seek also scientific discoveries amidst these unknown and undescribed regions of the west. His well-known love of science, and his hitherto scrupulous conduct, afford strong presumption that such was the real purpose of his mission.

He pursued his journey, undisturbed by any extraordinary events, till, on the 29th of January, 1846, he arrived in the neighborhood of Monterey, California. To avoid suspicion, or collision, he left his party about one hundred miles from Monterey, and proceeded alone to that place to explain the object of his visit. Here he proceeded to the house of the American consul, (Mr. Larkin,) and then called upon the governor, De Castro. The governor complained that he (Fremont) was bringing an armed force into the province with hostile views. To this Captain Fremont replied, that he was not even an officer of the line, but belonged to the Topographical Corps, and that his object was to survey a new route to Oregon in a more southerly direction, his visit being peaceful, and that he desired to winter in the valley of the San Joaquin. To this the governor assented. Captain Fremont then returned and brought his men nearer to the town, when he was informed that the governor was raising troops to attack him, and warned by Mr. Larkin (the consul) of his danger. Thus warned, he took post, with his small party of sixty men, on the summit of the *Sierra*, at a point about thirty miles from Monterey, and overlooking that town. Here, in the clear sky of the Pacific, and on this height, he could observe De Castro preparing his men to march upon the American camp. Here he hoisted the flag of the United States, and informed the Mexican that he would defend the post to the last. His intention was, if attacked and defeated, there to die with his companions on the spot where they had hoisted the flag, and leave to their country to avenge their death and vindicate their conduct.[1] This fate was fortunately avoid-

[1] Benton's Letter to the President, published in the "Union," November 9th, 1846.

ed. De Castro marched out, but did not attack them. Fremont, finding himself not attacked, marched out of his position on the 10th of March, by the valley of San Joaquin, and commenced his march, by slow degrees, towards Oregon. On the following morning De Castro took possession of his camp, and finding some old vessels or other camp luggage, boasted of the flight of the Americans!

On the 1st of April Fremont had reached lat. 40° in the valley of the Sacramento. On the 14th of May he was on the direct route to Oregon. On the 15th he arrived at the Great Tlamath Lake. Here he found the mountains of the Sierra Nevada in front covered with snow, and himself and party surrounded by hostile Indians. In this condition of affairs he determined to return back by the river Sacramento. On his arrival at the Bay of Francisco, he learns that Governor de Castro is at Zanona, on the opposite side, preparing an expedition against the American settlers. Under all the circumstances of the case he determined, on the 6th day of June, to overturn, if possible, the Mexican government in California. At that time the war with Mexico actually existed, and two battles had been fought on the Rio Grande; but with this fact Captain Fremont was not acquainted. He formed his judgment on the circumstances around him, and not on any of the previous events connected with military operations.[1]

A party of De Castro's men having crossed the Bay, Fremont's men captured fourteen, with two hundred mules. On the 1st of June he surprised and took the

---

[1] Colonel Benton's Letter to the President

military post at Zanona. Colonel Vallejo and several officers were taken, with nine cannon, and two hundred and fifty stand of arms. From this he proceeded to the Rio de los Americanos for assistance. There he heard that De Castro was about to attack his little garrison of only fourteen men, at Zanona. On the 23d of June he started with ninety mounted riflemen to their aid. Riding night and day he arrived on the 25th, a distance of eighty miles. De Castro's vanguard of seventy men was attacked and defeated by twenty Americans. About this time two Americans were taken by Torre, the commander of the Mexican party, and cut to pieces. In return, Fremont took and shot three of Torre's men.

On the 4th of July Fremont assembled the Americans in that neighborhood at Zanona, and after making a speech, he and his companions declared the Independence of California. A few days after this news came from Commodore Sloat, that the American flag was hoisted at Monterey. Fremont then set out with one hundred and sixty riflemen in pursuit of De Castro, who was retreating with four hundred men. From this he is recalled by Commodore Sloat. On his return to Monterey he found Stockton in command, who was preparing a new expedition by water. By sailing down the coast he thought he might cut off De Castro's retreat, who was moving southwardly to the lower posts.[1] On the 26th of July Fremont sailed in the sloop-of-war Cyane, with one hundred and sixty riflemen and seventy marines, the object being the port of San Diego, which it was supposed would be reached in time to cut off De Castro.

---

[1] Colonel Benton's Letter.

At this time Governor de Castro was encamped at Mera, three miles from Ciudad de los Angelos. In a few days after the departure of Fremont, Stockton sailed in the frigate Congress for the position of De Castro. When the latter heard of the approach of the American forces, he broke up his camp and proceeded to Mexico, while his officers and men were scattered in different directions. On the 13th of August, 1846, Stockton being joined by Captain (now Colonel) Fremont, with Mr. Larkin, late American consul, entered the City of Angels, the capital of the Californias.[1] Thus was completed, in a brief campaign, and with scarcely any bloodshed, the conquest of the Californias.

On the coast, the squadron under Commodore Sloat had taken the initial, and on the 6th of July, 1846, had hoisted the flag of the United States at Monterey. On the 22d of July, Commodore Stockton assumed the command of the naval forces, and he, with Fremont, completed, as we have seen, the overturn of the Mexican government in California. General Kearney did not arrive from his overland journey till these transactions were completed. Since then, controversies have arisen between the distinguished commanders on that station—Fremont and Kearney—in relation to their respective duties and commands. The events in which they were engaged have become memorable from their connection with the first footsteps and conquering march of that great nation which claims from destiny the dominion of the North American continent. In the traceway of these wild wilderness paths, some historian of after times may discover the steps by

---

[1] Niles's Register, 71, p. 185.

which a nation, ascended to imperial grandeur and liberty, pursued the stream of civilization round the earth.

The object of the American government, so far as the President can control its operations, is discovered in the instructions to its officers. While disclaiming conquest as the motive or object of the war, the executive of the United States furnished recorded proof that *permanent conquest* was intended to be its result. In the summer of 1846, a regiment of volunteers was raised in the city of New York, commanded by Colonel J. D. Stevenson. The object of this regiment was for some time unknown to the public. It was at length embarked for California. In the correspondence of the War Department subsequently published, a letter from the Secretary (Marcy) disclosed the intentions of the President. Speaking of the composition of this regiment, the Secretary says:—"The President expects, and indeed requires, that great care should be taken to have it composed of suitable persons—I mean of good habits; as far as practicable of various pursuits, *and such as would be likely to remain*, at the end of the war, either in Oregon or *in any other territory in that region of the globe which may then be a part of the United States*."[1] This regiment, then, were to act as pioneers in the work of conquest and colonization.

The directions given by Secretary Marcy to General Kearney, in forming the new government, assimilate themselves to this purpose. In his letter of the 3d June, 1846, he says—"You will establish *temporary civil governments* therein, abolishing all arbitrary restrictions that may

[1] Appendix to the Congressional Globe, 1845-6, p. 809

exist, so far as it can be done with safety." You may "continue existing officers, if they will *take the oath of allegiance* to the United States."—"Assure them it is the wish and *design of the United States to provide for them a free government.*"—"They will then be *called upon* to exercise the rights of freemen."[1]

At this time Mexico was a free country, so far as a written republican Constitution could make her so. To offer the people of that country freedom, then, could have no possible meaning, unless it was meant to bring it within the limits of the peculiar government of the United States. Much less could any other construction be put upon the phrase—"called upon to exercise the rights of freemen."

The oath of allegiance, too, which by the laws of nations could not be deprived of its legal virtue by any action of a foreign nation, and, by the Constitution of the United States, could not be made void in this country, except by an act of naturalization, was thus, by the order of a President, to be made void by a compulsory oath to the United States! The novelty of such a doctrine, if not its utter contempt of the civil law of this country and the public law of nations, attracted the attention of grave statesmen and of earnest patriots. It was sought, by the friends of the President, to explain the meaning of these documents, so that they might not appear in opposition to the theory and Constitution of American government; but, however explained, these orders and proclamations yet remain among the most extraordinary movements of an extraordinary war.[2]

---

[1] Marcy's Letter, 3d June, 1846.

[2] General Scott, in his official orders, while complying with the gen-

The conquest of New Mexico, which we have seen completed under General Kearney, though apparently bloodless, was yet to be attended by conflicts, if less sanguinary, yet more interesting than the common events of war. On the 19th of January, 1847, a violent and totally unexpected insurrection against the American authorities took place at Taos, in New Mexico. The origin and progress of this outbreak appears, by evidence subsequently given, to have been this:—In pursuance of the principles stated in the proclamations before referred to, and of orders expressly given by the President, Kearney had proceeded to organize a *civil government.* He had appointed a governor, sheriff, district attorney, and other functionaries; as if the general of an army, in the service of the United States, *could* have any other than military authority, or become by any means the source of a civil authority which, in the very nation he represented, could be conferred only through the laws. These civil functionaries, thus appointed, went quietly to work, as if they were in one of the States of the American Union: unconscious that the passions of a hostile people, the jealousy of displaced officers, or the violation

---

eral direction of the President to *occupy* the country, seems to have discreetly avoided *in his language* the absurdity involved in these proclamations, and in the order of Marcy on which they were founded. In Scott's Order to Kearney, dated November 3d, 1846, he says:—"You will erect and garrison durable defences for *holding* the bays of Monterey and San Francisco, together with such other important points in the same province as you may deem it necessary to *occupy*."—"You will *not*, however, formally *declare the province to be annexed.* Permanent incorporation of the territory must *depend on the government of the United States.*" In this language General Scott avoids the absurdities of the proclamation, and recognises the fundamental distinction between the orders of the President and the *legislation of Congress.*

of national usages, could arouse the indignation of the invaded people, or expose them to more than common dangers! They were mistaken in fact, as they were incautious in conduct. The displaced officers and the national pride occasioned a conspiracy to overthrow the American power in New Mexico. It appears from testimony that Thomas Cortez, Diego Archillette, Pino, Armijo, and others formed a plan for a general insurrection and overthrow of the Americans on Christmas night. This failed, or rather, was postponed. On the 15th of January, however, a tragedy occurred which startled the Americans, both in New Mexico and in the United States. On that night, Governor Charles Bent, with Elliott the sheriff, and twenty-three others, were murdered in the town of San Fernando de Taos. Seven others were killed at Turley's, eight miles from Taos, in the valley of the Moro.[1] In a short time the insurrection became general, and Col. Sterling Price, who commanded the troops at Santa Fé, learned that a strong body of Mexicans and Indians were advancing against the place. Mustering nearly four hundred troops—cavalry, infantry, and artillery—he marched out to meet them on the 23d of January. He found them posted, in a strong position, on the heights and in houses below, in front of the village of Covoda. The battle commenced with a cannonade and general firing, which lasted for an hour and a half. Colonel Price then ordered a general discharge upon the houses and lines of the enemy. They were soon dispersed in every direction.[2] The Mexican force engaged was supposed to be fifteen hundred

---

[1] Lt. Abert's Letter of February 20th, in the Union.

[2] Colonel Price's Despatch, 15th February, 1847.

men. Their loss was thirty-six. That of the Americans two killed and six wounded.

On the 27th of January Colonel Price marched to Luceros, on the Rio Grande, and on the 29th to La Joya, a strong pass, situated in a *canon*, or deep pass of the mountains, where the men could scarcely move abreast. Along the slopes of the mountains the enemy were posted, and there they were attacked by a detachment under Captain Burgwin of one hundred and eighty men, who, after a short conflict, dislodged them, with the loss to the Mexicans of twenty killed and sixty wounded.[1] On the 1st of February the main body of the forces, under Colonel Price, reached the top of the Taos mountain, which was covered with snow two feet deep. On the 2d they quartered at Rio Chiciti. On the 3d they entered the town of Don Fernando de Taos, which was the scene of the massacre of Governor Bent and party. The Mexican village was abandoned by the enemy, who had taken post at the Indian town of Pueblo de Taos. This was a strongly-fortified post. The key to the position was a large church, and two large buildings ascending in a pyramidal form, six or seven stories high, and pierced with embrasures for rifles. Around these was a wall, and within them the enemy had taken post. The Americans brought up a six-pounder and a howitzer, with which they battered the church and walls for two hours; but their ammunition-wagons not having come up, they retreated to Fernando.

On the morning of the 4th, at nine A. M., the Americans again advanced, determined to take the place. The six-pounder and two howitzers, commanded by Lieutenant

[1] Colonel Price's Despatch, 15th February, 1847.

Dyer, of the Ordnance, were brought to bear against the church on one side, and two howitzers on another side. After battering for two hours a charge was made by Captain Burgwin, of the Dragoons, with two companies in one line, and Captain Angrecy, with three companies in another line.[1] In this assault Captain Burgwin, a lieutenant of volunteers, and several dragoons were killed. The church walls were still unpenetrated by the Artillery. Ladders were made, and a small hole cut with axes; through that, fire was thrown into the church. A new assault was made upon the church door, which failed, with loss.[2] The six-pounder was then run up, at half-past three P. M., within sixty yards, and a breach made large enough to admit four men abreast. A storming party then entered the church, which was found full of smoke. The enemy still occupied the two large buildings; but early next morning, the aged men and women, bearing their children, images, and crosses, came out to meet the army, begging for mercy. The request was granted. In this battle the Americans were about four hundred and fifty; the Mexicans about six hundred. The American loss was fifty-four killed and wounded; that of the Mexicans one hundred and fifty-two killed and many wounded. Taken, as a whole, the short campaign of Colonel Price, with Captain Burgwin and others, from the 20th of January to the 5th of February, 1847, was one of the best exhibitions of military gallantry which has occurred in the minor parts of the war. Marching in midwinter over snow-covered ground, they three times

[1] Letter of Lieutenant A. B. Dyer.

[2] Colonel Price's Report, 15th February, 1847.

engaged the enemy; and in the last conflict, stormed and carried a very strong military position against superior numbers.

During the winter of 1846–7 the Californians, either not properly understanding or not impressed with the value of an oath of allegiance to the government of the United States, also rose in insurrection. At the City of Angels, and other points, the flag of the United States was torn down, and that of Mexico hoisted in its place. In November, 1846, an action occurred at Domingos Rancho, between a party from the United States frigate Savannah and a portion of the Californians. The latter were fortified, and supported by artillery. They gained an advantage over the sailors, who were on foot, which raised their courage and excited their hopes. In December, Commodore Stockton, having landed at Diego, advanced to the City of Angels, and again re-established the American dominion.

Soon after this a battle occurred between the Americans under General Kearney and the Mexicans at San Gabriel. In this engagement the Mexicans were defeated with loss; but on the American side several were killed, and General Kearney wounded.

In New Mexico and California, the inhabitants appear to have been much more interested in regaining their country by popular insurrection, than they had been in defending it against the advance of the invaders. Either they had been at first surprised, and yielded to an unexpected necessity, or the American army, and the new governments instituted among them had not impressed their minds with an idea of superiority and excellence. Both may in some measure have been true. But the lesson taught by these insurrections is, that the Mexican inhabitants of New Mexico and California remain under the dominion of the United States only as a conquered people; not from any adhesion to oaths of allegiance, or to any admiration for the free institutions which were proclaimed among them.

In the interval between the conquest of New Mexico by Kearney, and the march of Scott from Vera Cruz, there occurred, in the northern provinces of Mexico, one of those military adventures which convert the realities of history into the brilliant and enticing scenes of romance. This was the march of Colonel Doniphan's corps through the wild and unknown regions of Northern Mexico. When the American army, under Kearney, had reached Santa Fé, it was already nine hundred miles from the point of its departure. The great part of this distance had been passed over vast prairie plains, over arid deserts, in the valleys of streams, where no town or habitation was seen, and over hills like the Raton, from whose lofty summit no sign of civilization could be seen, and the distant horizon was limited only by the towering peaks of the Rocky Mountains. At Santa Fé there was but little real interruption to this wilderness prospect. New Mexico contained fifty thousand square miles, but only one hundred thousand inhabitants. The States of Chihuahua, Durango, and Coahuila, below, scarcely contained a greater population in proportion. Here and there a Mexican town appeared, and at intervals spots of beautiful culture, of vineyards and fruits; but, for the most part, there were uninhabited regions, unknown to the Americans, and almost untrodden by travellers.

In the early part of December Colonel Doniphan left

Santa Fé with eight hundred men, in three divisions, destined for Chihuahua. The object of the expedition was to join General Wool in the heart of Northern Mexico. Wool, as has been detailed, marched with what was called the Army of the Centre from San Antonio de Bexar for Chihuahua. The latter point he never reached; but Colonel Doniphan now supposed him either at Chihuahua or on his route. Doniphan, accordingly, marched south to form a junction. On the 21st of December his corps reached Brozitos, and the troops were dispersed getting wood, when a large force of the enemy, supposed to be a thousand strong, appeared in sight. The Americans immediately formed in line. The Mexicans were composed of Lancers and Infantry. A Mexican officer rode out on a fine charger, displaying a black flag. Their column immediately charged, and were received by the Americans with a well-directed fire of rifles. This determined the engagement. The Mexicans fled. Doniphan then pursued his march at his leisure.

On the 27th of December Doniphan's corps entered El Paso del Norte without opposition. This is a considerable town on the Rio del Norte, or rather Rio Grande, the former being the name of that river in New Mexico. This town contains about five thousand inhabitants; but there are about eleven thousand settled along the river for twenty-five miles. It is on the road to Chihuahua, and at one of the principal crossings of the Rio Grande.

Here Colonel Doniphan was compelled to wait for reinforcements, and also to hear from General Wool. The Americans were surrounded with a hostile population, and continually expecting an attack. One who was present writes, "Here we have spent a month in anxiety, drudgery, and toil."[1] Nothing, however, was heard from Wool; and it was long before reinforcements arrived. At length, on the 1st of February, Captain Weightman arrived with the Artillery, and Doniphan's command was increased to the amount of about nine hundred men.

In the latter part of February he set out from El Paso, and on the 23d the American forces were at Carmen, one hundred miles from Chihuahua. In the mean time, General Heredia, who commanded the Mexican forces in Chihuahua, having heard of the approach of the American army, despatched General Conde with eight hundred cavalry to watch the Americans. On the 21st General Heredia himself took position with additional troops near the Sacramento river, and awaited the approach of Colonel Doniphan.

The forces of Heredia were thus composed:—

Conde's Cavalry - - -	800	men
7th Regular Infantry - - -	70	"
Chihuahua Battalion - - -	250	"
National Guards - - -	180	"
Dragoons - - - - -	50	"
Ten pieces of artillery - -	119	"
Corps of other cavalry - -	106	"
Total of Heredia's army -	1575	"

Many of these troops were the new levies of the country —National Guards and Volunteers.[2]

On the 28th of February the American army discovered

[1] Letter in the Missouri Republican.

[2] General Jose Heredia's Report, March 2d, 1847, in the "Union," April 19th.

the enemy intrenched near the Rancho Sacramento, on the river Sacramento. The position was a very strong one. It was in a valley about four miles in width, having a range of mountains on each side. The Rio Sacramento, and Arroyo Seco, both crossed the valley here ; and the main road to Chihuahua, pursuing the valley, crosses the Sacramento at the Rancho Sacramento. The Mexican intrenchments were on a ridge between these streams, and completely commanding the road. Their right rested on the Cerro Frijoles, with high precipitous sides, on which was a battery commanding the surrounding country and the pass leading to Chihuahua, through the Arroyo Seco. On their left was the Cerro Sacramento, a pile of immense volcanic rocks, surmounted by a battery which commanded the main road to Chihuahua.[1]

A passage was found practicable across the Arroyo Seco, within reach of the enemy's fire ; and the American column having reached the ground between the Seco and Sacramento, commenced deploying towards the table-land occupied by the Mexicans. The column of General Conde's cavalry, opposed to the American right, now commenced a charge, which was returned by the fire of the Artillery Battery, consisting of six pieces, under the command of Major Clark. At the third fire the enemy's cavalry gave way and dispersed.[2] They fell back to the Mexican camp, and rallied behind a redoubt. This the Americans attacked with artillery, Captain Weightman rapidly advancing with two howitzers, supported by Captain Reed's company of horse, and then by Lieutenant-

---

[1] Report of Major Clark to Colonel Doniphan, March 2d, 1847

[2] Heredia's Report.

colonel Mitchell, delivering his fire with great effect, the enemy were driven from the redoubt. The Mexicans were pursued towards the mountains by Lieutenant-colonel Mitchell, Lieutenant-colonel Jackson, and Major Gilpin, accompanied by Weightman with his section of howitzers. In the mean time the Mexicans had carried their cannon to the Cerro Sacramento, to cover their retreat. The fire of the American artillery soon silenced these, and the Rancho Sacramento was then attacked. At length the Mexicans were driven from their last position, and the victory was complete.[1] The Mexicans lost one hundred men and ten pieces of artillery.

Colonel Doniphan and his little army entered the city of Chihuahua, the fruit of this victory, in divisions, on the 1st and 2d of March. This town is the capital of one of the most important States of Mexico, and contains more than forty thousand inhabitants. It lies on a branch of the Conchas river, two hundred and fifty miles south of El Paso. On the east lies the Rio Grande, and on the west the lofty summits of the Sierra Madre. The country is diversified with mountains and vales. The army passed rugged cliffs of basaltic rock on one side, and on the other fields rich with the finest wheat. In the clear atmosphere of this elevated region, the mountain-tops would seem, in the distance, blue as the skies above ; or, near by, would darkly frown in the cold gray aspect of its granite rock. Chihuahua, too, is the centre of rich and various mines. Not more than twelve miles from it are silver mines supposed to be the richest in Mexico. These mines are generally owned by private companies,

---

[1] Clark's Report.

composed of English or Spanish proprietors. At Chihuahua, in this rich country and pleasant climate, the army of Doniphan rested in the bright days of spring. They had departed so far from the American lines of intelligence, as to be ignorant of the situation or place of the American forces. The expedition had been planned with the idea that the corps of Doniphan would find the army of Wool at Chihuahua; but that army was not there. The reason we have already seen. Wool had encountered beyond Monclova the lofty ridges of the Sierra Madre, and been compelled to change his course to the south, and eventually to Saltillo.[1] After waiting in vain for any appearance of Wool, and having remained six weeks at Chihuahua,[2] the army at last took its line of march. Colonel Doniphan moved his corps from Chihuahua in three divisions, on the 25th, 26th, and 28th of April. Marching southwardly, through Cerro Gordo, Mapimi, and Parras, they reached Saltillo, three hundred and fifty miles further, on the 22d of May, 1847. Remaining but three days, on the 25th day of May they marched to Monterey. Pursuing their journey with rapid steps, they descended the Rio Grande, navigated the Gulf of Mexico, and arrived at New Orleans on the 15th of June. Here the volunteers were mustered out of the service of the United States, embarked on steamboats, and were soon returned to their homes in Missouri. In a little more than a year, this corps of volunteers, mustered from private life, had, by land and by water,—over mountain-tops and sandy plains,—

[1] See Chapter 5th.

[2] For a full and most interesting account of Doniphan's expedition, see "Doniphan's Expedition," by J. T. Hughes. Published by J. A. James & Co., Cincinnati.

in snow and in rain, and in hot deserts,—amidst the homes of civilization and the wilds of savages,—amidst the fires of battle, the sports of the camp, and the adventures of the wild wilderness, pursued their unchecked career for five thousand miles! Nor was this all. One detachment of this same corps, previous to the departure of the main body from Santa Fé, had marched another thousand miles in still wilder scenes and greater adventure. This was the detachment of Lt. Col. Gilpin, who was sent out towards the Rocky Mountains to overawe the Navajos Indians. This was a tribe which, unlike most tribes of Indians, lived in the pastoral state, and inhabited the great unknown country lying between New Mexico and the Colorado of the south. General Kearney had promised the New Mexicans protection from the incursions of this tribe. To carry out this intention, Gilpin's detachment was sent into their country. This command actually crossed the Rocky Mountains, and descended into the valley of the Colorado of the south. Their march was full of new scenery, new dangers, and new adventures. Tribes of Indians unknown to the people of the United States were found and observed. The grizly bear, supposed to inhabit chiefly the polar regions, was here found a common tenant of the mountains. After this party had thus pursued its novel and most interesting march through the spurs and rivers, and wild tribes and wilder animals of the Rocky Mountains, it returned in time to join the long and adventurous march of Doniphan to Chihuahua and the Gulf of Mexico.[1]

[1] See the "Expedition of Doniphan," by J. T. Hughes, mentioned before. The narrative of Mr. Hughes may be relied upon for accuracy, and is a graphic account of these remarkable adventures.

CHAPTER VII.

General Scott ordered to Mexico.—Letter of the Secretary of War to General Taylor.—Letter of the Secretary of War to General Scott.—General Scott leaves Washington.—His Letter to General Taylor.—Plan of appointing a Lieutenant-General.—Scott reaches the Rio Grande.—Condition of things there.—Withdraws a part of Taylor's Troops in compliance with the Orders of the War Department.

On the 18th of November, General Scott was directed by the Secretary of War to hold himself in readiness to assume the command of the army destined to make a descent on Vera Cruz. The purpose of organizing a force for this object was communicated to General Taylor in a letter from the Secretary of War, dated Washington, Oct. 22, 1846:

"I informed you in my last despatch, that in connection with an invasion of Tamaulipas and attack on Tampico, an expedition against Vera Cruz was then under advisement. Upon a more full consideration of the subject, it is believed that Vera Cruz may be taken, and having possession of that city, the castle of San Juan de Ulloa might possibly be reduced or compelled to surrender. If the expedition could go forth without the object being known to the enemy, it is supposed that four thousand troops would be sufficient for the enterprise, receiving as they would the co-operation of our naval force in the gulf; but *at least fifteen hundred or two thousand of them should be of the regular army, and under the command of officers best calculated for such an undertaking.* In looking at the disposition of the troops, *it appears to be scarcely possible to get the requisite number of regulars without drawing some of those now with you at Monterey,* or on the way to that place. Should you decide against holding military possession of any place in Coahuila or Chihuahua, and order the troops under General Wool to join you, it is presumed that the requisite force for the expedition to Vera Cruz could be detached without interfering with your plans of operation.

"You will therefore, unless it materially interferes with your own plan of operations, or weakens you too much in your present position, make the necessary arrangements for having four thousand men, of whom fifteen hundred or two thousand should be regular troops, ready to embark for Vera Cruz, or such other destination as may be given them, at the earliest practicable period. The place of embarkation will probably be the Brazos Santiago, or in that vicinity."

On the 23d of November General Scott received the following order from the Secretary of War:—

WAR DEPARTMENT, WASHINGTON,
November 23d, 1846.

SIR—The President, several days since, communicated in person to you his orders to repair to Mexico, to take the command of the forces there assembled, and particularly to organize and set on foot an expedition to operate on the Gulf coast, if, on arriving at the theatre of action, you shall deem it to be practicable. It is not proposed to control your operations by definite and positive instructions, but you are left to prosecute them as your judgment, under a full view of all the circumstances, shall dictate. The work is before you, and the means provided, or to be provided, for accomplishing it, are committed to you, in the full confidence that you will use them to the best advantage.

The objects which it is desirable to obtain have been indicated, and it is hoped that you will have the requisite force to accomplish them.

Of this you must be the judge, when preparations are made, and the time for action arrived.

Very respectfully,
Your obedient servant,
W. L. Marcy,
Secretary of War.

General Winfield Scott.

General Scott immediately made all the arrangements to carry the plan into full effect. The requisite number of transports were to be provided, surf-boats for the landing of the troops constructed, a train of siege ordnance was to be collected and sent forward, and ten new regiments were to be added to the line of the army, at the earliest possible moment after the meeting of Congress. In a very few days all the preliminary arrangements were completed, and General Scott left Washington on the 24th November, in the full belief that he enjoyed the confidence of the government, and that the conduct of the war, under general instructions, had been entirely confided to his discretion and judgment.

The only reluctance which he felt in accepting the high trusts confided to him by the President, arose from an unwillingness to interfere, in the slightest degree, with the command of an old friend and brother soldier; and this feeling was strongly expressed to General Taylor in a letter written from New York, November 25th, 1846.

"I left Washington late in the day yesterday, and expect to embark for New Orleans the 30th inst. By the 12th of December I may be in that city, at Point Isabel the 17th, and Camargo, say the 23d—in order to be within easy corresponding distance from you. It is not probable that I may be able to visit Monterey, and circumstances may prevent your coming to me. I shall much regret not having an early opportunity of felicitating you in person upon your many brilliant achievements; but we may meet somewhere in the interior of Mexico.

"I am not coming, my dear general, to supersede you in the immediate command on the line of operations rendered illustrious by you and your gallant army. My proposed theatre is different. You may imagine it; and I wish very much that it were prudent, at this distance, to tell you all that I expect to attempt or hope to execute. I have been admonished that despatches have been lost, and I have no special messenger at hand. Your imagination will be aided by the letters of the Secretary of War, conveyed by Mr. Armistead, Major Graham, and Mr. M'Lane.

"But, my dear general, I shall be obliged to take from you most of the gallant officers and men, (regulars and volunteers,) whom you have so long and so nobly commanded. I am afraid that I shall, by imperious necessity—the approach of yellow fever on the Gulf coast—reduce you, for a time, to stand on the defensive. This will be infinitely painful to you, and, for that reason, distressing to me. But I rely upon your patriotism to submit to the temporary sacrifice with cheerfulness. No man can better afford to do so. Recent victories place you on the high eminence; and I even flatter myself that any benefit that may result to me, personally, from the unequal division of troops alluded to, will lessen the pain of your consequent inactivity.

"You will be aware of the recent call for nine regiments of new volunteers, including one of Texas horse. The President may soon ask for many more; and we are not without hope that Congress may add ten or twelve to the regular establishment. These, by the spring, say April, may, by the aid of large bounties, be in the field—should Mexico not earlier propose terms of accommodation; and, long before the spring, (March,) it is probable you will be again in force to resume offensive operations.

"It was not possible for me to find time to write from Washington, as I much desired. I only received an intimation to hold myself in preparation for Mexico, on the 18th instant. Much has been done towards that end, and more remains to be executed.

"Your detailed report of the operations at Monterey, and reply to the Secretary's despatch, by Lieutenant Armistead, were both received two days after I was instructed to proceed south."

Before ordering General Scott to Mexico, as subsequently appeared by the statements of Senator Benton, the President had decided to create the office of lieutenant-general, and thus supersede, not only the scar-marked hero of Chippewa and Niagara, but also to tear the fresh laurels of Palo Alto and Resaca de la Palma from the brow of the gallant Taylor. After this plan had been finally arranged, the President sent for General Scott, and confided to him the command of the army in Mexico, and gave to him the most solemn assurance of his confidence and support.

Immediately on the opening of Congress the project of creating a higher military grade was brought forward, and the friends of generals Scott and Taylor saw with alarm, that a plan was maturing by which they were both to be degraded to subordinate stations, and the entire direction of affairs in Mexico confided to other and untried hands. The friends of General Scott now saw that his apprehensions of an attack "from the rear," and which had been frankly expressed in his former letters, were indeed but too well founded; and that notwithstanding the assurance given on his departure from Washington for the army, of the full and cordial support of the government, the plan of wresting from him the command, at the earliest possible day, was then matured, and ready for speedy execution. In view of all the circumstances, it is, perhaps, not uncharitable to suppose that he was selected for that command, for the purpose of stirring up a spirit of rivalry between his friends and those of General Taylor, and thus affording a plausible pretext for superseding them both.

On the 30th of November General Scott sailed from New York, in the fullest confidence that the government was acting in good faith, and that every means would be furnished him for the prosecution of the war. Little did he then suppose, that before he could reach the theatre of active operations the government which had selected and sent him, would attempt to degrade him in the eyes of the world, by declaring, in effect, that he was unfit for the very place to which he had been so recently appointed.

With the generous confidence of a brave soldier, who had often met the enemy in deadly conflict, he received through the President the plighted faith of the nation that all was right. The President saw him depart in the fulness of this confidence, and yet before he reached the army, the proposition to supersede him was already there. Yes, the very army into which he was to breathe the inspiration of hope—which he was to train and prepare for the deadly conflicts that awaited them—was informed, in advance, that the President had no confidence in their commander-in-chief.

General Scott reached the Rio Grande about the first of January. Early in the month it became evident that some of the principal arrangements for the attack on Vera Cruz were not likely to be carried out by the government. The bill for raising the ten additional regiments was lost sight of by the administration, in the desire to carry their favorite project of placing a political partisan at the head of the army; and this bill, which ought to have been passed in the first week of the session, was not finally disposed of till a day or two before the adjournment.

What was the condition of things in Mexico at this critical period?

Santa Anna, with a force of twenty-two thousand men, was at San Luis Potosi, a fortified city containing sixty thousand inhabitants, and about equally distant from Monterey, Vera Cruz, and Mexico.

General Taylor was in the vicinity of Monterey, in the command of a force of about eighteen thousand men, occupying the long line from Saltillo to Camargo, and thence to the mouth of the Rio Grande, where General Scott had just arrived with a small force, for the purpose of attacking Vera Cruz as soon as possible. He well knew that the *vomito* makes its appearance there in the early spring, and that delay would be fatal. The transports.

stores, and munitions, were beginning to arrive. What was to be done? Was the expedition against Vera Cruz to be abandoned, or was General Scott to go forward and do the best he could under circumstances so discouraging? He adopted the latter alternative. He reviewed all the disposable forces within his command, and carefully weighed chances and probabilities. He forwarded to General Taylor a full plan of his proposed operations. By the capture and assassination of Lieutenant Ritchie, the bearer of these despatches, the plans were fully disclosed to Santa Anna, and he became apprized that Vera Cruz was to be the main point of attack. At Vera Cruz, and its immediate vicinity, there were six or seven thousand men, and a much larger number could be collected from the adjoining country on a short notice. Would Santa Anna break up his camp at San Luis Potosi, and march on Vera Cruz—fill the city and castle with his best troops, and oppose the landing of General Scott with a selected army of forty thousand men? Or, was he likely to abandon the town and castle to their fate, thus leaving open the road to Mexico, and march with his whole force against General Taylor, over a desert of one hundred and fifty miles, with a certainty of having to encounter his enemy either in the defiles of the mountains or from behind the impregnable battlements of Monterey?

Under such circumstances it became the duty of General Scott so to divide the forces of the Rio Grande as would be most likely to meet any contingency that might arise. He collected the regular infantry—for these might be necessary to carry with the bayonet the fortified city and castle of Vera Cruz. He left within the limits of General Taylor's command, about ten thousand volun teers and several companies of the best artillery of the regular army. These General Taylor might have concentrated at Monterey, and General Scott suggested to him, in his instructions, to do so, if it became necessary. With this comparatively small force, General Taylor not only maintained all the posts within his command, but with the one half of it achieved the memorable victory of Buena Vista.

General Scott assigned twelve thousand men to the expedition against Vera Cruz, and had Santa Anna concentrated his forces at that point, the disparity of numbers would have been much greater than at Buena Vista. These remarks are not made for the purpose of comparing the skill, or the conduct, or the claims to public gratitude of the two distinguished generals who have so well fulfilled every trust reposed in them by their country; but simply to show that in the disposition of the forces made by General Scott, he did not take a larger portion for his own command than the interests of the service imperatively demanded.

CHAPTER VIII.

General Taylor's Movements.—Taylor's Position.—Santa Anna's Advance.—Importance of the event.—Battle of Buena Vista.—Retreat of the Mexicans.—Taylor's Official Account.—Santa Anna's Report.

In pursuance of orders from the War Department, General Taylor, in the month of November, ordered the divisions of Generals Twiggs, Quitman, and Pillow from Monterey to Victoria, for the purpose of joining at Tampico the expedition against Vera Cruz. In the latter part of December, General Patterson's division left Matamoras for the same destination, by the route through Victoria; while General Worth's division proceeded from Saltillo to Comargo, thence to Matamoras, and joined General Scott at the Brazos.

At Victoria, on the 30th of December, 1846, General Taylor received information of Scott's departure for Mexico. Santa Anna, in the mean time, was at San Luis Potosi, with an army of twenty-two thousand men.

In the latter part of January, 1847, General Taylor left Victoria and established his headquarters at Monterey, and early in February his whole force at this point, including the volunteers who had recently joined him, amounted to between six and seven thousand men.

Soon after reaching Monterey, he received intelligence

that a party of dragoons under Colonel May had been surprised at Encarnacion, in the early part of February, and that Cassius M. Clay and Majors Borland and Gaines were taken prisoners by General Minon, at the head of fifteen hundred men. These circumstances induced General Taylor to believe that Santa Anna intended advancing with his whole army, and he determined to proceed at once to Saltillo and give him battle.

Leaving a force of fifteen hundred men, he departed from Monterey on the 31st of January, and reached Saltillo on the 2d of February. Having, in the mean time, been reinforced by five hundred men, his effective force was about five thousand. On the 4th of February he advanced to Agua Nueva, a strong position on the road leading from Saltillo to San Luis. Here he remained until the 21st, when he received intelligence that Santa Anna was advancing with his whole army. Having carefully examined the strong mountain-passes, he decided that Buena Vista, a strong mountain-pass eleven miles nearer Saltillo, was the most favorable point to make a stand against a force so overwhelming. He therefore fell back to that place; and having formed his army in order of battle, calmly awaited the approach of the enemy.

The position of the American army at this moment was most critical. The regular troops had been withdrawn, with the exception of four companies of artillery, and even these had been filled up by new levies. The volunteers, of which the army was mainly composed, had received some instruction in the regular duties of the camp, but had not attained that perfection in discipline which gives confidence in military operations.

The army of Santa Anna was admirably equipped. It was composed of the flower of the Mexican nation, and numbered more than four to one of the army which it came to conquer. Hope and dire necessity both urged them to victory. Those who remembered that the American arms had triumphed at Palo Alto, Resaca de la Palma, and Monterey, well knew that the regular soldiers, who had contributed so largely to those victories, had been ordered to distant fields of operations; and that even courage and enthusiasm, without discipline, are unavailing against multiplied numbers.

The commander, Santa Anna, had well considered the advantages he would derive from this movement, if successful, and all the chances were in his favor. Could he have driven General Taylor from his position at Buena Vista, he would have swept down to Comargo, and over the whole valley of the Rio Grande. All the munitions of war, provisions, camp equipage, and public property of every description would have fallen into his hands, and the American troops would have been driven from every inch of ground which they occupied in the Mexican territory.

If defeated, Santa Anna well knew that his moral power over his army would be broken. The desert in his rear, and over which he had just passed, could not be traversed by a retreating and dispirited army without great loss and suffering. The fate of his country seemed suspended on the issue of a single battle. His own fame, his place in history, were both to be decided in the coming conflict.

On the 22d of February, a day memorable in American history, General Taylor saw the Mexican host approach

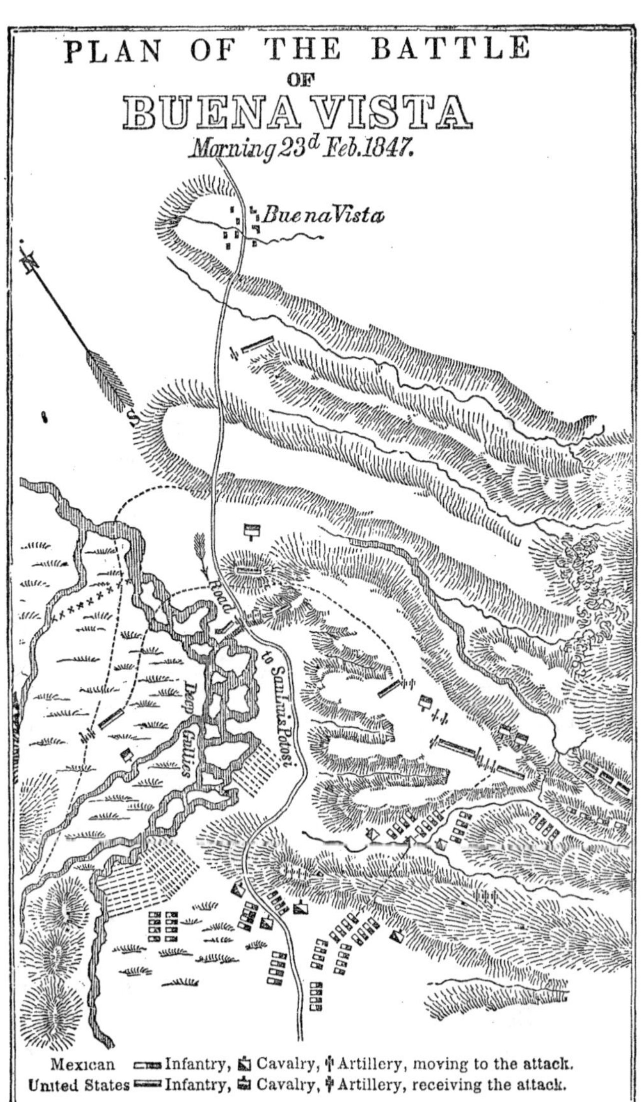
PLAN OF THE BATTLE
OF
BUENA VISTA
Morning 23d Feb. 1847.
Buena Vista
N
S
Road to San Luis Potosi
Deep Gullies
Mexican Infantry, Cavalry, Artillery, moving to the attack.
United States Infantry, Cavalry, Artillery, receiving the attack.

the narrow mountain-pass which he had selected as the Thermopylæ of his army.

The position of the two armies at, and soon after the commencement of the battle, is shown by the map. The enemy's right, opposite to our left, is concentrated in columns of attack behind a spur of the mountain, and his riflemen are on the side of the inaccessible mountain firing across a deep gully at our riflemen on the same mountain. A small eminence and spur of the mountain between them is unoccupied by either party. On our extreme left is the 2d Indiana regiment, supported by three pieces of artillery, one of which was lost in the onset of the morning; next, is the 2d Illinois regiment, with a piece of artillery on either flank; next, two pieces of artillery and a squadron of dragoons; next, two pieces of artillery and the 2d Kentucky foot; next, four companies of the 1st Illinois regiment on a spur of the plateau, at the foot of which is a parapet across the road, behind which are four pieces of artillery and two companies of the 1st Illinois regiment. A little to the rear is the 3d Indiana regiment on an eminence, behind which is a squadron of dragoons; and still further to the rear, near the rancho of Buena Vista, is the 1st Mississippi regiment, and one piece of artillery just arrived from Saltillo under General Taylor. In rear of our extreme left, on the edge of the plateau, are the Kentucky and Arkansas cavalry.

General Taylor, in reviewing his army, could not but recollect that the troops which formed his first encampment at Corpus Christi, and had shared with him the toils and triumphs of the campaign of 1846, were not in his line of battle. New men had come to replace them. Would these, as those, stand firm amid sheets of flame, the roar of artillery, and the impetuous rush of the charge? Were they worthy successors of the old guards, who would die at their posts, facing the enemy? These are questions which must have agitated the mind of the commander on the eve of that great battle. Fortunately for the country they have been all rightly answered. His own great example appears to have supplied the want of discipline, and inspired the troops with heroic enthusiasm. The volunteer is changed into the regular soldier; the citizen of yesterday becomes the veteran of to-day; and the American arms are everywhere triumphant.

The solid Mexican phalanx of twenty-two thousand men, armed and equipped for victory, have melted away before the steady fire of the artillery, and the deadly aim of the American rifle. When the last struggle for victory is made, and Santa Anna rallies his broken columns for a final charge; when the American regiments occupying the advance yield to superior numbers and fall back in confusion on the reserves, and the day seems lost; the commanding general hurries to the point where the battle is to be decided, orders the artillery to face about and unlimber, and gives the emphatic order, "A little more grape, Captain Bragg!" This saves the day. The Mexican columns now waver and halt. The curtains of night close down over the battle-field; the wounded and the dying rest in their gory bed; and the wearied officer and exhausted soldier sink together to repose.

The importance of this victory to the American arms cannot be exaggerated. It secured the whole frontier of the Rio Grande, and struck terror and dismay into the hearts of the Mexican nation. It was, in fact, the first great turning point of the war.

N. CARR & RICHARDSON, N.Y.

American Army 4,500 men.
Mexican Army 20,000 men

BATTLE OF BUENA VISTA,

Fought February 23d 1847.

The American Army under Gen. Taylor Completely Victorious

American Loss, 264 Killed.
450 Wounded.
26 Missing.
Mexican Loss, estimated in Killed

To the commander, General Taylor, the thanks of the country have been tendered in many ways for his signal ability, courage, and steadiness under circumstances so critical and trying. The general himself, with a magnanimity and modesty equalled only by his merits, has expressed his obligations to those who acted under him, of all grades of service. To them he has said that the country owes much. Their patient endurance of fatigue and privation; their cheerful submission to the rigorous discipline of the camp; their noble bearing in the hour of danger; their gallant conduct on the battle-field, gave to the army its efficiency and ensured its final triumph.

The following is General Taylor's official Report:

"HEADQUARTERS, ARMY OF OCCUPATION,
"Agua Nueva, March 6th, 1847.

"TO THE HON. SECRETARY OF WAR:

"SIR:—I have the honor to submit a detailed report of the operations of the forces under my command, which resulted in the engagement of Buena Vista, the repulse of the Mexican army, and the reoccupation of this position.

"The information which reached me of the advance and concentration of a heavy Mexican force in my front, had assumed such a probable form as to induce a special examination far beyond the reach of our pickets to ascertain its correctness. A small party of Texan spies, under Major McCullough, despatched to the hacienda of Encarnacion, thirty miles from this, on the route to San Luis Potosi, had reported a cavalry force of unknown strength at that place. On the 20th of February, a strong reconnoissance, under Lieutenant-colonel May, was despatched to the hacienda of Hecliondo, while Major McCullough made another examination of Encarnacion. The result of these expeditions left no doubt that the enemy was in large force at Encarnacion, under the orders of General Santa Anna, and that he meditated a forward movement and attack upon our position.

"As the camp of Aguá Nueva could be turned on either flank, and as the enemy's force was greatly superior to our own, particularly in the arm of cavalry, I determined, after much consideration, to take up a position about eleven miles in rear, and there await the attack. The army broke up its camp and marched at noon on the 21st, encamping at the new position a little in front of the hacienda of Buena Vista. With a small force I proceeded to Saltillo, to make some necessary arrangements for the defence of the town, leaving Brigadier-General Wool in the immediate command of the troops.

"Before these arrangements were completed, on the morning of the 22d, I was advised that the enemy was in sight, advancing. Upon reaching the ground it was found that his cavalry advance was in our front, having marched from Encarnacion, as we have since learned, at eleven o'clock the day previous, and driving in a mounted force left at Agua Nueva to cover the removal of public stores. Our troops were in position, occupying a line of remarkable strength. The road at this point becomes a narrow defile, the valley on its right being rendered quite impracticable for artillery by a succession of deep and impassable gullies, while on the left a succession of rugged ridges and precipitous ravines extends far back towards the moun tain which bounds the valley. The features of the ground were such as nearly to paralyze the artillery and cavalry of the enemy, while his infantry could not derive all the advantage of its numerical superiority. In this position we prepared to receive him. Captain Washington's battery (Fourth artillery) was posted to command the road, while the First and Second Illinois regiments, under Colonels Hardin and Bissell, each eight companies, (to the latter of which was attached Captain Conner's company of Texas volunteers,) and the Second Kentucky, under Colonel McKee, occupied the crests of the ridges on the left and in rear. The Arkansas and Kentucky regiments of cavalry, commanded by Colonels Yell and H. Marshall, occupied the extreme left near the base of the mountain, while the Indiana brigade, under Brigadier-General Lane, (composed of the Second and Third regiments, under Colonels Bowles and Lane,) the Mississippi riflemen, under Colonel Davis, the squadrons of the First and Second dragoons, under Captain Steene and Lieutenant-colonel May, and the light batteries of Captains Sherman and Bragg, Third artillery, were held in reserve.

"At eleven o'clock I received from General Santa Anna a summons to surrender at discretion, which, with a copy of my reply, I have already transmitted. The enemy still forebore his attack, evidently waiting for the arrival of his rear columns, which could be distinctly seen by our look-outs as they approached the field. A demonstration made on his left caused me to detach the Second Kentucky regiment and a section of artillery to our right, in which position they bivouacked for the night. In the mean time the Mexican light troops had engaged ours on the extreme left, (composed of parts of the Kentucky and Arkansas cavalry dismounted, and a rifle battalion from the Indiana brigade under Major Gorman, the whole commanded by Colonel Marshall,) and kept up a sharp fire, climbing the mountain side, and apparently endeavoring to gain our flank. Three pieces of Captain Washington's battery had been detached to the left, and were supported by the Second Indiana regiment. An occasional shell was thrown by the enemy into this part of our line, but without effect. The skirmishing of the light troops was kept up with trifling loss on our part until dark, when I became convinced that no serious attack would be made before the morning, and returned, with the Mississippi regiment and squadron of Second dragoons, to Saltillo. The troops bivouacked without fires, and laid upon their arms. A body of cavalry, some fifteen hundred strong, had been visible all day in rear of the town, having entered the valley through a narrow pass, east of the city. This cavalry, commanded by General Minon, had evidently been thrown in our rear to break up and harass our retreat, and perhaps make some attempt against the town, if practicable. The city was occupied by four excellent companies of Illinois volunteers, under Major Warren, of the First regiment. A field-work, which commanded most of the approaches, was garrisoned by Captain Webster's company, First artillery, and armed with two twenty-four pound howitzers, while the train and head-quarter camp was guarded by two companies of Mississippi riflemen, under Captain Rogers, and a field-piece, commanded by Captain Shover, Third artillery. Having made these dispositions for the protection of the rear, I proceeded on the morning of the 23d to Buena Vista, ordering forward all the other available troops. The action had commenced before my arrival on the field.

"During the evening and night of the 22d, the enemy had thrown a body of light troops on the mountain side, with the purpose of outflanking our left; and it was here that the action of the 23d commenced at an early hour. Our riflemen, under Colonel Marshall, who had been reinforced by three companies under Major Trail, Second Illinois volunteers, maintained their ground handsomely against a greatly superior force, holding themselves under cover, and using their weapons with deadly effect. About eight o'clock, a strong demonstration was made against the centre of our position, a heavy column moving along the road. This force was soon dispersed by a few rapid and well-directed shots from Captain Washington's battery. In the mean time the enemy was concentrating a large force of infantry and cavalry under cover of the ridges, with the obvious intention of forcing our left, which was posted on an extensive plateau. The Second Indiana and Second Illinois regiments formed this part of our line, the former covering three pieces of light artillery, under the orders of Captain O'Brien—Brigadier-General Lane being in the immediate command. In order to bring his men within effective range, General Lane ordered the artillery and Second Indiana regiment forward. The artillery advanced within musket-range of a heavy body of Mexican infantry, and was served against it with great effect, but without being able to check its advance. The infantry ordered to its support had fallen back in disorder, being exposed, as well as the battery, not only to a severe fire of small-arms from the front, but also to a murderous cross-fire of grape and canister, from a Mexican battery on the left. Captain O'Brien found it impossible to retain his position without support, but was only able to withdraw two of his pieces, all the horses and cannoniers of the third piece being killed or disabled. The Second Indiana regiment, which had fallen back as stated, could not be rallied, and took no farther part in the action, except a handful of men, who, under its gallant colonel, Bowles, joined the Mississippi regiment, and did good service, and those fugitives who, at a later period in the day, assisted in defending the train and depot at Buena Vista. This portion of our line having given way, and the enemy appearing in overwhelming force against our left flank, the light troops which had rendered such good service on the mountain were compelled to withdraw, which they did, for the most part, in good order. Many, however, were not rallied until they reached the depot at Buena Vista, to the defence of which they afterwards contributed.

"Col. Bissell's regiment, (Second Illinois,) which had been joined by a section of Captain Sherman's battery, had become completely outflanked, and was compelled to fall back, being entirely unsupported. The enemy was now pouring masses of infantry and cavalry along the base of the mountain on our left, and was gaining our rear in great force. At this moment I arrived upon the field. The Mississippi regiment had been directed to the left before reaching the position, and immediately came into action against the Mexican infantry which had turned our flank. The Second Kentucky regiment, and a section of artillery under Captain Bragg, had previously been ordered from the right to reinforce our left, and arrived at a most opportune moment. That regiment, and a portion of the First Illinois, under Colonel Hardin, gallantly drove the enemy, and recovered a portion of the ground we had lost. The batteries of Captains Sherman and Bragg were in position on the plateau, and did much execution, not only in front, but particularly upon the masses which had gained our rear. Discovering that the enemy was heavily pressing upon the Mississippi regiment, the Third Indiana regiment, under Colonel Lane, was despatched to strengthen that part of our line which formed a crotchet perpendicular to the first line of battle. At the same time Lieutenant Kilburn, with a piece of Captain Bragg's battery, was directed to support the infantry there engaged. The action was for a long time warmly sustained at that point—the enemy making several efforts both with infantry and cavalry against our line, and being always repulsed with heavy loss. I had placed all the regular cavalry and Captain Pike's squadron of Arkansas horse under the orders of Brevet Lieutenant-colonel May, with directions to hold in check the enemy's column, still advancing to the rear along the base of the mountain, which was done in conjunction with the Kentucky and Arkansas cavalry, under Colonels Marshall and Yell.

"In the mean time our left, which was still strongly threatened by a superior force, was farther strengthened by the detachment of Captain Bragg's and a portion of Captain Sherman's batteries to that quarter. The concentration of artillery-fire upon the masses of the enemy along the base of the mountain, and the determined resistance offered by the two regiments opposed to them, had created confusion in their ranks, and some of the corps attempted to effect a retreat upon their main line of battle. The squadron of the First dragoons, under Lieutenant

Rucker, was now ordered up the deep ravine which these retreating corps were endeavoring to cross, in order to charge and disperse them. The squadron proceeded to the point indicated, but could not accomplish the object, being exposed to a heavy fire from a battery established to cover the retreat of those corps. While the squadron was detached on this service, a large body of the enemy was observed to concentrate on our extreme left, apparently with the view of making a descent upon the hacienda of Buena Vista, where our train and baggage were deposited. Lieutenant-colonel May was ordered to the support of that point, with two pieces of Captain Sherman's battery under Lieutenant Reynolds. In the mean time, the scattered forces near the hacienda, composed in part of Majors Trail and Gorman's commands, had been to some extent organized under the advice of Major Munroe, chief of artillery, with the assistance of Major Morrison, volunteer staff, and were posted to defend the position. Before our cavalry had reached the hacienda, that of the enemy had made its attack; having been handsomely met by the Kentucky and Arkansas cavalry under Colonels Marshall and Yell. The Mexican column immediately divided, one portion sweeping by the depot, where it received a destructive fire from the force which had collected there, and then gaining the mountain opposite, under a fire from Lieutenant Reynolds' section, the remaining portion regaining the base of the mountain on our left. In the charge at Buena Vista, Colonel Yell fell gallantly at the head of his regiment; we also lost Adjutant Vaughan, of the Kentucky cavalry—a young officer of much promise. Lieutenant-colonel May, who had been rejoined by the squadron of the First dragoons and by portions of the

Arkansas and Indiana troops, under Lieutenant-colonel Roane and Major Gorman, now approached the base of the mountain, holding in check the right flank of the enemy, upon whose masses, crowded in the narrow gorges and ravines, our artillery was doing fearful execution.

"The position of that portion of the Mexican army which had gained our rear was now very critical, and it seemed doubtful whether it could regain the main body. At this moment I received from General Santa Anna a message by a staff officer, desiring to know what I wanted. I immediately despatched Brigadier-general Wool to the Mexican general-in-chief, and sent orders to cease firing. Upon reaching the Mexican lines, General Wool could not cause the enemy to cease their fire, and accordingly returned without having an interview. The extreme right of the enemy continued its retreat along the base of the mountain, and finally, in spite of all our efforts, effect ed a junction with the remainder of the army.

"During the day, the cavalry of General Minon had ascended the elevated plain above Saltillo, and occupied the road from the city to the field of battle, where they intercepted several of our men. Approaching the town, they were fired upon by Captain Webster, from the redoubt occupied by his company, and then moved off towards the eastern side of the valley, and obliquely towards Buena Vista. At this time, Captain Shover moved rapidly forward with his piece, supported by a miscellaneous command of mounted volunteers, and fired several shots at the cavalry with great effect. They were driven into the ravines which lead to the lower valley, closely pursued by Captain Shover, who was farther supported by a piece of Captain Webster's battery, under Lieutenant Donaldson, which had advanced from the redoubt, supported by Captain Wheeler's company of Illinois volunteers. The enemy made one or two efforts to charge the artillery, but was finally driven back in a confused mass, and did not again appear upon the plain.

"In the mean time, the firing had partially ceased upon the principal field. The enemy seemed to confine his efforts to the protection of his artillery, and I had left the plateau for a moment, when I was recalled thither by a very heavy musketry fire. On regaining that position, I discovered that our infantry (Illinois and Second Kentucky) had engaged a greatly superior force of the enemy—evidently his reserve—and that they had been overwhelmed by numbers. The moment was most critical. Captain O'Brien, with two pieces, had sustained this heavy charge to the last, and was finally obliged to leave his guns on the field—his infantry support being entirely routed. Captain Bragg, who had just arrived from the left, was ordered at once into battery. Without any infantry to support him, and at the imminent risk of losing his guns, this officer came rapidly into action, the Mexican line being but a few yards from the muzzle of his pieces. The first discharge of canister caused the enemy to hesitate; the second and third drove him back in dis order and saved the day. The Second Kentucky regiment, which had advanced beyond supporting distance in this affair, was driven back and closely pressed by the enemy's cavalry. Taking a ravine which led in the direction of Captain Washington's battery, their pursuers became exposed to his fire, which soon checked and drove them back with loss. In the mean time the rest of our artillery had taken position on the plateau, covered by the

Mississippi and Third Indiana regiments, the former of which had reached the ground in time to pour a fire into the right flank of the enemy, and thus contribute to his repulse.

"In this last conflict we had the misfortune to sustain a very heavy loss. Colonel Hardin, First Illinois, and Colonel McKee and Lieutenant-colonel Clay, Second Kentucky regiment, fell at this time, while gallantly leading their commands.

"No farther attempt was made by the enemy to force our position, and the approach of night gave an opportunity to pay proper attention to the wounded, and also to refresh the soldiers, who had been exhausted by incessant watchfulness and combat. Though the night was severely cold, the troops were compelled for the most to bivouac without fires, expecting that morning would renew the conflict. During the night the wounded were removed to Saltillo, and every preparation made to receive the enemy, should he again attack our position. Seven fresh companies were drawn from the town, and Brigadier-general Marshall, with a reinforcement of Kentucky cavalry and four heavy guns, under Captain Prentiss, First artillery, was near at hand, when it was discovered that the enemy had abandoned his position during the night. Our scouts soon ascertained that he had fallen back upon Agua Nueva. The great disparity of numbers, and the exhaustion of our troops, rendered it inexpedient and hazardous to attempt pursuit. A staff officer was despatched to General Santa Anna, to negotiate an exchange of prisoners, which was satisfactorily completed on the following day. Our own dead were collected and buried, and the Mexican wounded, of which a large number had been left upon the field, were removed to Saltillo, and rendered as comfortable as circumstances would permit.

"On the evening of the 26th, a close reconnoissance was made of the enemy's position, which was found to be occupied only by a small body of cavalry, the infantry and artillery having retreated in the direction of San Luis Potosi. On the 27th, our troops resumed their former camp at Agua Nueva, the enemy's rear-guard evacuating the place as we approached, leaving a considerable number of wounded. It was my purpose to beat up his quarters at Encarnacion early the next morning, but upon examination, the weak condition of the cavalry horses rendered it unadvisable to attempt so long a march without water. A command was finally despatched to Encarnacion, on the 1st of March, under Colonel Belknap. Some two hundred wounded, and about sixty Mexican soldiers were found there, the army having passed on in the direction of Matehuala, with greatly reduced numbers, and suffering much from hunger. The dead and dying were strewed upon the road and crowded the buildings of the hacienda.

"The American force engaged in the action of Buena Vista is shown, by the accompanying field report, to have been three hundred and thirty-four officers, and four thousand four hundred and twenty-five men, exclusive of the small command left in and near Saltillo. Of this number, two squadrons of cavalry and three batteries of light artillery, making not more than four hundred and fifty-three men, composed the only force of regular troops. The strength of the Mexican army is stated by General Santa Anna, in his summons, to be twenty thousand; and that estimate is confirmed by all the information since obtained.

Our loss is two hundred and sixty-seven killed, four hundred and fifty-six wounded, and twenty-three missing. Of the numerous wounded, many did not require removal to the hospital, and it is hoped that a comparatively small number will be permanently disabled. The Mexican loss in killed and wounded may be fairly estimated at one thousand and five hundred, and will probably reach two thousand. At least five hundred of their killed were left upon the field of battle. We have no means of ascertaining the number of deserters and dispersed men from their ranks, but it is known to be very great.

"Our loss has been especially severe in officers, twenty-eight having been killed upon the field. We have to lament the death of Captain George Lincoln, assistant adjutant-general, serving in the staff of General Wool—a young officer of high bearing and approved gallantry, who fell early in the action. No loss falls more heavily upon the army in the field than that of Colonels Hardin and McKee, and Lieutenant-colonel Clay. Possessing in a remarkable degree the confidence of their commands, and the last two having enjoyed the advantage of a military education, I had looked particularly to them for support in case we met the enemy. I need not say that their zeal in engaging the enemy, and the cool and steadfast courage with which they maintained their positions during the day, fully realized my hopes, and caused me to feel yet more sensibly their untimely loss.

"I perform a grateful duty in bringing to the notice of the government the general good conduct of the troops. Exposed for successive nights, without fires, to the severity of the weather, they were very prompt and cheerful in the discharge of every duty; and finally displayed conspicuous steadiness and gallantry in repulsing, at great odds, a disciplined foe. While the brilliant success achieved by their arms releases me from the painful necessity of specifying many cases of bad conduct before the enemy, I feel an increased obligation to mention particular corps and officers, whose skill, coolness, and gallantry in trying situations, and under a continued and heavy fire, seem to merit particular notice.

"To Brigadier-general Wool my obligations are especially due. The high state of discipline and instruction of several of the volunteer regiments was attained under his command, and to his vigilance and arduous service before the action, and his gallantry and activity on the field, a large share of our success may justly be attributed. During most of the engagement he was in immediate command of the troops thrown back on our left flank. I beg leave to recommend him to the favorable notice of the government. Brigadier-general Lane (slightly wounded) was active and zealous throughout the day, and displayed great coolness and gallantry before the enemy.

"The services of the light artillery, always conspicuous, were more than usually distinguished. Moving rapidly over the roughest ground, it was always in action at the right place and the right time, and its well-directed fire dealt destruction in the masses of the enemy. While I recommend to particular favor the gallant conduct and valuable services of Major Munroe, chief of artillery, and Captains Washington, Fourth artillery, and Sherman and Bragg, Third artillery, commanding batteries, I deem it no more than just to mention all the subaltern officers. They were nearly all detached at different times, and in every situation exhibited conspicuous skill and gallantry

Captain O'Brien, Lieutenants Brent, Whiting, and Couch, Fourth artillery, and Bryan, topographical engineers, (slightly wounded,) were attached to Captain Washington's battery. Lieutenants Thomas, Reynolds, and French, Third artillery, (severely wounded,) to that of Captain Sherman; and Captain Shover and Lieutenant Kilburn, Third artillery, to that of Captain Bragg. Captain Shover, in conjunction with Lieutenant Donaldson, First artillery, rendered gallant and important service in repulsing the cavalry of General Minon. The regular cavalry, under Lieutenant-colonel May, with which was associated Captain Pike's squadron of Arkansas horse, rendered useful service in holding the enemy in check and in covering the batteries at several points. Captain Steene, First dragoons, was severely wounded early in the day, while gallantly endeavoring, with my authority, to rally the troops which were falling to the rear.

"The Mississippi riflemen, under Colonel Davis, were highly conspicuous for their gallantry and steadiness, and sustained throughout the engagement the reputation of veteran troops. Brought into action against an immensely superior force, they maintained themselves for a long time unsupported and with heavy loss, and held an important part of the field until reinforced. Colonel Davis, though severely wounded, remained in the saddle until the close of the action. His distinguished coolness and gallantry at the head of his regiment on this day, entitle him to the particular notice of the government. The Third Indiana regiment, under Colonel Lane, and a fragment of the Second, under Colonel Bowles, were associated with the Mississippi regiment during the greater portion of the day, and acquitted themselves creditably in repulsing the attempts of the enemy to break that portion of our line. The Kentucky cavalry, under Colonel Marshall, rendered good service dismounted, acting as light troops on our left, and afterwards, with a portion of the Arkansas regiment, in meeting and dispersing the column of cavalry at Buena Vista. The First and Second Illinois, and the Kentucky regiments, served immediately under my eye, and I bear a willing testimony to their excellent conduct throughout the day. The spirit and gallantry with which the First Illinois and Second Kentucky engaged the enemy in the morning, restored confidence to that part of the field, while the list of casualties will show how much these three regiments suffered in sustaining the heavy charge of the enemy in the afternoon. Captain Conner's company of Texas volunteers, attached to the Second Illinois regiment, fought bravely, its captain being wounded and two subalterns killed. Colonel Bissell, the only surviving colonel of these regiments, merits notice for his coolness and bravery on this occasion. After the fall of the field-officers of the First Illinois and Second Kentucky regiments, the command of the former devolved upon Lieutenant-colonel Weatherford; that of the latter, upon Major Fry.

"Regimental commanders and others who have rendered reports, speak in general terms of the good conduct of their officers and men, and have specified many names, but the limits of this report forbid a recapitulation of them here. I may, however, mention Lieutenants Rucker and Campbell of the dragoons, and Captain Pike, Arkansas cavalry, commanding squadrons; Lieutenant-colonel Field, Kentucky cavalry; Lieutenant-colonel Roane, Arkansas cavalry, upon whom the command devolved after the fall of Colonel Yell; Major Bradford, Captain Sharpe, (severely wounded,) and Adjutant Griffith, Mississippi regiment; Lieutenant-colonel Hadden, Second Indiana regiment, and Lieutenant Robinson, aid-de-camp to General Lane; Lieutenant-colonel Weatherford, First Illinois regiment; Lieutenant-colonel Morrison, Major Trail, and Adjutant Whiteside, (severely wounded,) Second Illinois regiment; and Major Fry, Second Kentucky regiment, as being favorably noticed for gallantry and good conduct. Major McCulloch, quartermaster in the volunteer service, rendered important services before the engagement, in the command of a spy company, and during the affair was associated with the regular cavalry. To Major Warren, First Illinois volunteers, I feel much indebted for his firm and judicious course, while exercising command in the city of Saltillo.

"The medical staff, under the able direction of Assist ant-surgeon Hitchcock, were assiduous in attention to the wounded on the field, and in their careful removal to the rear. Both in these respects, and in the subsequent organization and service of the hospitals, the administration of this department was every thing that could be wished.

"Brigadier-general Wool speaks in high terms of the officers of his staff, and I take pleasure in mentioning them here, having witnessed their activity and zeal upon the field. Lieutenant and Aid-de-camp McDowell, Colonel Churchill, inspector-general, Captain Chapman, assistant-quartermaster, Lieutenant Sitgreaves, topographical engineers, and Captains Howard and Davis, volunteer service, are conspicuously noticed by the General for their gallantry and good conduct. Messrs. March, Addicks, Potts, Harrison, Burgess, and Dusenbery, attached in various capacities to General Wool's headquarters, are likewise mentioned for their intelligent alacrity in conveying orders to all parts of the field.

"In conclusion, I beg leave to speak of my own staff, to whose exertions in rallying troops and communicating orders I feel greatly indebted. Major Bliss, assistant-adjutant-general, Captain J. H. Eaton, and Lieutenant R. S. Garnett, aids-de-camp, served near my person, and were prompt and zealous in the discharge of every duty. Major Munroe, besides rendering valuable service as chief of artillery, was active and instrumental, as were also Colonels Churchill and Belknap, inspectors-general, in rallying troops and disposing them for the defence of the train and baggage. Colonel Whiting, quartermaster-general, and Captain Eaton, chief of the subsistence department, were engaged with the duties of their departments, and also served in my immediate staff on the field. Captain Sibley, assistant-quartermaster, was necessarily left with the headquarter camp near town, where his services were highly useful. Major Mansfield and Lieutenant Benham, engineers, and Captain Linnard and Lieutenants Pope and Franklin, topographical engineers, were employed before and during the engagement in making reconnoissances, and on the field were very active in bringing information and in conveying my orders to distant points. Lieutenant Kingsbury, in addition to his proper duties as ordnance officer, Captain Chilton, assistant-quartermaster, and Majors Dix and Coffee, served also as extra aids-de-camp and were actively employed in the transmission of orders. Mr. Thomas L. Crittenden, of Kentucky, though not in service, volunteered as my aid-de-camp on this occasion, and served with credit in that capacity. Major Craig, chief of ordnance, and Surgeon Craig, medical director, had been detached on duty from headquarters, and did not reach the ground until the morning of the 24th—too late to participate in the action, but in time to render useful services in their respective departments of the staff."

In this battle the American arms acquired new glory, and the commanding general won imperishable laurels. His cool courage—his presence at every point where duty called him—his self-possession and apparent confidence in the final result, inspired a heroic ardor, and contributed largely to those daring and sustained efforts which finally turned back and overwhelmed the Mexican hosts.

We here add Santa Anna's final report:

"In my despatch from the battle-field of Angostura, dated the 23d, I promised to give you details of the action of the 23d, so soon as I should effect the movement which our entire lack of water and of all supplies made indispensable. In those engagements the army and the nation have restored the lustre of their arms, by overcoming obstacles inconceivable to all save those who witnessed them. These arose, not only from the difficulties of this contest, and of our own situation, but also from the rigor of the season, and the exhaustion of the country along an almost desert route of over fifty leagues, that was destitute of good water, and of all save the most limited supplies.

"The supreme government was informed by communications made before my leaving San Luis, that the army under my command would not commence its operations till the end of winter, as I knew by experience the severe climate of the region, which was also scant of habitations, provisions, shelter, and even of fuel. I therefore resolved to go on organizing, drilling, arming, and clothing the army; and, in a word, to put into a military shape the forces which had just been assembled. My intentions, however, could not be maturely realized.

"The want of pecuniary resources embarrassed all my dispositions. The soldiers, though well disposed to combat with the enemy, had been badly supplied for a month, and would soon have been in want even of food, but that the exertions of the commanders of corps prevented that destitution from driving them from their ranks. While those meritorious men were suffering all kinds of privation, certain writers, from ignorance, want of reflection, party spirit, or, perhaps, from mistaken patriotism, were zealously engaged in thwarting the plans which might otherwise have proved successful. This they did by unjust charges against the army and particular individuals, whom they abused for not marching to the conflict, accusing them of want of decision, and asserting that the position of the army at San Luis was more threatening to our liberties than to the enemy. In the clubs of that capital they labored with assiduity to make the army the instrument of a revolt; but I frustrated their intrigues by timely steps. There was one writer who had the audacity to intimate that I was in collusion with the enemy. Yes, I, to whom they may attribute errors, but whose whole previous course has shown the most elevated patriotism! Traitors are they, who seek not only to traduce me, but, by their detraction of the army, to unnerve its vigor for the service of the country. It seems as if a fatality directs the destinies of this nation, and interdicts a unanimity of the public will for its defence; and from this fatal blindness, the moment when every heart and every aspiration should be directed to one object, is the very juncture when division and distrust are disseminated. Behold me, then, compelled by every circumstance to change my plans. Desertion had already commenced to a shameful extent; and I was fully persuaded that if the scarcity should continue, the army would be dishonorably frittered away. I therefore resolved that, if annihilated, it should be with glory. Having no supplies, I, to obtain them, compromited my private fortune and the credit of myself and friends. All this procured me the sum of one hundred and eighty thousand dollars, with which I was able to furnish the needful supplies to the army for twelve days. I knew well the country we had to cross, and the necessity there would be for carrying provisions; and I sympathized in anticipation with the soldier for what he would endure from the rigor of the season; but to render good service to the country, and save its honor, I had to overlook all this.

"The army moved from San Luis by brigades, so as to render available the scanty resources afforded by the country we were to cross. The force consisted of thirteen thousand four hundred and thirty-two infantry, divided into twenty-eight battalions; four thousand three hundred and thirty-eight cavalry, in thirty-nine squadrons; and a train of artillery of three twenty-four pounders, three sixteen-pounders, five twelve-pounders, five eight-pounders, and a seven-inch howitzer, all served by four hundred and thirteen artillerymen—the total being eighteen thousand one hundred and thirty-three men. Of this force there remained behind, the garrison of the works at San Luis, and others which I allotted to the towns on the route; as also two squadrons to escort our small and only reserve of ammunition; a brigade of infantry, of two battalions, under General Don Ciriaco Vasquez, which remained as a corps of reserve in Matehuala, and of observation upon Tula; as also a brigade of cavalry, under General Don Jose Urrea. The latter was intended to pass Tula, and move through Tamaulipas to the neighborhood of Monterey, so as to call the enemy's attention to that quarter. The point of concentration for the brigades ought necessarily to be near this place, so that in the region through which they had to move, many troops might not be at once thrown together. I therefore fixed on the hacienda of Encarnacion for that point, it being, as I calculated, the last stage but one of my march. I there held a review of the army, which had already lost a thousand men by sickness and desertion. The former was caused by the scantiness and bad quality of food, and still more of water, which was brackish as well as scarce, as also by snow-storms and the exposure of the troops, who had always to be in bivouac and without fuel. These snow-storms obliged me to suspend the march two days, till the weather became more settled; for the cold had already caused the death of several men and horses, and I felt bound by every means to diminish the losses we were incurring. These hardships will account for the number of desertions which occurred up to our arrival at Encarnacion, and which afterwards even increased. It must also be remembered, that almost the whole army had been recently formed, and, as is well known, of men taken by violence from their homes.

"We had advices that the enemy were fortified in the hacienda of Agua Nueva, with six thousand men and thirty pieces, resolved to defend the defiles known by the names of the passes of Canero and Agua Nueva. The Americans did not know the precise point on which our march was directed; for, though they exchanged some shots with our advance in Encarnacion, and had frequent small skirmishes with us in the above passes, they supposed our troops to be scouting-parties of the first brigade of cavalry, under Don Jose V. Minon, whom I had advanced as far as the hacienda of Potosi. These were the impressions when I made my dispositions.

"It was my intention to place my forces between the enemy and Saltillo, so as to oblige him to fight under the disadvantage of having his communication cut off, or, if he would not leave his works, to enable me to besiege him in Agua Nueva. The plan might be carried out in three different ways. One was by marching twenty leagues by the direct road; another by moving to the right by La Hedionda, so as to occupy Buena Vista; and the third, by moving to the left by La Punta de Santa Elena, so as to occupy the hacienda of La Banqueria, and thereafter the road to Saltillo. The two last movements were at this time impracticable, for they would either of them require three or four days' march, while we were without provisions, forage, or water. I therefore resolved to operate by the direct road, force the positions, and, after passing the last defile, make a diversion by the left, and occupy the rancho of Encantada, with the view of obtaining water, none of which was to be had for more than eighteen leagues. All this was favored by the enemy's ignorance of our march; but misfortune still followed us. A deserter from the regiment of Coraceros, a native of Saltillo, named Francisco Valdes, passed over from Encarnacion to the enemy, and gave him information of the movement. The execrable treason of this infamous wretch frustrated the best combinations.

"On the 21st, at noon, I ordered the march to commence, the four light battalions, under General Don Pedro Ampudia, forming the vanguard. I had not hesitated to allow that general, and other officers who had been court-martialed for the affair of Monterey, to participate in these operations, not only because I did not consider them culpable, but also on account of the zeal they manifested. This brigade was followed by one of artillery, of sixteen-pounders, with the regiments of engineers and their train, and those by the park of the regiment of hussars. Then came the First division, commanded by General Don Manuel Lombardini, with four twelve-pounders and the park. The Second division, under General Don Francisco Pacheco, followed next, with four eight-pounders and their park; after these the whole of the cavalry, under Don Julian Juvera; and then the remainder of the general park and baggage, the rear being covered by a brigade of cavalry under General Don Manuel Andrade.

"In this order of march the troops were ordered to make the first fourteen leagues, between Encenada and a plain called De la Guerra, which is in front of the first defile called the Pass of the Pinones; and to pass the night on that plain in the same order of column. The troops having eaten their rations, order was given for carrying water, as none could be met with till the day following, after having overcome the enemy at Agua Nueva, three leagues beyond the aforesaid pass. I, with my staff and the regiment of engineers, occupied the front, a little behind the light troops. On arriving at the plain De la

Guerra, I continued the march in order to pass the defile of Pinones, which was accomplished; and I ordered the light brigade to take a position in the pass of Carnero, where it had a skirmish with an advance of the enemy. Under these dispositions we passed the night.

"At dawn on the 22d the army continued its march, with the idea of carrying by force of arms the pass of Agua Nueva, which I supposed would be defended by the enemy; but I found to my surprise that it had been abandoned. I then concluded that the American forces had retired to their fortifications in the hacienda, to concentrate their defence under cover of the intrenchments, which I had heard they had there thrown up. Under this idea I continued the march, in order to turn by the right to the rancho of Encantada, which, as I have before mentioned, is on the Saltillo road, being between that city and Agua Nueva, and four or five leagues from each. Till that time no one had appeared to give me information, nor did any one after, except a servant from Agua Nueva, who told me that the enemy had been evacuating his position since the day previous, and falling back towards Saltillo; and that on that same morning, the hacienda had been wholly abandoned, by the retreat of a small detachment which escorted a large quantity of munitions. By this movement my first plans and dispositions, founded on an expected resistance, were rendered abortive; but I still did not despair of a successful result, for I had in anticipation directed General Minon, with his cavalry brigade, twelve hundred strong, to occupy, on the morning of the 22d, the hacienda of Buena Vista, distant three short leagues from Saltillo. This force might arrest the enemy's march, or, at least, make a diversion that would give time for the army to come up. I therefore continued my march, without losing more time than would allow the soldiers to drink water on the road. The light brigade came within sight of the enemy's rear-guard, and I ordered them to charge in conjunction with the hussar regiment. I had reason to believe the enemy were making a precipitate retreat, as they left several articles on the road, such as carts, forge implements, extra wheels, and other things, which we gathered while marching. In consequence of the different reports I received, I ordered the cavalry to advance; I thought we would be able to reach their rear-guard, and placed myself at the head of those troops.

"On arriving at a place called Angostura, I found the main body of the enemy awaiting me in position. The road from the pass of Pinones to Saltillo runs between two chains of mountains, which form that pass and those of Carnero and Agua Nueva. The ridges open beyond the hacienda and approach each other again at Angostura, where the road turns to the right. At this place there is a succession of ridges, which run out towards the line of our route, and at right angles with it, and between them are ravines which form the drains of the mountains on the right. They are more or less passable, but all very difficult. The enemy's position was in front and in rear of the road, his right and front being covered by ravines that were impassable, even for infantry, and a battery of four pieces being planted on the highest point. His battalions were formed on the heights with two other batteries, one of which was in a low part of the road, between two hills; and, to my view, their forces appeared to be about eight thousand men, with twenty pieces; but the prisoners taken from them report twenty-six pieces, and upwards of eight thousand combatants.

"I reconnoitred the position and situation of the enemy, and ordered the director of engineers, General Don Ignacio de Mora y Villamil, to do the same. After ascertaining the force of the invader, it was necessary either to await the infantry, to take position, or to fight, as might seem most advisable. At this interval, I observed that the enemy had neglected to occupy a height on his left flank; and, without losing a moment, I ordered General Ampudia's light brigade to take possession of, and hold it at every cost. As the brigade came up, I formed them in two lines on a rising ground that fronted the enemy, there being another eminence between our two positions: the first division of infantry was under the command of General Lombardini, and the second under the command of General Pacheco. I directed that General Mora y Villamil, in conjunction with the commanding general of artillery, Don Antonio Corona, should find a position for a battery of sixteen-pounders, to be sustained by the regiment of engineers. Two other batteries, of twelve and eight-pounders, were located by me. The cavalry, commanded by General Juvera, were placed on the right of our rear, and on our left flank. The regiment of hussars was also posted in the rear, and on the left flank aforesaid was a height which I ordered the battalion of Leon to occupy. The general park was in the rear, covered by the brigade of General Andrade, and between this park and the lines of battle I took my own position.

"The making of these dispositions, as may be supposed, occupied some time, for the troops arrived at their positions after a march of more than twenty leagues. It was therefore not an hour for combat, and the army lay on its arms. The enemy, however, so soon as he perceived that we had occupied the height that flanked his left and our right, despatched two battalions to dislodge us, which led to a warm engagement, that lasted all the afternoon and till after dark, when he was repulsed with a loss of four hundred men, according to the report of the prisoners. Ours was much less, as we had the advantage of the ground.

"At dawn on the 23d I mounted my horse; the enemy had not changed his previous dispositions, and was ready to receive us. I observed but one difference, which was, that on his right, and at some distance from his position, he had formed two bodies of infantry, with a battery of four pieces, as if with the intent of threatening our left flank; but I at once believed this to be a mere demonstration, for he would never have left in his rear the difficult ground which gave strength to that position, being the web of impassable ravines before referred to. I, therefore, gave no attention to this disposition of his forces, and resolved to move mine by the right. With this intention, I advanced the divisions of General Lombardini and General Pacheco in that direction. I ordered General Don Manuel Micheltorena to plant the battery of eight-pounders on our right flank, so as to rake obliquely the enemy's line, and to remain with the staff, of which he was chief, and await my orders. I directed that General Ampudia, with the light brigade, should charge by our left flank on the enemy's right, and that General Mora y Villamil should form a column of attack composed of the regiment of engineers, the 12th battalion, the *fijo de Mexico*, and the companies of Puebla and Tampico, commanded by Colonel

Don Santiago Blanco. At the same time, I directed General Corona, commanding the artillery, to place the battery of twelve-pounders in a more commanding position, while the 3d division remained in reserve under Brevet General Don Jose Maria Ortega.

"So soon as the enemy perceived our movements, he commenced the action at all points, attacked our troops with intrepidity, and maintained the conflict with great vigor. Our men received them with proper energy, driving back and following up the assailants. At this time my horse was disabled by a grape-shot, and it was some time before I could mount another. As the enemy had yielded ground, I ordered the cavalry to advance and charge, which was done with vigor. Suitable orders had been sent to the generals of division and brigade, among the rest to General Don Angel Guzman; but, though the officers and troops acted with great resolution, it was impossible to overcome the difficulties of the ground; and after a struggle which did them honor, they were obliged to fall back to their positions. After various alternations, the same occurred with the infantry.

"The battle, which commenced at seven in the morning, was prolonged for many hours, our loss every moment accumulating. Many officers and soldiers had already been killed, and a number of commanders and distinguished officers wounded, among whom were General Lombardini, Lieutenant-colonels Brito, Galloso, and others. Among the slain were Lieutenant-colonels Asonos, Berra, and other meritorious officers, whose loss the country will ever lament. The enemy maintained his ground with the utmost obstinacy, insomuch that some of our troops faltered in their attacks, and many of the raw recruits dispersed. This, however, ought to exalt the merit of those whose intrepidity was never paralyzed, and may also be cited to show how hotly contested was the action.

"Things were in this situation when I concluded to make the final effort. With this view I ordered that a battery of twenty-four pounders should be mounted; that the column of attack then posted on our left flank, where it had no object of operation, should be transferred to our right, and there be joined by the remains of the Eleventh regiment, the battalion of Leon, and the reserves, all under the command of Brevet-General Don Francisco Perez. I executed this in person, and afterwards sent for General Mora y Villamil, and made him acquainted with my final disposition. I had already directed Generals Perez and Pacheco, each with his command, to be prepared for an extreme struggle, and had ordered the battery of eight-pounders to advance and take the enemy's line in flank. The charge was made with daring valor, and was resisted with animated vigor, with a fire so heavy and rapid as to cause admiration; but the Americans could not sustain themselves—they were driven back and overcome, with the loss of three pieces of cannon and as many stands of colors. I sent two of the latter to the government with my last despatch; the other, which I then omitted to notice, will be presented to the honorable congress of the State of San Luis Potosi, as a testimonial of the army's gratitude for the patriotic services they had rendered, and the generous sacrifices they had made for its benefit. We moreover captured a travelling forge, and some smaller articles, which I will not enumerate. Our cavalry, which so bravely executed the order to charge, reached the enemy's rearmost positions; but, owing to the nature of the ground and the fatigue of the men and horses, I did not think it prudent to attempt to dislodge them from those. The battle closed at six in the evening, our troops being then formed on the ground which the Americans had occupied. Our last effort would have been decisive, if Gen eral Minon had done his part by attacking the enemy in the rear; but he omitted to do it, and I am under the painful necessity of subjecting his conduct to a court martial, that he may explain it. An action thus contested necessarily involved considerable loss. Ours in killed and wounded amounted to more than fifteen hundred men, and that of the enemy was much greater, for we had time to take a view of the great number of their dead.

"The plans of these two actions, and of the route from Agua Nueva to Saltillo, and the reports of the generals of the division and brigade, which I send with this to your excellency, will give the supreme government an idea of such details as I have not dwelt on, without making this report more diffuse; but this will still serve to attest the bravery of our troops, and the glory acquired by the nation during these days of action.

"In the order of the day, I expressed, as in duty bound, my satisfaction with the conduct of the officers, commanders of corps, and generals, and gave them thanks for it in the name of the republic. I could wish to announce in this report the names of many commanding officers, that their memory may be engraved on the gratitude of the nation, not only for their resolute and honorable deportment in both actions, but for the constancy with which they have overcome so many privations, sufferings, and fatigues, and given therein an example both of civic and military worth. Anxious to do this justice, I adopt as my own the authorship of those eulogies which the generals of brigade and division have bestowed on their subordinates. I would, moreover, place in view of the government, the merit manifested by the director-general of engineers, Don Ignacio Mora y Villamil, who fulfilled, to my entire satisfaction, all the duties I assigned to him, for which I consider him worthy of the highest praise, and of such remuneration as the supreme government may be pleased to award to his distinguished services. General Ampudia, to whom, from the favorable opinion which I had of him, I intrusted the command of the four light battalions, acquitted himself with gallantry. General Lombardini, who commanded the First division of infantry, conducted himself with valor, and was wounded. General Pacheco, commanding the Second division of infantry, came up to my orders and his duties, and fought to my satisfaction. General Juvera comported himself honorably, and had his horse killed under him. Brevet-General Torrejon received a contusion, and General Guzman displayed the gallantry for which he was already distinguished, and was wounded. Brevet-General Micheltorena, as head of the staff, duly performed all that belonged to his station; and I also confided to his special charge the battery of eight-pounders, which was the most in advance. General Perez acted as might be expected from his accustomed gallantry, and for this I intrusted to his command the troops I have before mentioned, with which he contributed to disorder the line of the enemy at five in the evening. I would also commend General Ortega, who commanded the Third division of foot, and performed his duties to my satisfaction, as also Brevet general Uraga, and Generals Parrodi, Portilla, Vasquez, Jauregui, Terres, and Sanchez.

"It is entirely due to the commanding general of artillery, Don Antonio Corona, that I should commend him for carrying out my dispositions, as might be expected from him, and for laboring assiduously at San Luis, in the heaviest duties of his branch of service; and it is a pleasing duty for me to laud the merit acquired by Colonel Banencli, and Colonel Brito, who was wounded; Colonel Aldrade, of the hussars, who, to my satisfaction, evinced his usual bravery; Colonel S. Blanco, who commanded a column of attack on the left, and acted well, and Colonel M. Blanco—both of the last being of the engineers—as also Colonel Obando, of the flying artillery, and Colonel Garay.

"The report of the killed and wounded, which I also send, will show what has been our loss. I should be lacking in justice, and not express my own feelings, were I not most earnestly to request that attention be paid, as is by law provided, to the cases of the widows, orphans, and such of the wounded as may be permanently disabled.

"The formidable position which the enemy occupied, was all that saved him; the victory would otherwise have been decisive, notwithstanding his obstinate resistance. Still this triumph will have favorable results to the national cause, as it will show to every one what can be accomplished when all hearts are united, and with one aim.

"The army has done more than could be expected under the laws of nature. It had just been formed, and as yet had not acquired discipline or military habits; yet in marching to the combat, it overcame difficulties which might have subdued the stoutest heart. After a march of twenty leagues, sixteen of them without water, and without other food than a single ration, which was dealt out at Encarnacion, it endured the fatigue of combat for two days, and finally triumphed. With all this, its physical powers were exhausted. My knowledge of this, and the duty I felt in attending to such a number of wounded, constrained me, after remaining a few hours on the field of battle, to fall back upon Agua Nueva, for the relief and refreshment of the troops.

"From the impression we had made on the enemy, he did not appear before us for three days. The bearer of a flag of truce, however, arrived with a proposition from General Taylor for an exchange of prisoners, and for our sending for the wounded who had remained on the field. He also expressed to me the desire which the Americans felt for the re-establishment of peace. I replied, in order that he might say the same to his general, that we sustained the most sacred of causes—the defence of our territory, and the preservation of our nationality and rights; that we were not the aggressors, and that our government had never offended that of the United States. *I observed, that we could say nothing of peace while the Americans were on this side of the Bravo, or occupied any part of the Mexican territory, or blockaded our ports;* and that we were resolved to perish or vindicate our rights; that fortune might not be always favorable to the enemy, and their experience of the 22d and 23d should convince them that it could change; I added, that the Americans waged against us a war of vandalism, whose excesses outraged those sentiments of humanity which one civilized nation ought to evince towards another; and that if he would go outside of the apartment he would still see smoking, which was the fact, the dwellings of Agua Nueva, recently a flourishing, though a small settlement; that the same vestiges of desolation marked the route of his retreat; and that if he would go a little farther on, to Catana, he would hear the moans of the widows and orphans of innocent victims who had been sacrificed without necessity.

"With respect to the wounded, whom I was invited to send for, I replied that there could be none save those who had been too much hurt to rise from the field, or those most in the advance, who had remained in the ravines; and that as I had not means for their conveyance, the enemy might take them to Saltillo, under the protection of the laws of nations. As for the prisoners which he offered to exchange, I told him I did not know who they could be, unless it were some of our dispersed troops, or some who, from the fatigue of the two previous days, had remained asleep when we moved. In answer to the courtesy the enemy's general had shown with respect to our wounded, I consented, in the name of the nation, to release all the prisoners we had—those taken both in the battle and at Encarnacion. At the same time I allowed the bearer of the flag, who was a superior officer, of prepossessing appearance and manners, to take the bandage from his eyes, and informed him that it was for him personally that the honor of this concession was meant. I did it also that he might see our camp and our troops.

"As I have said in the preceding paragraph, we remained at the hacienda three days; but the only supply we could obtain was ninety beeves, and these were consumed on the 25th. The horses were also without forage, and notwithstanding all the efforts or provisions that I could make, many of the wounded had been but once attended to, and some not at all. From the rigor of the climate, the badness and scantiness of the sustenance, the entire want of bread, and the bad quality of the water used in our former bivouacs, a bowel complaint had broken out in the army, and rendered ineffective at least one-half of it. I knew that a retrograde movement to our former positions had become inevitable; but though every thing around me proclaimed this necessity, my feelings revolted against it, solely because I foresaw that from ignorance, malice, or presumption, the countermarch would be condemned, and that those who did not witness our situation would imagine the possibility of the army's continuing its operations.

"Six days before, when the troops had not suffered so much, nor fought for two successive days, nor been embarrassed with sick and wounded, but were still sound in morale and in health, I had not deemed it prudent to augment the labors and difficulties of the army by moving to the right or to the left; how then would it have been possible to go on operating after all that subsequently occurred? But let detractors say what they will, the army as well as myself will always answer by an appeal to our conduct, our wishes, and the notorious impossibility of carrying them out. Notwithstanding my conviction, I wished to hear the opinion of the generals and some of the commanders of corps, and to ascertain if they could point out any resource which had not occurred to me. Without disclosing my own ideas on the subject I lis tened to theirs, and they all unanimously, and each one by his opinion separately expressed, showed and demonstrated in various ways, that however good their will to remain, the countermarch of the army had become indispensable, but that this necessity was not forced upon us by the enemy. It was not till I had heard their opinions that I announced my own accordant resolution, and the proceedings of the council being drawn up, I had the honor of remitting them to your excellency on the 25th.

"On the 26th, after I had ordered General Minon to follow the movement, the army commenced its retreat with the view of occupying the first peopled localities, where resources might be obtained, such as Vanegas Catorce, El Cadral, and Matehuala, as also Tula; but I doubt if in those places proper attention can be given to the sick and wounded—or the losses we have sustained in those laborious movements be remedied.

"The nation, for which a triumph has been gained at the cost of so many sufferings, will learn that, if we were able to conquer in the midst of so many embarrassments, there will be no doubt as to our final success in the struggle we sustain, if every spirit but rallies to the one sacred object of common defence. A mere determined number of men will not, as many imagine, suffice for the prosecution of war: it is indispensable that they be armed, equipped, disciplined, and habituated, and that a systematized support for such an organized force be provided. We must bear in mind that we have to combat in a region deficient of all resources, and that every thing for subsistence has to be carried along with the soldiery: the good-will of a few will not suffice, bu the co-operation of all is needed; and if we do not cast aside selfish interests, and petty passions, we can expect nothing but disaster. The army, and myself who have led it, have the satisfaction of knowing that we have demonstrated this truth"

CHAPTER IX.

Advance of the Army to Lobos; thence to Antonio Lizardo.—Siege and Capture of Vera Cruz.—Official Despatches.—March to the Interior.—Battle of Cerro Gordo.—Official Despatches.—Capture of Puebla.

General Scott having been joined by the troops from the Upper Rio Grande, halted for a few days at the mouth of the river. Every thing being in readiness, they were taken on board transports, and proceeded to join others who had made their rendezvous at the island of Lobos, about 125 miles north and west of the city of Vera Cruz. The troops being thus collected, the whole armament proceeded to Antonio Lizardo.

On the morning of the 7th of March, General Scott, in a steamer, with Commodore Connor, reconnoitred the city, for the purpose of selecting the best landing-place for the army. The spot selected was the shore west of the island of Sacrificios. The anchorage was too narrow for a large number of vessels, and on the morning of the 9th of March the troops were removed from the transports to the ships of war. The fleet then set sail—General Scott in the steamship Massachusetts, leading the van. As he passed through the squadron, his tall form, conspicuous on the deck, attracted the eyes of soldier and of sailor; a cheer burst spontaneously forth, and from vessel to vessel was echoed, and answered through the line. The voices of veterans, and of new recruits—of those who had been victorious at Monterey, and of those who hoped for victories in the future—were mingled in loud acclamation for him, whose character inspired confidence, and whose actions were already embodied in the glorious history of their country!

Near Sacrificios the landing commenced. It must be observed at this point, that every man expected to be met at the landing; for such, in military judgment, should have been the course of the enemy, and such would have been the case had the landing been made at the point where the enemy expected it, and where his forces were collected. Preparations were therefore made for any possible contingency. Two steamers and five gunboats, arranged in line, covered the landing. Five thousand five hundred troops embarked in sixty-seven surf-boats. The signal-gun was fired. The seamen bent to their oars, and in a magnificent semicircle the boats swept rapidly towards the beach. Every man is anxious to be first. They plunge into the water before they reach the shore! they rush through the sand-hills! and with loud shouts they press forward! They wave the flag of their country in the land of the Aztecs! Where are their comrades? They also soon embark—they hurry through the water—they land in safety—they rejoin their companions—they return shout for shout, to friends in the vessels and friends on shore. Safely, but hurriedly, they then pass through this exciting crisis.

In the meanwhile, the sun shines down in the brilliance of his light, the waters are but just ruffled by a breeze, while the deep waves are calm and the sky serene. Full in view lies the city of Vera Cruz, and near is the renowned castle of San Juan d'Ulloa! The harbor is crowded with foreign vessels, and decks and rigging are filled with wondering spectators! Never, says one, shall I forget the excitement of that scene!

The first division of troops had landed a little before sunset, the second and third followed in succession, and before ten o'clock the whole army (numbering twelve thousand men) was landed, without the slightest accident and without the loss of a single life!

Thus, at the distance of more than three hundred years, was renewed the landing and march of Cortez! Both were brilliant, and remarkable in history and conduct. The Spanish hero came to encounter and subdue, on unknown shores, the Aztectic-American civilization. The Anglo-American came to meet and prevail against the Spanish-Aztec combination. Both came with inferior numbers, to illustrate the higher order and vastly superior energies of moral power. Both came agents controlled by an invisible spirit, in carrying forward the drama of Divine Providence on earth. In vain do we speculate as to the end; it will be revealed only when the last curtain is drawn from the deep, mysterious Future.

The landing at Vera Cruz, as a military operation, deserves a credit which is seldom awarded to bloodless achievements. It is common to measure military operations by the current of blood which has flowed. But why? Is he not the best general who accomplishes the greatest results with the least loss? Or must we adopt the savage theory, that the greatest inhumanity is the greatest heroism? Mere animal bravery is a common quality. Why, then, should the exhibition of so common a quality, in an open battle, give distinction, when it is skill only that is valuable, and science only that is uncommon? This skill and science were exhibited in a

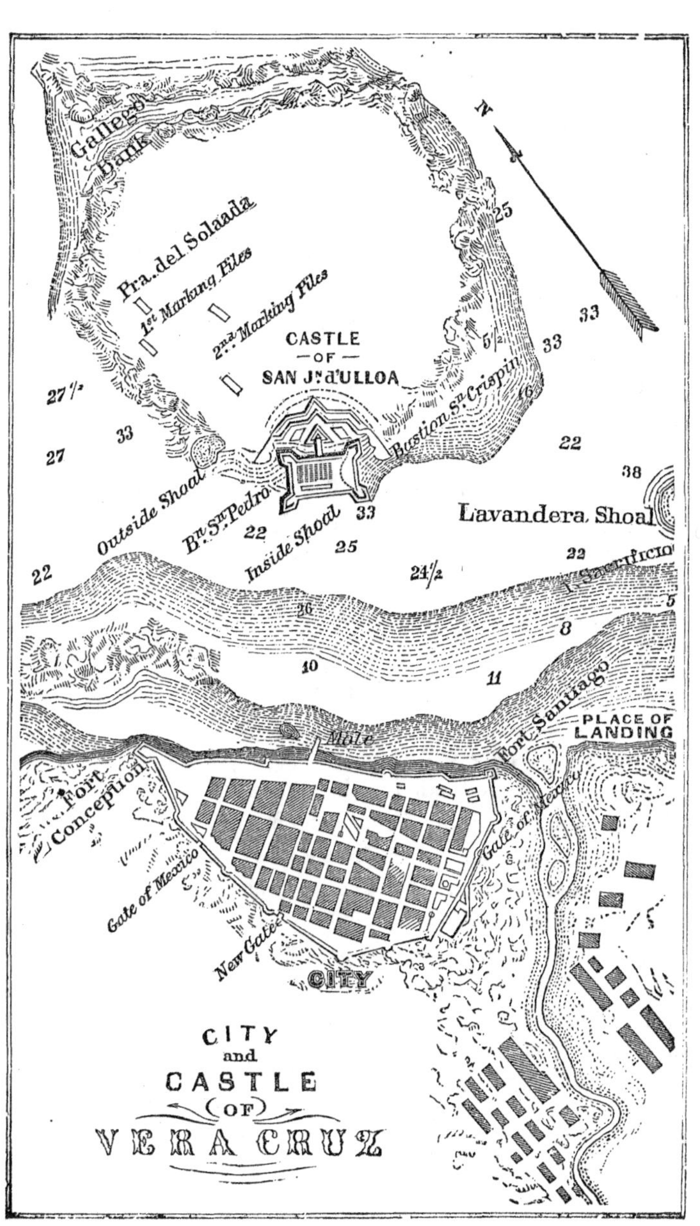

N
Gallego Bank
Pra. del Solaada
1st Marking Files
2nd Marking Files
CASTLE
— OF —
SAN Jn d'ULLOA
Bastion Sn Crispin
Outside Shoal
Bn Sn Pedro
Inside Shoal
Lavandera Shoal
I. Sacrificio
Fort Santiago
PLACE OF LANDING
Mole
Fort Concepcion
Gate of Mexico
Gate of Mexico
New Gate
CITY
CITY
and
CASTLE
OF
VERA CRUZ

most singular and felicitous manner, in the pre-arrangements, combinations, and success, which attended the landing of the American army under the walls of Vera Cruz.

Of this landing, as compared with a similar one by the French at Algiers, the *New Orleans Bulletin*, of March 27th, makes the following correct and interesting remarks:

"The landing of the American army at Vera Cruz has been accomplished in a manner that reflects the highest credit on all concerned, and the regularity, precision, and promptness with which it was effected, has probably not been surpassed, if it has been equalled in modern warfare.

"The removal of a large body of troops from numerous transports into boats in an open sea—their subsequent disembarkation on the sea-beach, on an enemy's coast, through a surf, with all their arms and accoutrements, without a single error or accident, requires great exertion, skill, and sound judgment.

"The French expedition against Algiers, in 1830, was said to be the most complete armament in every respect that ever left Europe; it had been prepared with labor, attention, and experience, and nothing had been omitted to ensure success, and particularly in the means and facilities for landing the troops. This disembarkation took place in a wide bay, which was more favorable than an open beach directly on the ocean, and (as in the present instance) without any resistance on the part of the enemy—yet, only nine thousand men were landed the first day, and from thirty to forty lives were lost by accidents, or upsetting of boats; whereas, on the present occasion, twelve thousand men were landed in one day, without, so far as we have heard, the slightest accident or the loss of a single life."

No troops of the enemy made direct opposition to the American army on reaching the beach, but the guns of the castle and city kept up a constant firing with round shot and thirteen-inch shells. The several corps immediately occupied the lines of investment to which they had been respectively assigned by General Scott's orders.[1] These orders pointed out the most minute particulars, and were based on *prior information*, obtained by the engineer and topographical departments, and carefully analyzed and thoroughly studied, by the commander-in-chief. This information was so accurate, and so well understood by the commander, the engineers, and the chief of the staff, that they made no mistakes. They found all as they anticipated: their arrangements resulted as they intended, and the regiments and companies took their respective places as quietly and orderly as if they were parading on the green banks of the Potomac! Parties of the enemy appeared, and skirmishes took place, but nothing seriously interrupted the progress of investment. On the 12th instant, the entire army had completely occupied its positions.[2]

All this was not done without labor, fatigue, and exposure of the severest kind. The carts, horses, and mules, except a very few,[3] had not yet arrived. Innumerable

---

[1] General Orders, No. 47.

[2] General Scott's Official Report, dated 12th of March, 1847.

[3] There had then arrived but fifteen carts and one hundred draught-horses.

nills of loose sand, and almost impassable thickets of chapparal, covered the ground of operations. Through these, by their own hands, and on their backs, soldiers, both regular and volunteer, dragged their provisions, their equipments, and munitions of war, under the rays of a sun already hot in a tropical climate. The sands of this peculiar region are so light, that during the existence of a "norther," (a so-called wind of the Gulf,) if a man would lie down for an hour or two, he would inevitably be buried in the floating drifts! He must therefore, at this season, seek shelter in chapparals. In such circumstances—under the distant fire of the enemy's fortresses, and in the midst of sharp skirmishes—the investment was completed. The lines of siege were five miles in length, and on that whole distance provisions must be carried and communications kept up with dépôts, and with ships at sea. In this the officers and seamen of the navy co-operated with those of the army in the most gallant and skilful manner.

During this part of the siege a "norther" prevailed, which rendered it impossible to land heavy ordnance. On the 17th a pause occurred in the storm, and ten mortars, four twenty-four-pound guns, and some howitzers were landed. On the night of the 18th the trenches were opened, and, the engineers with the sappers and miners leading the way, the army gradually closed in nearer the city.

On the 22d of March—seven of the ten-inch mortars being in battery, and other works in progress—General Scott summoned the governor of Vera Cruz to surrender the city. The governor, who was also governor of the castle, chose to consider the summons to surrender that, as well as the city, and rejected the proposition. On the return of the flag, the mortar-battery, at the distance o. eight hundred yards from the city, opened its fire on the city, and continued to fire during the day and night.

On the 24th the batteries were reinforced with twenty-four-pounders and paixhan guns. On the 25th all the batteries were in "awful activity." Terrible was the scene! The darkness of night was illuminated with blazing shells circling through the air. The roar of artillery and the heavy fall of descending shot were heard through the streets of the besieged city. The roofs of buildings were on fire. The domes of churches reverberated with fearful explosions. The sea was reddened with the broadsides of ships. The castle of San Juan returned, from its heavy batteries, the fire, the light, the smoke, the noise of battle. Such was the sublime and awfully terrible scene, as beheld from the trenches of the army, from the 22d to the 25th of March, when the accumulated science of ages, applied to the military art, had, on the plains of Vera Cruz, aggregated and displayed the fulness of its destructive power.

On the evening of the 25th instant, the consuls of European powers residing in Vera Cruz, made application, by memorial, to General Scott for a truce, to enable them and the women and children of the city to retire. To this General Scott replied—that a *truce* could only be granted on application of General Morales, the governor, with a view to surrender;[1] that safeguards had already been sent to the foreign consuls, of which they had refused to avail themselves; that the blockade had been left open to consuls and neutrals to the 22d proximo; and

[1] Scott's Official Report of March 25, 1847.

BOMBARDMENT OF VERA CRUZ AND CASTLE.

that the case of women and children, with their hardships and distresses, had been fully considered before one gun was fired.

The memorial represented that the batteries had already a terrible effect on the city—and by this, and other evidence, it was now clear that a crisis had arrived. The city must either be surrendered, or it must be consigned to inevitable and most melancholy destruction.

Accordingly, early on the morning of the 26th of March, General Landero, on whom the command had been devolved by General Morales, made overtures of surrender. Arrangements had been made by Scott for carrying the city by assault on that very day. The proposition of the Mexican general made this unnecessary, and Generals Worth and Pillow, with Colonel Totten, that distinguished officer of the engineer corps, who had conducted the siege, were appointed commissioners on the part of the Ameri can army, to treat with others appointed by the governor of Vera Cruz. Late on the night of the 27th the articles of capitulation were signed and exchanged.

On the 29th of March the official despatch of General Scott announced that the flag of the United States floated over the walls of Vera Cruz and the castle of San Juan d'Ulloa. The regular siege of the city had continued from the day of *investment*, the 12th of March, to the day the articles of capitulation were signed, the 27th, making a period of *fifteen days*, in which active, continuous, and vigorous operations were carried on. During this time our army had thrown three thousand ten-inch shells, two hundred howitzer shells, one thousand paixhan shot, and two thousand five hundred round-shot, weighing on the whole about *half a million of pounds!* Most effective and most terrible was the disaster and destruction they caused within the walls of the city, whose ruins and whose mourning attested both the energy and the sadness of war.

By some it was thought strange that the governor of Vera Cruz should have surrendered so soon; but, on a full exhibition of the facts of the siege, surprise gives place to admiration at the progress, power, and development of military science. The thirty years which had elapsed since the fall of Napoleon, had not been idly passed by military men. They had acquired and systematized new arts and new methods in the art of war. Nor were American officers inattentive to this progress. They had shared in it all, and when the siege of Vera Cruz was undertaken, this new power and method were fully displayed. The city was environed with cords of strength, in which all its defences must be folded and crushed. The result was inevitable. The officers of Vera Cruz saw this, and although the castle of San Juan might have held out a few days longer, for what purpose would it have been? There is no rule of military science which requires fighting when fighting is useless. There is no law of humanity which would not be violated by the wanton exposure of towns and inhabitants when defence was impossible. The surrender was, therefore, alike just to victors and defenders, both of whom had arrived at an inevitable end,—the result of progress in high civilization, and of the highest military skill and accomplishments.

By the terms of capitulation, all the arms and munitions of war were given up to the United States; five thousand prisoners surrendered on parole; near five hundred pieces of fine artillery were taken; the best port of Mexico captured and possessed; and the famed castle of San Juan, said to be impregnable, and which had been refitted and equipped in the best possible manner, yielded its defences to the superior skill and energy of the Anglo-Americans. At 10 A. M., on the morning of the 29th, that people, who centuries before had, with a small band, marched through the Aztec empire, and, with the pride of power, supplanted its ancient dominion, struck their flags and quietly submitted to another and a newer race, who had come over the Atlantic later than themselves, but who had imbibed other principles, and been impelled by stronger energies, in the colder regions of the north. On the castle of San Juan, on the forts of Santiago and Conception, the banner of the American Union gracefully ascended, and, amidst the shouts and cheers of warriors on sea and shore, bent its folds to the breeze, and looked forth over the Mexican Gulf.

In this great and successful enterprise, the American arms met with but little loss. Two officers,[1] (valuable, however, to their corps and country,) with a few soldiers, were all the deaths. So great a result, obtained with so little loss, may be sought in vain among the best campaigns of the best generals of modern times. There are those who think victory brightest when achieved in the carnival of death, and the laurel greenest which is plucked from a crimson tree. But this is not the estimate of the humane, the honorable, or the intelligent. They, in this age of the world, will deem that achievement greatest which costs the least, where skill has been substituted for death, and science for the brave but often wasted energy of bodily force.

---

[1] Captains Alburtis and Vinton, both distinguished officers, were killed, with several private soldiers.

Some incidents of this siege are related, which illustrate the character of General Scott and the nature of the war. On one occasion, when the general was walking along the trenches, the soldiers would frequently rise up and look over the parapet. The general cried out, "Down—down, men!—don't expose yourselves." "But, general," said one, "*you* are exposed." "Oh!" said Scott, "*generals*, now-a-days, can be made out of anybody, but *men* cannot be had."

Something has been severely said, as to the loss of women and children by the bombardment of the city; but this is unjustly said. Scott, as appears by the official papers, gave ample notice of the danger to consuls, neutrals, and non-combatants in the city, and ample time for them to remove. That they, or at least many of them, did not avail themselves of that notice, was their own fault; and, by the laws of war, it was both unnecessary and impossible that the siege should be delayed, or given up, on account of the inhabitants within, who had long known that the United States army would land there, and who had received from the commander full notice of danger.

We add General Scott's official despatches.

HEADQUARTERS OF THE ARMY,
Camp Washington, before VERA CRUZ,
March 12th, 1847.

SIR:—The colors of the United States were triumphantly planted ashore, in full view of this city and castle, and under the distant fire of both, in the afternoon of the 9th inst. Brevet Brigadier-general Worth's brigade of regulars led the descent, quickly followed by the division of United States volunteers under Major-general Patterson, and Brigadier-general Twiggs' reserve brigade of regulars. The three lines successively landed in sixty-seven surf-boats, each boat conducted by a naval officer, and rowed by sailors from Commodore Connor's squadron, whose lighter vessels flanked the boats so as to be ready to protect the operation by their cross-fire. The whole army reached the shore in fine style, and without direct opposition, (on the beach,) accident, or loss, driving the enemy from the ground to be occupied.

The line of investment, according to General Orders, No. 47, was partially taken up the same night; but has only been completed to-day, owing to the most extraordinary difficulties: 1. The environs of the city, outside of the fire of its guns and those of the castle, are broken into innumerable hills of loose sand, from 20 to 250 feet in height, with almost impassable forests of chapporal between; and, 2. Of all our means of land-transportation—wagons, carts, pack-saddles, horses, and mules, expected to join us from Tampico and the Brazos, weeks ago—but 15 carts and about 100 draught-horses have yet arrived. Three hundred pack-mules are greatly needed to relieve the troops in taking subsistence alone, along the line of investment of more than five miles, as, at present, our only depot is south of the city. On the cessation of the present raging Norther, which almost stifles the troops with sand, sweeping away hills and creating new, I hope to establish a second depot north of the city, which will partially relieve the left wing of the army.

In extending the line of investment around the city, the troops for three days have performed the heaviest labors in getting over the hills and cutting through the intervening forests—all under the distant fire of the city and castle, and in the midst of many sharp skirmishes with the enemy. In these operations we have lost in killed and wounded several valuable officers and men. Among the killed I have to report Brevet Capt. Alburtis, of the United States 2d Infantry, much distinguished in the Florida war, and a most excellent officer. He fell on the 11th inst.; and Lieut. Col. Dickenson, of the South Carolina Regiment, was badly wounded in a skirmish the day before. Two privates have been killed in these operations, and four or five wounded. As yet I have not been able to obtain their names.

As soon as the subsistence of the troops can be assured, and their positions are well established, I shall, by an organized movement, cause each brigade of regulars and volunteers to send detachments, with supports, to clear its front, including sub-bourgs, of the enemy's parties, so as to oblige them to confine themselves within the walls of the city.

I have heretofore reported that but two-sevenths of the siege-train and ammunition had reached me. The remainder is yet unheard of. We shall commence landing the heavy metal as soon as the storm subsides, and hope that the five-sevenths may be up in time.

The city being invested, would, no doubt, early surrender, but for the fear that, if occupied by us, it would immediately be fired upon by the castle. I am not altogether without hope of finding the means of coming to some compromise with the city on this subject.

So far, the principal skirmishing has fallen to the lot of Brigadier-general Pillow's and Quitman's brigades. Both old and new volunteer regiments have conducted themselves admirably. Indeed, the whole army is full of zeal and confidence, and cannot fail to acquire distinction in the impending operations.

To Commodore Connor, the officers and sailors of his squadron, the army is indebted for great and unceasing assistance, promptly and cheerfully rendered. Their co-operation is the constant theme of our gratitude and admiration. A handsome detachment of marines, under Capt. Edson, of that corps, landed with the first line, and is doing duty with the army.

March 13.—The enemy, at intervals, continues the fire of heavy ordnance, from the city and castle, upon our line of investment, both by day and night, but with little or no effect.

The norther has ceased, which has renewed our communication with the store-ships at anchor under Sacrificios. We shall immediately commence landing the few pieces of heavy ordnance, with ordnance stores, at hand, and hope soon to have the necessary draught-mules to take them to their positions. Any farther delay in the arrival of those means of transportation will be severely felt in our operations.

I have the honor to remain, sir, with high respect, your most obedient servant,

WINFIELD SCOTT.

Hon. Wm. L. Marcy, Secretary of War.

Headquarters of the Army,
Camp Washington, before Vera Cruz,
March 23, 1847.

Sir:—Yesterday, seven of our 10-inch mortars being in battery, and the labors for planting the remainder of our heavy metal being in progress, I addressed, at two o'clock, P. M. a summons to the Governor of Vera Cruz, and within the two hours limited by the bearer of the flag, received the Governor's answer. Copies of the two papers (marked respectively A and B) are herewith enclosed.

It will be perceived that the Governor, who, it turns out, is the commander of both places, chose, against the plain terms of the summons, to suppose me to have demanded the surrender of the castle and of the city; when in fact, from the non-arrival of our heavy metal—principally mortars—I was in no condition to threaten the former.

On the return of the flag with that reply, I at once ordered the seven mortars, in battery, to open upon the city. In a short time the smaller vessels of Commodore Perry's squadron—two steamers and five schooners—according to previous arrangement with him, approached the city within about a mile and an eighth, whence, being partially covered from the castle—an essential condition to their safety—they also opened a brisk fire upon the city. This has been continued uninterruptedly by the mortars, and only with a few intermissions, by the vessels, up to 9 o'clock this morning, when the Commodore, very properly, called them off from a position too daringly assumed.

Our three remaining mortars are now (12 o'clock, A. M.) in battery, and the whole ten in activity. To-morrow, early, if the city should continue obstinate, batteries Nos. 4 and 5 will be ready to add their fire: No. 4, consisting of four 24-pounders and two 8-inch Paixhan guns, and No. 5 (naval battery) of three 32-pounders and three 8-inch Paixhans—the guns, officers, and sailors, landed from the squadron—our friends of the navy being unremitting in their zealous co-operation, in every mode and form.

So far, we know that our fire upon the city has been highly effective, particularly from the batteries of 10-inch mortars, planted at about 800 yards from the city. Including the preparation and defence of the batteries, from the beginning—now many days—and notwithstanding the heavy fire of the enemy, from city and castle, we have only had four or five men wounded and one officer and one man killed, in or near the trenches. That officer was Captain John R. Vinton, of the United States third artillery, one of the most talented, accomplished, and effective members of the army, and who was highly distinguished in the brilliant operations at Monterey. He fell last evening in the trenches, where he was on duty as field and commanding officer, universally regretted. I have just attended his honored remains to a soldier's grave—in full view of the enemy and within reach of his guns.

Thirteen of the long-needed mortars—leaving twenty-seven, besides heavy guns, behind—have arrived, and two of them landed. A heavy norther then set in (at meridian) that stopped that operation, and also the landing of shells. Hence the fire of our mortar batteries has been slackened, since two o'clock to day, and cannot be reinvigorated until we shall again have a smooth sea. In the mean time I shall leave this report open for journalizing events that may occur up to the departure of the steam ship-of-war, the Princeton, with Com. Connor, who, I learn, expects to leave the anchorage of Sacrificios, for the United States, the 25th inst.

March 24.—The storm having subsided in the night, we commenced this forenoon, as soon as the sea became a little smooth, to land shot, shells, and mortars.

The naval battery No. 5, was opened with great activity, under Capt. Aulick, the second in rank of the squadron, at about 10 A. M. His fire was continued to 2 o'clock, P. M., a little before he was relieved by Capt. Mayo, who landed with a fresh supply of ammunition, Capt. A. having exhausted the supply he had brought with him. He lost four sailors, killed, and had one officer, Lieut. Baldwin, slightly hurt.

The mortar batteries, Nos. 1, 2, and 3, have fired but languidly during the day for want of shells, which are now going out from the beach.

The two reports of Col. Bankhead, chief of artillery, both of this date, copies of which I enclose, give the incidents of those three batteries.

Battery No. 4, which will mount four 24-pounders and two 8-inch Paixhan guns, has been much delayed in the hands of the indefatigable engineers by the norther that filled up the work with sand nearly as fast as it could be opened by the half-blinded laborers. It will, however, doubtless be in full activity early to-morrow morning.

March 25.—The Princeton being about to start for Philadelphia, I have but a moment to continue this report.

All the batteries, Nos. 1, 2, 3, 4, and 5, are in awful activity this morning. The effect is, no doubt, very great, and I think the city cannot hold out beyond to-day. To-morrow morning many of the new mortars will be in a position to add their fire, when, or after the delay of some twelve hours, if no proposition to surrender should be received, I shall organize parties for carrying the city by assault. So far the defence has been spirited and obstinate.

I enclose a copy of a memorial received last night signed by the consuls of Great Britain, France, Spain, and Prussia, within Vera Cruz, asking me to grant a truce to enable the neutrals, together with Mexican women and children, to withdraw from the scene of havoc about them. I shall reply, the moment that an opportunity may be taken, to say—1. That a truce can only be granted on the application of Gov. Morales, with a view to surrender. 2. That in sending safeguards to the different consuls, beginning so far back as the 13th inst., I distinctly admonished them—particularly the French and Spanish consuls—and of course, through the two, the other consuls, of the dangers that have followed. 3. That although at that date I had already refused to allow any person whatsoever to pass the line of investment either way, yet the blockade had been left open to the consuls and other neutrals to pass out to their respective ships of war up to the 22d instant; and, 4. I shall enclose to the memorialists a copy of my summons to the Governor, to show that I had fully considered the impending hardships and distresses of the place, including those of women and children, before one gun had been fired in that direction. The intercourse between the neutral ships of war and the city was stopped at the last-mentioned date by Commodore Perry, with my concurrence, which I placed on the ground that that intercourse could not fail to give to the enemy *moral aid and comfort.*

It will be seen from the memorial, that our batteries have

already had a terrible effect on the city, (also known through other sources,) and hence the inference that a surrender must soon be proposed. In haste,

I have the honor to remain, sir, with respect, your most obedient servant,

WINFIELD SCOTT.

Hon. Wm. L. Marcy, Secretary of War.

Headquarters of the Army,
Vera Cruz, March 29, 1847.

Sir—The flag of the United States of America floats triumphantly over the walls of this city and the castle of San Juan d'Ulloa.

Our troops have garrisoned both since 10 o'clock: it is now noon. Brig. Gen. Worth is in command of the two places.

Articles of capitulation were signed and exchanged at a late hour night before last. I enclose a copy of the document.

I have heretofore reported the principal incidents of the siege up to the 25th instant. Nothing of striking interest occurred till early in the morning of the next day, when I received overtures from General Landero, on whom General Morales had devolved the principal command. A terrible storm of wind and sand made it difficult to communicate with the city, and impossible to refer to Commodore Perry. I was obliged to entertain the proposition alone, or to continue the fire upon a place that had shown a disposition to surrender; for the loss of a day, or perhaps several, could not be permitted. The accompanying papers will show the proceedings and results.

Yesterday, after the norther had abated, and the commissioners appointed by me early the morning before had again met those appointed by General Landero, Commodore Perry sent ashore his second in command, Captain Aulick, as a commissioner on the part of the navy. Although not included in my specific arrangement made with the Mexican commander, I did not hesitate, with proper courtesy, to desire that Captain Aulick might be duly introduced and allowed to participate in the discussions and acts of the commissioners who had been reciprocally accredited. Hence the preamble to his signature. The original American commissioners were, Brevet Brigadier-general Worth, Brigadier-general Pillow, and Colonel Totten. Four more able or judicious officers could not have been desired.

I have to add but little more. The remaining details of the siege—the able co-operation of the United States squadron, successively under the command of Commodores Connor and Perry—the admirable conduct of the whole army, regulars and volunteers—I should be happy to dwell upon as they deserve; but the steamer Princeton, with Commodore Connor on board, is under way, and I have commenced organizing an advance into the interior. This may be delayed a few days, waiting the arrival of additional means of transportation. In the mean time, a joint operation, by land and water, will be made upon Alvarado. No lateral expedition, however, shall interfere with the grand movement towards the capital.

In consideration of the great services of Col. Totten, in the siege that has just terminated most successfully, and the importance of his presence at Washington, as the head of the engineer bureau, I intrust this despatch to his personal care, and beg to commend him to the very favorable consideration of the department.

I have the honor to remain, sir, with high respect, your most obedient servant,

WINFIELD SCOTT.

Hon. Wm. L. Marcy, Secretary of War

The following were the terms of capitulation finally agreed upon:—

Generals W. J. Worth and G. J. Pillow, and Col. J. G. Totten, chief engineer, on the part of Major-general Scott, general-in-chief of the armies of the United States; and Col. Jose Gutierrez de Villanueva, Lieut. Colonel of the engineers, Manuel Robles, and Col. Pedra de Herrera, commissioners appointed by General of brigade Don Jose Juan Landero, commanding in chief, Vera Cruz, the castle of San Juan d'Ulloa and their dependencies—for the surrender to the arms of the United States of the said forts, with their armaments, munitions of war, garrisons, and arms.

1. The whole garrison, or garrisons, to be surrendered to the arms of the United States, as prisoners of war, the 29th inst., at 10 o'clock, A. M.; the garrisons to be permitted to march out with all the honors of war, and to lay down their arms to such officers as may be appointed by the general-in-chief of the United States, and at a point to be agreed on by the commissioners.

2. Mexican officers shall preserve their arms and private effects, including horse and horse furniture, and to be allowed, regular and irregular officers and also to rank and file, five days to retire to their respective homes, on parole, as hereinafter prescribed.

3. Coincident with the surrender, as stipulated in article one, the Mexican flags of the various forts and stations shall be struck, saluted by their own batteries; and, immediately thereafter, forts Santiago and Conception and the castle of San Juan d'Ulloa, occupied by the forces of the United States.

4. The rank and file of the regular portion of the prisoners to be disposed of, after surrender and parole, as their general-in-chief may desire, and the irregular to be permitted to return to their homes. The officers, in respect to all arms and descriptions of force, giving the usual parole, that the said rank and file, as well as themselves, shall not serve again until duly exchanged.

5. All the *materiel* of war, and all public property of every description found in the city, the castle of San Juan d'Ulloa, and their dependencies, to belong to the United States; but the armament of the same (not injured or destroyed in the further prosecution of the actual war) may be considered as liable to be restored to Mexico by a definitive treaty of peace.

6. The sick and wounded Mexicans to be allowed to remain in the city, with such medical officers of the army as may be necessary to their care and treatment.

7. Absolute protection is solemnly guarantied to persons in the city, and property, and it is clearly understood that no private building or property is to be taken or used by the forces of the United States, without previous arrangement with the owners, and for a fair equivalent.

8. Absolute freedom of religious worship and ceremonies is solemnly guarantied.

We must now resume the march of Scott's army to the capital of Mexico. Worth is appointed (for the time) governor of Vera Cruz. The army is organized for an advance on the Jalapa road—but wagons are wanting. Eight thousand men are to be thrown forward into the heart of Mexico. Quantities of ammunition, provisions, cannon, arms, are to be carried. Yet the wagons, horses, and mules which are to do this service, are not yet arrived. A little while since, and they were two thousand miles off, in the heart of the United States. But they will come. They are descending the Ohio and the Mississippi. They will be here. One by one, dozen by dozen, they arrive. On the 8th of April, ten days after the surrender of Vera Cruz, the veteran Twiggs, with his heroic division, takes the Jalapa road. Other divisions rapidly follow. In three days they reach the foot of the mountains, from whose heights may be seen the splendid vision of Orizaba, and its snow-crowned tops, along whose ridges the road continues to the ancient capital of the Montezumas; and from whose almost impregnable summits looks down Santa Anna with fifteen thousand men. The Mexican chief, defeated at Buena Vista, had rapidly traversed the interior provinces with the greater part of his army, and now sought to defend the heights of Cerro Gordo, formidable by nature, with batteries and intrenchments.

Here Twiggs makes a reconnoissance on the 12th, and determines to attack the enemy next morning. In the meanwhile Patterson arrives with volunteers, and delays the attack till the arrival of the general-in-chief. Scott makes a new reconnoissance, and perceives that an attack in front would be in vain, for the batteries there are commanded by the still higher ones on the summits of Cerro Gordo. He orders a road to be cut to the right of the American army, but to the left of Cerro Gordo, which winds round the base of the mountains and ascends them in the rear of the Mexican forts, there rejoining the Jalapa road, and behind the whole Mexican position. The labor, the skill, the courage of American soldiers accomplish it. For three days the Mexicans do not discover it. It is nearly done on the 17th, when they fire with grape and musketry on the working parties. Twiggs again advances to the storm. He carries the hill below Cerro Gordo, but above the new road. All is safe now, and all is ready for the coming battle. On the 17th of April Scott issues his celebrated order, dated Plan del Rio. It details, with prophetic accuracy, the movements of the following day—the positions, the attack, the battle, the victory, and the hot pursuit, till the spires of Jalapa should appear in sight. It is an order most remarkable in history. Here it is :—

GENERAL ORDERS, No. 111.

HEADQUARTERS OF THE ARMY,
Plan del Rio, April 17, 1847.

The enemy's whole line of intrenchments and batteries will be attacked in front, and at the same time turned, early in the day to-morrow—probably before ten o'clock, A. M.

The second (Twiggs') division of regulars is already advanced within easy turning distance towards the enemy's left. That division has instructions to move forward before daylight to-morrow, and take up a position across the national road in the enemy's rear, so as to cut off a retreat towards Xalapa. It may be reinforced to-day, if unexpectedly attacked in force, by regiments—one or two taken from Shields' brigade of volunteers. If not, the two volunteer regiments will march for that purpose at daylight to-morrow morning, under Brigadier-general Shields, who will report to Brigadier-general Twiggs, on getting up with him, or the general-in-chief, if he be in advance.

The remaining regiment of that volunteer brigade will receive instructions in the course of this day.

The first division of regulars (Worth's) will follow the movement against the enemy's left at sunrise to-morrow morning.

As already arranged, Brigadier-general Pillow's brigade will march at six o'clock to-morrow morning along the route he has carefully reconnoitred, and stand ready as soon as he hears the report of arms on our right, or sooner if circumstances should favor him, to pierce the enemy's line of batteries at such point—the nearer the river the better—as he may select. Once in the rear of that line, he will turn to the right or left, or both, and attack the batteries in reverse;

or, if abandoned, he will pursue the enemy with vigor until further orders.

Wall's field battery and the cavalry will be held in reserve on the national road, a little out of view and range of the enemy's batteries. They will take up that position at nine o'clock in the morning.

The enemy's batteries being carried or abandoned, all our divisions and corps will pursue with vigor.

This pursuit may be continued many miles, until stopped by darkness or fortified positions towards Xalapa. Consequently, the body of the army will not return to this encampment, but be followed to-morrow afternoon, or early the next morning, by the baggage trains of the several corps. For this purpose, the feebler officers and men of each corps will be left to guard its camp and effects, and to load up the latter in the wagons of the corps. A commander of the present encampment will be designated in the course of this day.

As soon as it shall be known that the enemy's works have been carried, or that the general pursuit has been commenced, one wagon for each regiment and one for the cavalry will follow the movement, to receive, under the directions of medical officers, the wounded and disabled, who will be brought back to this place for treatment in general hospital.

The Surgeon-general will organize this important service and designate that hospital, as well as the medical officers to be left at it.

Every man who marches out to attack or pursue the enemy, will take the usual allowance of ammunition, and subsistence for at least two days.

By command of Maj. Gen. Scott,

H. L. SCOTT, A. A. A. General.

The order thus given was realized to the letter, with the exception that General Pillow's brigade was repulsed

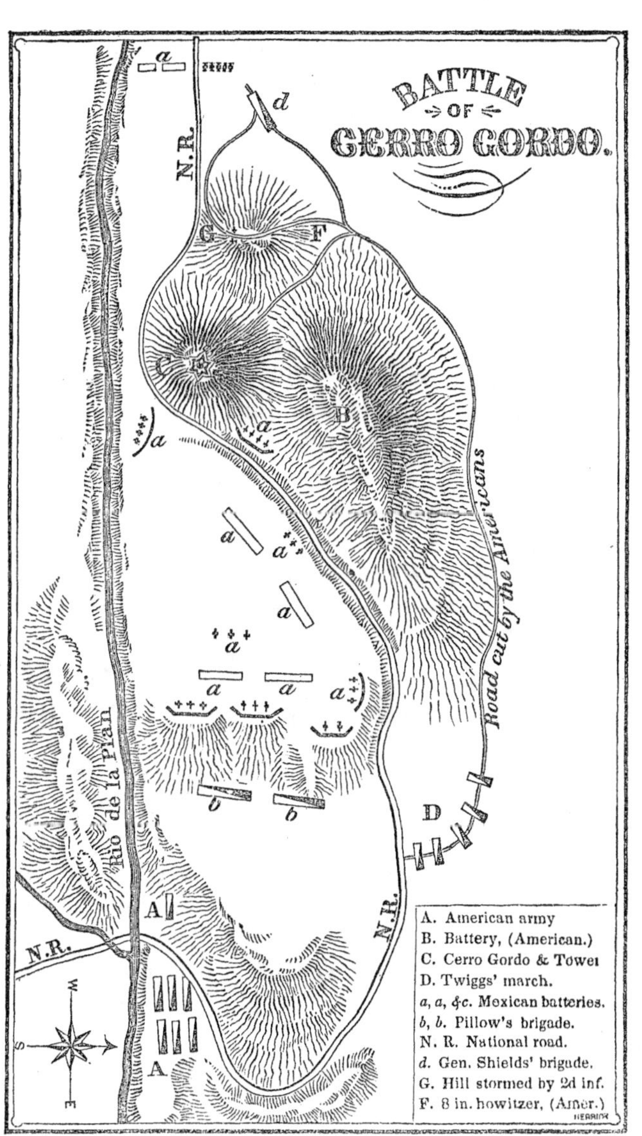
BATTLE
OF
CERRO GORDO.
N.R.
Rio de la Plan
Road cut by the Americans
A. American army
B. Battery, (American.)
C. Cerro Gordo & Towei
D. Twiggs' march.
a, a, &c. Mexican batteries.
b, b. Pillow's brigade.
N. R. National road.
d. Gen. Shields' brigade.
G. Hill stormed by 2d inf.
F. 8 in. howitzer, (Amer.)

in the attack on the batteries in front. They were, however, taken, and their garrisons made prisoners, by the advanced corps of the army, at the close of the battle. In each particular—of march, battle, victory, and pursuit—the order of Scott was prophetically correct. It proves the confidence of the commander in the indomitable energy of his troops. On the night of that day, (the 17th,) the enemy's position appears almost impregnable. On their right rolls a deep river. Along its side rises a chain of mountains one thousand feet in height. On these, heavy batteries frown down on all below. Over all rises the summit and tower of Cerro Gordo. Winding among the gorges of these mountains, and at last turning between the highest battery and the river below, is the National road, by which only the American army must pass. The Anglo-American soldier looks out from his camp at Plan del Rio, and sees this deep river on the side, this rampart of mountains in front, the high batteries beyond, and knows that the Mexican chief, with fifteen thousand men, is encamped on these mountains thus strongly defended. How shall he be attacked? The general order points out each step in the way.

On the night of the 17th, a thousand men of Twiggs' division are detailed on their route to plant an American battery on the captured hill below Cerro Gordo. A heavy twenty-four-pounder was brought up, and two twenty-four-pound howitzers. These were dragged by main force up the hill, hundreds of feet high, in a night of total darkness. A fire is built below, and the officers and men are told to take the cannon straight up. They are already fatigued, exhausted, and parched with thirst; but they stop not for these. They are divided into two parties, of five hundred men each, for relief. They drag the pieces up with the hands. Here they stop, block up, and chain the wheels, till they are relieved by the other division. Again they go on, and again they relieve. Thus they go on from seven in the evening till three in the morning. The ground is covered with exhausted soldiers, some to sleep and some to rest. But the cannon are carried up. The morning finds them on the hill, and as the rosy light blushes in the heavens, the soft music of the Mexican reveillee is heard summoning their men to the muster. The batteries and encampments are revealed. The fine body of Mexican lancers, in splendid uniforms, and with an unfurled standard, are moving along. Here battalions of artillery, and there a dense column of infantry, arrest the attention. Below and above are batteries darkly threatening to open their fire. This captured position thus commands all the defences but Cerro Gordo. But *that* is above. *That* can fire down upon *every position* which could be taken. It is plain, then, that the fort of Cerro Gordo is the key position of all the rest. This the discriminating eye of military science had clearly seen. Scott sees it, and has prepared for it. Hence the new road was made, winding, as you see, around the base of the mountain to our right, but to the left of Cerro Gordo, so that this citadel of the Mexican camp may be stormed from the flank, and the retreat of the troops by the National road cut off. Hence, Pillow's brigade is to attack their batteries on the front hill rampart, and either take them, or divert their attention from our flank movement. Hence, the night work of our men, so that our new hill-fort may command these batteries of the enemy, and at the right moment compel their surrender. All is well done. All is ready. The night-watch is past. Twiggs' division, which has rested on its arms, is rousing itself at the first light. The gallant artillerymen and engineers on the hill cut away the light brush in front of their guns, and now the heavy cannon begin their fire on the hill batteries. Their thunder tones are echoed from the mountain sides, and returned from the pieces of the enemy. The division of Twiggs is marching. The volunteers of Shields are hurrying on to seize the Jalapa road in rear of Santa Anna. Cerro Gordo now opens its plunging fire on Twiggs, and the issue has come. Cerro Gordo must be stormed. The storm is led by the gallant Harney. They fight under the eye of Scott. Here march the rifles, the 1st artillery, the 7th infantry; and near them, and with them storming the heights, are the 2d and the 3d infantry, and the 4th artillery. These are the regulars of Twiggs, and here they march up the rocky ascent, so steep that they must climb as they go, and with no covering but the very steepness of the hill. They receive a plunging fire in front and a rolling fire on the flanks—but, on they go. On—on, Harney leads his men. The front rank melts away before the shot; but they stop not till the hill is gained, and then a long and loud shout echoes from the mountain sides—Cerro Gordo is gained! Vasquez, the Mexican general, is killed in the fortress. Now the flags of the 1st artillery and 7th infantry are planted on the batteries, and now Sergeant Henry hauls down the national standard of Mexico. The Anglo-American again unfurls the flag of his country, and again renews the victories of Cortez. But where are the volunteers? Yet further to the right, and hastening to the Jalapa road, They storm a fort in front—the heroic Shields is shot through the lungs—but the fort is taken—the road is gained—and the flying army of Santa Anna is pursued in all directions.

On the river batteries in front, Pillow's attack is not successful. The batteries enfilade our men, and after bravely fighting, they are drawn back; but their effort is not lost. The corps of General La Vega is kept employed till Cerro Gordo has fallen. Then he surrenders, with three thousand men prisoners of war. Santa Anna, with Almonte, Canalizo, and eight thousand have escaped, leaving carriages and baggage behind, and are now on the road to Jalapa. The sun is at noon, and the battle is ended; but the pursuit continues. The reserve division of Worth comes up, passes Twiggs, and hurries rapidly on after the confused and flying Mexicans; nor does he stop till Jalapa appears in sight!

On the 19th of April, from Plan del Rio, Scott announces to the War Department, that he is embarrassed with the results of victory! Three thousand prisoners, forty-three pieces of bronze artillery manufactured at Seville, five thousand stand of arms, five generals, with the munitions and materials of an army, captured in a single battle, are the fruits of victory, and demand the earnest care of the conquering general! The men must be paroled; the small-arms must be destroyed; we have not men to take care of them.

Such was THE BATTLE OF CERRO GORDO. In the skill with which it was planned, in the formidable defences to be surmounted, in the heroism of the attack, and in the magnitude of results, with which of American battles will it not compare? There were almost impassable obstacles, surmounted by skill; there were almost impregnable batteries, stormed by valor; there were thousands of prisoners captured, and an army destroyed; there was a road to the capital laid open, and towns and cities taken in the long vista of a victorious march! The Mexican empire lies under the feet of the conqueror, and again is the Aztec compelled to witness the triumphs of power, and utter by the ruins of the Past, the mournings of the Present!

Look around you upon the battle-field, now that the dark chariot of war has driven by! Hear the description of one who has been to look upon the dead.

"A dragoon we encountered on the way kindly offered to be our guide, and from him we learned the positions of the different armies, their divisions and subdivisions. As winding around the hills by the National road, the enemy's intrenchments, their barricaded heights, strong forts, and well-defended passes came in view, we halted, and gazed for several moments in mute amazement. No one, from reading the newspaper accounts or the reports of the generals, can form a proper idea of the advantages possessed by the enemy in his chosen position. The battle, I knew it had been fought and won by our troops; yet it seemed, in its bare, still reality, a dream. I could not shake off this feeling as I rode along the enemy's lines of intrenchments, entered his dismantled forts and magazines, and looked from his chosen heights upon the paths up which our troops rushed into the jaws of death. * * *

"Passing down the ravine where the National Guard had three times attempted to dislodge the mounted riflemen, who, supported by the howitzer battery, literally rained death among their ranks, I was obliged to turn back and retrace my steps. The gorge was choked up with the mangled bodies of the flower of the Mexican army. The wolf-dog and the buzzard howled and screamed as I rode by, and the stench was too sickening to be endured. Returning to the National road, we passed a large number of cannon taken by our troops, and saw piles of muskets charred with fire in heaps, where they had been heaped and burned. * * * * *

" All along the road were the bodies of Mexican lancers and their horses, cut down by Colonel Harney's dragoons, when these fire-eaters chased Santa Anna and his retreating troops into and beyond Jalapa. Almost every man's skull was literally split open with the sabres of our horsemen, and they lay stretched upon the ground in ghastly groups."

From this sad scenery of war, as exhibited in the relics of a battle-field, we must hasten on with the gallant general, who renewed with yet deeper verdure the laurels of Niagara on the summits of Cerro Gordo. Scott was no distant spectator of the combat. He had called others to the field, and he shared its dangers himself. Having prepared all things for the storm of the tower, (called by the Mexicans the Telegraph,) he took post at the point Col. Harney charged, and under the heavy fire of the enemy's artillery. There he witnessed the gallant charge and there he encouraged the troops. It was then that he thus addressed Colonel Harney, (between whom and himself there had been some coolness :) " Colonel Harney, I can not now adequately express my admiration of your gallant achievement, but at the proper time I shall take great pleasure in thanking you in proper terms." Harney, with the modesty of true valor, claimed the praise as due to his officers and men.

At this time Captain Patten, an excellent officer of the

SCOTT COMPLIMENTING COLONEL HARNEY

3d infantry, was wounded, losing a part of his left hand. It was in the midst of the thunder-crash of battle, when the dying fell thickest, and when the crisis was at hand. It was a plunging fire; and after thus wounding Captain Patten, the ball struck a rock which it broke into fragments, one of which cut down and wounded the second sergeant of Captain Patten's company.

While Captain Patten was yet in the field, holding with his right hand the arm of the shattered left, General Scott rode slowly by, "under a canopy," to use Captain Patten's expression, "of cannon-balls." Seeing a wounded man, and supposing him to be a soldier, he exclaimed, slacking his pace, "There is a brave soldier badly wounded, I fear;" and then, being told by an officer that it was Captain Patten, the general halted, and called to Captain Patten to inquire the nature of the wound; but in the roar of battle he was not heard.

Captain Patten spoke with enthusiasm as well of the calm and soldierly bearing of his gallant commander, amid the thickest and hottest of this murderous cannonade, as of his ready sympathy with, and attention to the wounded men and officers.

When the battle was closed, the hoped-for victory had become reality, and the future no longer absorbed all the mind, Scott hastened to the side of the wounded. It was from a hospital of wounded and sick, that his first official report, dated April 19th, was despatched. An officer who was present in these scenes, relates that General Scott visited in person the wounded, and saw, himself, that they were attended in the best manner. His men were in all cases, when the events of the campaign allowed him any time for thought on other subjects, his first care. He was ever as humane as heroic. He attended the bedside of the sick with cholera in the Northwest, and he now visited and aided, in the hospitals of the wounded of Cerro Gordo. Soon after this event, and on the occupation of Jalapa, he caused the removal of the wounded and sick to the more comfortable and healthier quarters in that town. Among these was the brave Shields, in whose dangerous condition he deeply sympathized.

It will be recollected that Santa Anna's carriage, with a large amount of specie, was captured, just after the Mexican army fled from the field. Whatever of this property belonged personally to Santa Anna, Scott was most careful to return to his agent and man of business. It was a principle with General Scott, which he has most carefully carried out, that war was not a scheme for robbery, but the honorable contest of nations for national rights. He suffers no plunder of private property, no aggression on the rights of citizens, and he is most anxious to vindicate the American soldier and the American name from that barbarism which would convert war into the pillage of plunderers, and the glory of victory into the grossness of brutality. The following is the official despatch of the commander-in-chief:—

HEADQUARTERS OF THE ARMY,
PLAN DEL RIO, 50 miles from Vera Cruz,
April 19, 1847.

SIR: The plan of attack, sketched in General Orders, No. 111, forwarded herewith, was finely executed by this gallant army, before two o'clock P. M. yesterday. We are quite embarrassed with the results of victory—prisoners of war, heavy ordnance, field batteries, small-arms, and accoutrements.

About 3,000 men laid down their arms, with the usual

proportion of field and company officers, besides five generals, several of them of great distinction—Pinson, Jarrero, La Vega, Noriega, and Obando. A sixth general, Vasquez, was killed in defending the battery (tower) in the rear of the whole Mexican army, the capture of which gave us thos. glorious results.

Our loss, though comparatively small in numbers, has been serious. Brigadier-general Shields, a commander o. activity, zeal, and talent, is, I fear, if not dead, mortally wounded. He is some five miles from me at the moment. The field of operations covered many miles, broken by mountains and deep chasms, and I have not a report, as yet, from any division or brigade.

Twiggs' division, followed by Shields' (now Col. Baker's) brigade, are now at or near Xalapa, and Worth's division is in route thither, all pursuing, with good results, as I learn, that part of the Mexican army—perhaps six or seven thousand men—who had fled before our right had carried the tower, and gained the Xalapa road.

Pillow's brigade alone, is near me at this depot of wounded, sick, and prisoners; and I have time only to give from him the names of 1st Lieut. F. B. Nelson, and 2d C. G. Hill, both of the 2d Tennessee foot, (Haskell's regiment,) among the killed, and in the brigade 106, of all ranks, killed or wounded.

Among the latter, the gallant Brigadier-general himself has a smart wound in the arm, but not disabled; and Major R. Farqueson, 2d Tennessee, Captain H. F. Murray, 2d Lieut. G. T. Sutherland, 1st Lieut. W. P. Hale, Adjutant, all of the same regiment, severely, and 1st Lieut. W. Yearwood, mortally wounded. And I know, from personal observation on the ground, that 1st Lieut. Ewell, of the rifles, if not now dead, was mortally wounded in entering, sword in hand, the intrenchments around the captured tower.

2d Lieut. Derby, topographical engineers, I also saw, at

the same place, severely wounded, and Captain Patten, 2d United States Infantry, lost his right hand. Major Sumner, 2d United States dragoons, was slightly wounded the day before, and Capt. Johnston, topographical engineers, (now Lieut.-colonel of infantry,) was very severely wounded some days earlier while reconnoitring. I must not omit to add that Capt. Mason, and 2d Lieut. Davis, both of the rifles, were among the very severely wounded in storming the same tower.

I estimate our total loss, in killed and wounded, may be about 250, and that of the enemy at 350. In the pursuit towards Xalapa (25 miles hence) I learn we have added much to the enemy's loss in prisoners, killed, and wounded. In fact, I suppose his retreating army to be nearly disorganized, and hence my haste to follow, in an hour or two, to profit by events.

In this hurried and imperfect report I must not omit to say that Brigadier-general Twiggs, in passing the mountain-range beyond Cerro Gordo, crowned with the tower, detached from his division, as I suggested the day before, a strong force to carry that height, which commanded the Xalapa road at the foot, and could not fail, if carried, to cut off the whole, or any part of the enemy's forces, from a retreat in any direction.

A portion of the 1st artillery, under the often-distinguished Brevet Colonel Childs, the 3d infantry, under Captain Alexander, the 7th infantry, under Lieut.-colonel Plymton, and the rifles, under Major Loring, all under the temporary command of Colonel Harney, 2d dragoons, during the confinement to his bed of Brevet Brig.-general P. F. Smith, composed that detachment. The style of execution, which I had the pleasure to witness, was most brilliant and decisive.

The brigade ascended the long and difficult slope of Cerro Gordo, without shelter, and under the tremendous fire of artillery and musketry with the utmost steadiness, reached the breastworks, drove the enemy from them, planted the colors of the 1st artillery, 3d and 7th infantry—the enemy's flag still flying—and, after some minutes' sharp firing, finished the conquest with the bayonet.

It is a most pleasing duty to say that the highest praise is due to Harney, Childs, Plymton, Loring, Alexander, their gallant officers and men, for this brilliant service, independent of the great results which soon followed.

Worth's division of regulars coming up at this time, he detached Brevet Lieutenant-colonel C. F. Smith, with his light battalion, to support the assault, but not in time. The general, reaching the tower a few minutes before me, and observing a white flag displayed from the nearest portion of the enemy towards the batteries below, sent out Colonels Harney and Childs to hold a parley. The surrender followed in an hour or two.

Major-general Patterson left a sick-bed to share in the dangers and fatigues of the day; and after the surrender went forward to command the advanced forces towards Xalapa.

Brig.-general Pillow and his brigade twice assaulted with great daring the enemy's line of batteries on our left; and though without success, they contributed much to distract and dismay their immediate opponents.

President Santa Anna, with Generals Canalizo and Almonte, and some six or eight thousand men, escaped towards Xalapa just before Cerro Gordo was carried, and before Twiggs' division reached the National road above.

I have determined to parole the prisoners—officers and men—as I have not the means of feeding them here, beyond to-day, and cannot afford to detach a heavy body of horse and foot, with wagons, to accompany them to Vera Cruz. Our baggage train, though increasing, is not half large enough to give an assured progress to this army.

Besides, a greater number of prisoners would, probably escape from the escort in the long and deep sandy road without subsistence—ten to one—than we shall find again, out of the same body of men, in the ranks opposed to us. Not one of the Vera Cruz prisoners is believed to have been in the lines of Cerro Gordo. Some six of the officers, highest in rank, refuse to give their paroles, except to go to Vera Cruz, and thence, perhaps, to the United States.

The small-arms and accoutrements, being of no value to our army here or at home, I have ordered them to be destroyed; for we have not the means of transporting them. I am, also, somewhat embarrassed with the —— pieces of artillery, all bronze, which we have captured. It would take a brigade, and half the mules of our army, to transport them fifty miles.

A field battery I shall take for service with the army; but the heavy metal must be collected, and left here for the present. We have our own siege-train and the proper carriages with us.

Being much occupied with the prisoners, and all the details of a forward movement, besides looking to the supplies which are to follow from Vera Cruz, I have time to add no more—intending to be at Xalapa early to-morrow. We shall not, probably, again meet with serious opposition this side of Perote—certainly not, unless delayed by the want of the means of transportation.

I have the honor to remain, sir, with high respect, your most obedient servant,

WINFIELD SCOTT.

Hon. Wm. L. Marcy, Secretary of War.

From the field of Cerro Gordo the rout of the Mexican army was complete. Jalapa was entered on the 19th The strong position of La Hoya was abandoned, with its artillery and works; and on the 22d of April, Worth and his division occupied the strong castle and town of PEROTE! Here fifty-four pieces of cannon, and mortars, (both bronze and iron,) eleven thousand cannon-balls, fourteen thousand bombs, and five hundred muskets, swelled the vast amount of the munitions of war captured from the army of Mexico!

On the 15th of May, General Worth, after encountering but little resistance, entered the ancient city of Puebla. Thus, in a campaign which extended only from the 12th of March to the 15th of May, the city of Vera Cruz had been besieged and taken, the famed castle of San Juan d'Ulloa had fallen, the battle of Cerro Gordo was fought and won, the city of Jalapa taken, the castle and town of Perote captured, and the fine city of Puebla occupied! Ten thousand men made prisoners of war, seven hundred splendid cannon, ten thousand stand of arms, thirty thousand shells and shot, were the spoils of the triumphant victories which had attended the American army, in a campaign of only two months! History has few parallels for such rapid and such brilliant achievements! But a few months before, an unguarded expression had made WINFIELD SCOTT the mark of a ribald ridicule! Now, the government journal pronounces his campaign the rival of European splendor in war, eloquence is fervid in its declamatory praises, and the more just and grateful sentiment of the people renders back to the commander at Cerro Gordo, the admiration so gloriously won on the memorable plains of Niagara!

CHAPTER X.

Entrance of the American Army into Puebla.—Mexican Account.—American Officers.—Conduct of the Army.—Situation of Puebla.—Character of the Country.—The ancient Cholula.—Strength of the Army.—Scott's Proclamation.—Humanity of the Army.—Mission of Trist.—Reasons for remaining in Puebla.—Drilling of the Army.—Raising new Regiments.—New Volunteers.—Attack on the Train of M'Intosh.—Advance of Pierce.—Concentration of the Army.

In a morning of the beautiful month of May, and within the tropical zone, the American army of the north entered the "City of the Angels;" in the Spanish tongue, *Puebla de los Angelos.* They came with the renown, sounding far in advance, of San Juan de Ulloa captured, and the heights of Cerro Gordo victoriously stormed. They had landed on the shores of the Mexican Gulf, intrenched themselves in the wind-driven sands, battered the defences of Vera Cruz, received the surrender of the castle, and marched two hundred miles into the land of the Spanish-Aztec Americans. The National Bridge had been passed, Jalapa had surrendered, Perote made no resistance, and now the bold invaders of Mexico approached a city surrounded by the monuments of ancient civilization, and deemed fit, in the warm imagination of southern climes, for celestial residents. It was natural that such an army, the heralds too of a new and extraordinary republic, should be received by the inhabitants with mingled feelings of fear, surprise, and curiosity.

Accordingly, the citizens of Puebla crowded the street and filled the balconies on the line with spectators. Near noon the division of Worth entered the city, the artillery and infantry forming in the square, and the train of wagons extending from the street of Mercadores to the bridge of Nocte Buena.[1] The troops were fatigued with their march, and needed both rest and refreshment. This weary aspect, the fact that many of them had been ill, the common gray undress uniform, and the plain truth that they were neither giants nor centaurs, disappointed the vivid imaginations of the Mexicans of Puebla, who had supposed that the conquerors of Cerro Gordo were something marvellous in appearance or superhuman in power. The spectators turned from the scene with surprise, and asked themselves, How have these men become the conquerors of Mexico?

One of the most intelligent of the Mexican citizens, writing from Puebla two days after the entrance of the American army, thus expresses his disappointment at the appearance of that army, and endeavors to solve the problem proposed by its achievements:—

"Nor does their armament seem to me any thing extraordinary. In a word, except the draught-horses, which are very good, I assure you, without exaggeration, that these men bring nothing that we have not seen a thousand times. Even the immense number of their wagons is not a proof of large stores. The wagons are all empty, and I understood their principal use to be for the transport of troops. How, then, have they done what they

---

[1] Letter from a native of Puebla, dated May 16th, and published in the London Times.

have? How have they continually beaten our army, which not only surpasses them in appearance—for that is unquestionable—but in my opinion has real and positive advantages over them? Every one asks this question, to which there is but one reply. Their leaders, and particularly the colonels of regiments, are old gray-haired men. Their gray hairs explain the phenomenon. This makes me still rely on our soldiers, and gives me for the future some hopes, which we require more than ever."[1]

This solution of the problem was at least partially correct. The officers of the American army have experience, skill, and science. Many of them served in the campaigns of 1813, 1814, and 1815, against the veteran soldiers of Great Britain; many of them were bred at the military school at West Point—the equal, and in some things the superior, of any school of military instruction in the world. All of them have been accustomed to the discipline of their profession, and are perfectly acquainted with the superior energies which the republican habits and intellectual vivacity of their countrymen have developed in war. The army of the United States is not intrusted to weak or ill-instructed hands; but to officers skilled in the science and experience of the duties of the military art—a fact as honorable to the legislative sagacity of the republic, as its achievements in arms have proved illustrious in history.

The soldiers piled their arms in the public square, and although surrounded by thousands of a hostile population, lay down to sleep, in perfect confidence that the enemy could not and dare not disturb them. No higher

[1] Letter of the native of Puebla.

evidence could be given of that sense of absolute superiority and of resistless energy, which is uniformly felt by American troops—the sense that they are predestined to victory, no matter by whom, in what numbers, or in what manner opposed. On the following day they took possession of the hills of Loreto and Guadaloupe, and artillery was sent to the hill of San Juan. General Worth paid the compliment of a visit to the Bishop of Puebla, and the bishop, in returning it, was received at the quarters of Worth with the honors paid to a general. Affably and respectfully did the American officers mingle with the people; and for a time the stern countenance of war seemed to be lighted up with the smiles of beneficence, and its fearful strifes deferred to a peaceful harmony.

The city of PUEBLA is situated on that vast plain which, in its height above the sea and the character of its productions, is the most singular portion of the earth.

This plain is seven thousand feet high, and although wholly within the *torrid zone*, is called the *tierras frias*, or the cold grounds. The climate of a country depends as much upon altitude as latitude, and hence these lofty plains are called cold, and really produce the grains and fruits of the most temperate climes.[1] Wheat of the finest quality, our Indian corn, barley, and fruits peculiar to this region, constitute the staple productions and elementary food of the inhabitants. Within this tropical but really temperate zone of lofty plains, and encircled by the sublime range of the Cordilleras, lies the province of Puebla. Its soil is scattered over with and partly composed of

---

[1] Humboldt's Travels in New Spain.

the volcanic remains of ancient convulsions.[1] The lava is strewed over the ground in different varieties, bearing a resemblance to the cinders of an iron-furnace. On the tops of the highest and most magnificent mountains may be found the craters whence in ages past have streamed out these rich but dangerous ingredients of the soil. Yet, with all this, the earth is there garnished with but little of that beauty of foliage and that abundance of vegetable production which so distinguishes the great alluvials of the United States of the north. The *cactus*, that discriminating inhabitant of barren lands, is still frequent, and, except within a few miles of Puebla, the whole road from Vera Cruz to that city presents but a few scrubby bushes, some palms, and this unproductive cactus, called in this country the prickly-pear.[2] In the neighborhood of Puebla, cultivated fields and waving grain indicate that husbandry has resumed its occupation, and that man, a resident of cities, has higher demands for food and luxury than the natural fruits or natural grasses can supply. He is still, however, the man of two thousand years ago. Time, which has revolutionized empires and established the supremacy of science in other lands, has left the Spanish Aztec, the unchanged image of his ancient fathers, in the indolence of his life and the fixedness of his habits. In vain has invention created arts, and genius startled a world with its wonderful achievements. He uses the plough of two thousand years since, employs oxen instead of horses, folds his arms in contemptuous pride, and sees the world, and its exhibitions of power

---

[1] Waddy Thompson's Recollections of Mexico, page 17.

[2] Ibid.

and wonder in science, pass by him, with the frigidity of indolence and the indifference of contempt! In this state was once one of the most numerous populations of the ancient Mexicans, yet it now scarcely contains fifty to a square mile—a number large compared with most of the provinces of Mexico, yet small compared with the populous nations which inhabited here in the time of Cortez.[1] It was then the seat of the Tlascalans and Cholulans—people who had advanced far in the arts, and whose monuments were among the greatest of the earth. Six miles from the present city of Puebla was the great city of Cholula, which once contained two hundred thousand inhabitants, and where Cortez beheld the towers of four hundred idol temples! Of this great city not a vestige remains! Not a brick nor a stone stands upon another! One monument stands in gloomy and solitary grandeur amidst the vast plain which surrounded it.[2] This is the great pyramid, truncated at top, and supposed to have been dedicated to the worship of the gods of the Aztecs. This pyramid is one of the most remarkable among the ruins of ancient nations. It is 1440 feet on the side, at the base, 177 feet in height, and 45,210 square feet on the summit.[3]

In the midst of these ruins of ancient empires, surrounded by these mountains, upon this high plain, looking out upon these lava-covered fields, and through the clear, vivid, brilliant atmosphere of tropical highlands, is the city of Puebla. It now contains about eighty thousand

---

[1] Cortez and Bernal Diaz.

[2] Waddy Thompson's Recollections of Mexico.

[3] Description of Humboldt.

inhabitants. It is a beautiful city, well built, with lofty houses, broad streets, and fine public buildings.[1] Here, at two hundred miles from the city of Vera Cruz on the Gulf of Mexico, and ninety from Mexico, the heart of the Aztec empire, the small but brave and glorious army of Scott arrived on the 15th of May, 1847. With complexions sallowed, and disabled by the unwholesome climate of Vera Cruz—in the gray undress uniform of the United States, and wearied with many miles of tedious march, the army entered this Mexican city, to surprise its inhabitants as much by the inferiority of its appearance as it had done by the greatness of its deeds. Were these indeed to be the conquerors of Mexico? Where were the far-famed heroes of Cerro Gordo? Time, however, was to convince the Pueblans, in a yet more startling manner, that the energy of the American soldier could be revived to greater actions, and the glory of former battles be obscured by the brightness of those to come.

The army, as it entered Puebla, was stated by a Mexican eye-witness to have numbered four thousand two hundred and ninety effective men, with thirteen pieces of artillery.[2] This was the *marching* force at that point. On that day and at that place the number given was very nearly correct. Scott's force at that time capable of marching on Mexico did not exceed *four thousand five hundred men.* A slight review of the preceding events and circumstances will explain this fact, and show that such was a necessary consequence of the measures taken by the government, and the losses necessarily sus

---

[1] Letter from a native of Puebla.

[2] Ibid

tained in a distant campaign in a foreign land. In May, 1846, Congress had authorized the President to call out fifty thousand volunteers. Twenty-three regiments had been called out in May and June. The time for which they were called out was but twelve months, and expired in May, 1847. Several of these regiments were in the army of Scott, and had been discharged on the way to Puebla. Sickness also had been rife among the troops. The camp dysentery, so common and so fatal among armies, had disabled many and destroyed others. At Vera Cruz, at Cerro Gordo, and in other engagements and skirmishes, not a few of the brave men who landed in Mexico had fallen a sacrifice to the bloody rites of war.

The army, when concentrated at the Island of Lobos, had numbered fourteen thousand men; but thus reduced by sickness, by discharges, and by death, in addition to the garrisons required, not more than five thousand (exclusive of the garrison of Jalapa) capable of moving in arms could be assembled to march against the capital of Mexico. What were they to do? Were the laurels of many battles and the glory of victorious campaigns to be risked, in the heart of a hostile nation, with so small a band? Already had complaints of delay been made and repeated by the unthinking friends of the administration. They seemed to imagine that armies had nothing to do but march and fight, and that these should be done, by Americans, with a speed which surpassed all human experience; that they neither required sleep nor bread, baggage nor transportation; but that, heedless of supplies and regardless of opposition, they should hurry on to the end, rivalling the winds and trusting in a predestined victory! Such a compliment was not undeserved by the skilful commander and heroic soldiers of the army of Mexico; but even they ought not to have been expected to perform such unprecedented achievements. With this small array, however, impelled by the natural ardor of a successful general, and in reliance upon the invincible energies of the American soldier, would Scott have proceeded at once to the city of Mexico, but for other and unexpected interferences.

The cabinet at Washington had from the commencement of the war professed an anxious desire to terminate the controversy with Mexico, in any way honorable to the United States. General Scott, animated by the same desire, and conscious that no useful end was to be gained by carrying the terrors of martial law among the people of Mexico, beyond that of securing a permanent peace, had already addressed from Jalapa, a humane and reasoning proclamation to the Mexican people, stating to them the plain facts in their own condition, the events of the war, the unskilfulness of their leaders, the burdens imposed upon them, and the already foreshadowed results of this drama of conquest. This document[1] is one of the finest specimens of military literature, both for the matter it contains and the manner of its composition. Having recited the civil and military events which preceded the battle of Cerro Gordo, the commander of the army proceeds to say—

Finally, the bloody event of Cerro Gordo has shown the Mexican nation what it may reasonably expect if it longer continues blind to the true situation in which it has been

---

[1] Scott's Proclamation, dated Jalapa, May 11, 1847.

placed by some generals, whom it has most distinguished and in whom it has most confided.

The hardest heart would be moved to grief in contemplating the battle-fields of Mexico a moment after the last struggle. Those generals whom the nation has, without service rendered, paid for so many years, with some honorable exceptions, have in the day of need betrayed it by their example or unskilfulness. On that field, among the dead and dying, are seen no proofs of military honor, for they are reduced to the sad fate of the soldier—the same on every occasion, from Palo Alto to Cerro Gordo—the dead to remain unburied, and the wounded abandoned to the charity and clemency of the conqueror. Soldiers who go to fight expecting such a recompense, deserve to be classed among the best in the world, since they are stimulated by no hope of ephemeral glory, of regret, of remembrance, or even of a grave.

Again, Mexicans of honorable pride—contemplate the lot of peaceful and laborious citizens in all classes of your society. The possessions of the Church menaced and held out as an incitement to revolution and anarchy; the fortune of the rich proprietors pointed out for plunder to the ill-disposed; the merchant and the artisan, the laborer and the manufacturer, burdened with contributions, excises, monopolies, taxes upon consumption, surrounded with restrictions and charged with odious internal customs; the man of letters and the statesman, the man of liberal knowledge who dares to speak, persecuted without trial by some factions or by the rulers who abuse their power; criminals unpunished and set at liberty, as were those of Perote—is this, then, Mexicans, the liberty which you enjoy?

I will not believe that the Mexicans of the present day are wanting in courage to confess errors which do not dishonor them, and to adopt a system of true liberty, of peace, and union with their brethren and neighbors of the north; neither will I believe that they are ignorant of the falsity of the calumnies of the press, intended to excite hostility. No! public sentiment is not to be created or animated by falsehood. We have not profaned your temples, nor abused your women, nor seized your property, as they would have you believe.

We say this with pride, and we confirm it by your own bishops, and by the clergy of Tampico, Tuspan, Matamoras, Monterey, Vera Cruz, and Jalapa, and by all the authorities civil and religious, and the inhabitants of every town we have occupied. We adore the same God, and a large portion of our army, as well as of the population of the United States, are Catholics, like yourselves. We punish crime wherever we find it, and reward merit and virtue.

The army of the United States respects, and will always respect, private property of every description, and the property of the Mexican church.

Mexicans! the past cannot be remedied, but the future may be provided for. Repeatedly have I shown you that the government and people of the United States desire peace, desire your sincere friendship.

Abandon, then, rancorous prejudices, cease to be the sport of individual ambition, and conduct yourselves like a great American nation; leave off at once colonial habits, and learn to be truly free, truly republican, and you will become prosperous and happy, for you possess all the elements to be so. Remember that you are Americans, and that your happiness is not to come from Europe.

I desire, in conclusion, to declare, and with equal frankness, that, if necessary, an army of one hundred thousand could promptly be brought, and that the United States would not terminate their differences with Mexico (if compelled to do so by force of arms) in any manner uncertain, precarious, or dishonoring to yourselves. I should insult the intelligent of this country if I had any doubt of their acquaintance with this truth.

The order to form guerilla parties to attack us, I assure you can procure nothing but evil to your country, and no evil to our army, which will know how to proceed against them; and if, so far from conciliating, you succeed in irritating, you will impose upon us the hard necessity of retaliation, and then you cannot blame us for the consequences which will fall upon yourselves.

I am marching with my army upon Puebla and Mexico—I do not conceal it; from those capitals I shall again address you. I desire peace, friendship, and union—it is for you to select whether you prefer war; under any circumstances, be assured I shall not fail my word.

WINFIELD SCOTT.

This proclamation contains one of the best and most correct pictures of the conduct of the Mexican army, and the real operations of its government, anywhere to be found. It is true that it was (with a few honorable exceptions) the Mexican officers and not the soldiers who had been wanting in skill, energy, or courage. The battle-fields, as here depicted, were strewed with the dead soldiers of the Mexican army; but in some instances the officers had retreated in haste, in some they were unwilling to fight, and in all they had shown a deficiency in military education, utterly incompetent to meet in successful contest the superior skill and the wonderfully developed power of modern military science. It was true, also, that the government of Mexico was one of unequal burdens and of unstable power. It depended rather upon the will of military chiefs than the affections of the people. It imposed burdens by caprice rather than principle. It fettered trade by restrictions alike unjust and unnecessary. It was true, and as honorable as true, that the army of Scott had signalized the humanity of modern warfare by a forbearance of all the barbarities of conquest. It had seized no individual property, destroyed no church structures, violated no private rights, and imposed no contributions upon a prostrate population. The armies of Mexico were indeed swept from its paths with the fearful might of destruction, but they were swept away only in pursuance of the acknowledged rights of war, and left behind no mournful evidences of a vindictive malice. It was war and not barbarism which bore over the fields of Mexico the unfolded banner of the North American republic.

Such was the professed disposition of the United States government towards Mexico, such the address of General Scott, and such the humane manner in which the war had been carried on, when an agent of the cabinet in Washington arrived in Mexico to negotiate peace. This person was Mr. Nicholas P. Trist, chief clerk in the department of state. From the hostile attitude of the two governments towards each other, he could not come in the character of a regularly appointed envoy—a character only consistent with a state of peace. He did come, however, with certain letters from the cabinet at Washington to persons in Mexico, and with powers, on certain terms, as a commissioner to conclude a treaty of peace.[1] Mr.

[1] Mr. Polk's official commission to Trist.

Trist arrived at Jalapa just before Scott's departure for Puebla, and immediately intimated a desire to transmit certain papers to the Mexican government. If the propositions they contained were acceptable to the authorities in Mexico, they necessarily implied a cessation of hostilities while the negotiations proceeded. Such was the condition of affairs at Puebla in the beginning of June. With the government commissioner anxious for peace, and actually seeking opportunities of negotiation, on the one hand, and with an army diminished (including all its disposable force) in effective men to less than five thousand, Scott, anxious to go forward, and looking with hope to the consummation of the campaign in the city of Mexico, was yet compelled, by considerations both civil and military. to remain in Puebla.

The *military reasons* why the army should remain at Puebla till reinforced, were of the strongest kind, and demanded the serious attention of the boldest commander, even if convinced of the entire infallibility of his troops. The event proved their force and the superior sagacity of the general, who, hopeful of the highest glory, and anticipating only victory, sacrificed this ardor of action to high prudential considerations. These reasons were: 1*st*. If the entire five thousand men then at Puebla could be placed at once in the city of Mexico, they were barely sufficient to constitute a common garrison, impotent to move in any direction, or to overawe the Mexican government by any demonstrative movement. 2*d*. In this defensive, shut-up position, they must remain for months, before reinforcements could arrive[1] sufficiently strong to

[1] The brigade of Pierce did not arrive at Puebla till the 5th of August. —See Scott's official despatch, (No. 34,) dated September 18th.

authorize any offensive movement. *3d.* The main body of the army of Santa Anna was yet unbroken, and at this period it would have been his policy to leave the American army to shut itself up in Mexico, while he fell, in succession, on the advancing bodies of new troops marching to reinforce Scott. In this, he would either have defeated them or have prevented their junction. *4th.* Alvarez, with a division of four thousand men, was within striking distance of Puebla,[1] and on the advance of Scott to Mexico would have taken possession of the post he left, and cut off all communication with his rear.[2] In fine, it is only remarkable that the commander or his officers should have at all entertained the idea of advancing with so small a force. That persons in the United States should have thought their delay singular, only proved that they were very little acquainted with military affairs, and that they believed, that by some extraordinary decree of Heaven the army was rendered invulnerable to misfortune, and predestined to inevitable victory. It has, indeed, realized such a destiny; but only by science the most accomplished, by sagacity the most penetrating, and by valor the most indomitable. The children of destiny are first made such by the energy of their own character, and the superiority of their own minds.

Such was the *necessity*, both civil and military, which constrained General Scott to restrain his desire to advance, and maintain the army at Puebla. Nor was it

---

[1] Mr. Kendall's letter, dated October 15th, 1847.

[2] Let the reader recollect, that notwithstanding all the reinforcements which arrived between May and September, General Scott's communications with Vera Cruz were cut off during the whole period for want of troops to keep them open!

unemployed or useless delay. Whatever gives an army discipline gives it strength. More than thirty years previous, Scott had, in the camp at Buffalo, availed himself of such an opportunity to drill and discipline the men whose valor and firmness had withstood the veteran troops of Great Britain on the fields of Chippewa and Niagara. Such experience was not lost. The divisions of Worth, Twiggs, and Quitman, were drawn out and constantly drilled on the plains bordering Puebla, till their discipline was complete.[1] Thus was perfected the only remaining element which was necessary to give an unexampled success to the arms of the United States in the republic of Mexico.

In the mean while, the cabinet at Washington had become awakened to the necessity of reinforcing the army of Scott, left alone in the midst of hostile millions. Congress had authorized the enlistment of ten new regiments, and the business of recruiting was rapidly carried on. Recruiting-stations were established in the principal interior towns of the United States, and the spirit of adventure, the high pay, and the bounty lands so liberally offered by the government, were rapidly filling the exhausted ranks of the army. New volunteer regiments were called out; but this resource was not taken till too late to supply the places of the levy of 1846, whose time expired in May. General Scott had been obliged to discharge the portion of these connected with his army, at Jalapa. The want of foresight in not preparing for this event was the real reason why the army of Scott was,

[1] Kendall's letter, of October 15th, 1847.

numerically, too small to advance, without hazard, at once from Puebla.

Soon after Scott arrived at that place the garrison of Jalapa was broken up, the army not being strong enough to spare such a detachment. Perote was made a dépôt, and the line of communication was left without defence —one of the few examples of a general trusting to the innate energies of his army, leaving it alone in an enemy's country, without any provision for retreat. This measure was, however, one of necessity; for, taking the received maxims of war as the rule, the garrisons alone necessary to keep open the line, would have consumed the entire army!

On the 5th of May a large train, under the command of Colonel M'Intosh, left Vera Cruz for the army. It consisted of one hundred and thirty-two wagons, six hundred pack-mules, and about eight hundred men. This corps was attacked by a strong body of guerillas at Passo de Ovejas. The guerillas were partially successful, although the detachment made good its defence. The Americans lost thirty men, killed and wounded, thirty-five wagons, and two hundred mules. This was a serious check; but was soon remedied by new reinforcements. On the 10th of May General Cadwallader marched to the aid of M'Intosh with six hundred men, from Vera Cruz, composed chiefly of the new regiment of voltigeurs, accompanied with six howitzers. A junction was made, and the detachment, now fourteen hundred strong, with its train, moved on, to join as soon as possible the main army.

On the 17th of May General Pillow left Vera Cruz with another detachment of about one thousand men

At a subsequent period General Pierce was also sent forward, with about two thousand five hundred. Thus, by successive additions of new recruits, the government was able, after two months' delay, to increase the army of General Scott to a number short of eleven thousand available men. With this number, in the early part of August, the army moved to the conquest of Mexico—the capital of the Spanish Aztec nation! Its progress, its victories, its heroic conduct, and its wonderful achievements, we must now pursue, record, and, as far as possible, spread out, for the admiration of all true lovers of the great and heroic in martial achievement.

BATTLE GROUNDS
around
MEXICO
Taken by permission from
Humboldt's Valley of Mexico
Christobal
Road to Tampico
Laguna de
Tezcuco
MEXICO
7.605 ft.
above the Ocean
Chapoltepec
Tacubaya
Acapalco Road
Coyoacan
Churubusco
S. Angel
Contreras
Battle
S. Antonio
S. Pablo
Istacalco
Iztapalapan
Mexicalzingo
Culhuacan
Road to Puebla & Veracruz
El Penon
Los Reyes
San Augustin
de las Cuevas
Road cut by Americans
Tepepa
Ajusco
Xochimilco
Nalivitas
S. Cruz
S. Gregorio
S. Luis
Tuliagualco
Laguna de Xochimilco
Tlapisahua
Ayotla
Venta de Chalco
Buenavista
Laguna de Chalco
S. Lucia
Chalco
Chimalpa
Tuiscingo
Teconuque
Road cut
by the Americans

CHAPTER XI.

Strength of the Army.—Reinforcements.—Divisions of the Army.—March from Puebla.—Hospitals of Puebla.—Volcano of Popocatapetl.—Pass of Rio Frio.—View of Mexico.—Valley of Mexico.—Lakes.—Inundations.—Topography of the Valley.—Position of the Army on the 13th of August.—Reconnaissance of the Rifles.—El Penon.—Mexicalcingo.—Turning of Lake Chalco.—March to San Augustine.—Skirmish at Buena Vista.—Concentration.—Position of the Army on the 18th.

We have already said that Scott's army in Puebla, on the 1st day of June, 1847, did not exceed five thousand *effectives*,—that is, capable of marching and fighting. From Vera Cruz to Puebla, the road had been strewed with the sick, or languishing—the convalescent invalids, or the wounded,—who had been left in depots or were in the moveable hospitals of the army. Here we should recollect, and consider carefully, the wide and important difference which exists between a mere detachment of an army, or light division moving rapidly through a country for temporary purposes, and a regularly organized army, equipped to remain in the midst of a hostile nation, and, therefore, obliged to supply all its own wants. The former being small, and moving rapidly for a short time, either has no sick and wounded, or depends upon transporting them in wagons or leaving them to the private kindness of the inhabitants of the country. On the other hand, a regularly organized army, subsisting in the heart of an enemy's country, must provide itself with hospitals and depots, either moveable or stationary; and must there leave all the provisions, guards, men, and equipments, which are necessary to maintain these depots, and secure their safety and comfort. If these are stationary in towns, (as they should be,) then garrisons must be left with them. If moveable, from camp to camp, they require a large number of wagons, a numerous body of teamsters, and a yet more numerous body of attendants. In either case, it is not too high an estimate to say, that an invading army, advanced within the territory of a hostile country, requires at least one-fourth of its original number to be enrolled as *non-combatants*. A part of these will be sick, a part wounded, and a large part engaged as attendants, convoys, or garrisons. If Scott had left Jalapa, then, with eight thousand effective men, he could not have had more than six thousand with which to leave Puebla. But far worse than this was the actual fact. The inhospitable climate of Mexico did not cease its ravages with the lowlands of the coast. The record of disease in the army has never been fully unfolded. In the more unhealthy positions on the Rio Grande, at Vera Cruz, Tampico, Perote,[1] and many other places—even at Puebla—disease pursued the troops, and in the space of one year hurried thousands to the grave. Hundreds and thousands of the volunteer regiments also disappeared from the army, from the effects of disease, which caused their discharge, from voluntary absences, and from being cut off in small parties. Nor was this all. Desertions

[1] The names were recently published of no less than seven hundred men, who died in a few months at Perote.

from the regular army were frequent. No less than seventeen hundred were reported in a little more than a year.[1]

Such were the causes which rapidly diminished the number of effective troops in the field; but which could not be properly estimated by those who looked only to the muster-rolls at Washington.

Three different bodies of reinforcements had left Vera Cruz for Puebla, and reached there in time for the march on Mexico. With these, and the garrison of Jalapa, the army of Scott, in the beginning of August, may be thus enumerated:

ARMY ON THE 6TH DAY OF AUGUST, 1847.

Scott's forces at Puebla, (including all,) . .	7,000
Cadwallader's Brigade, ...	1,400
Pillow's "	1,800
Pierce's Corps "	2,409
Garrison of Puebla, under Colonel Childs .	1,400
Total arrived at Puebla, ...	14,009
Deduct from this, Garrison of Puebla, with the sick in hospitals, .	3,261
Total marched from Puebla, ...	10,738

Nor was the want of men the only difficulty with the troops, in preparing for its march. Although the government (Congress) had, in the aggregate, provided amply for the troops; yet the difficulty of transmitting funds to distant posts, in a foreign country, without the

[1] Their names were recorded in the Police Gazette.

aid of mercantile arrangements, was so great, that the officers of the different departments, and of the line, were frequently much embarrassed for funds. The merchants of Puebla, and of Mexico generally, deal almost altogether with England and France. They were willing to buy drafts on those countries, but not on our own. The consequence was, that the officers of the quartermaster's and commissary's departments, had often to get money discounted at a heavy rate, for the purchase of such supplies, in the country, as were needed at the moment.

The following paragraph is from a letter written on the 6th of August, at Puebla:

"General Pierce came up to-day with his command, bringing eighty-five thousand dollars *in drafts*, but not one cent in money. The disappointment and vexation, both of the general-in-chief, and the quartermaster's and commissary's departments, is great in the extreme, and how they are to get along, is with them an unsolved problem. The paymaster's department is no better off; and the only way officers can get along to provide themselves with the necessaries of life, is to first procure a draft on one of the cities of our Union from the paymaster, and then have it shaved at the rate of twenty-five or thirty per cent. from its face. This is but a faint and imperfect sketch of the *financial operations* of our army."[1]

This was a consequence of one of the errors of the campaign,—not on the part of the army, or its commander, but in the War Department. This error was,

---

[1] Letter to the St. Louis Republican.

in leaving the army *too weak to maintain its communications*. It is a rule of common sense, not less than of the military art, that at every step made by the army, it should leave such defences and depots in its rear, that there may always be a direct communication with its source of supply at home. When the army of Scott had arrived at Jalapa, the volunteer corps enrolled in May and June, 1846, began to disappear. Their places were not supplied till months afterwards. Thus the army moved on towards Mexico, without being able to keep open its communications. In fact, many places, such as the National Bridge, which it was important to defend, were abandoned. The army was too weak to move forward and leave garrisons behind. The consequence of this condition of things was an inconvenient derangement in the transmission of funds. Specie could only be carried safely with the large trains; while drafts on the government treasuries in the towns of the United States were at a discount in Mexico. Such was the state of the military chest, when it was determined to march from Puebla to Mexico.

On the 5th of August a council of war was held, at which the heads of the different divisions and brigades were present; among whom were Major-Generals Worth, Quitman, and Pillow, with Brigadiers Twiggs, Shields, and Cadwallader. General Pierce did not arrive till next day. The general-in-chief (Scott) then laid down distinctly the plan of operations, the routes, and the mode, by which he proposed to reach, attack, and capture the city of Mexico and its defences. Subsequent events proved how ably and clearly these dispositions were made

We have said that Scott left Puebla with 10,738 men,[1] and that 3,261 were left in garrison and in hospitals. Of the last, the largest part were in the hospital, where were at one time no less than nineteen hundred sick! Of these, seven hundred found their graves at Puebla. Leaving this large body of sick with a very moderate garrison, under Col. Childs, the army commenced its march for the valley of Mexico on the 7th of August.

The army, under the directions of the general-in-chief, was arranged in four divisions, with a cavalry brigade. The divisions comprehended a large number of regiments, but their numbers were reduced one-half. Some of them were the mere skeletons of what they should be, under the regular organization.

The divisions were very nearly as follows:

Cavalry Brigade, Col. Harney.	1st Dragoons, Capt. Kearney, 2d do. Major Sumner, 3d do. Capt. McReynolds,	Parts.

1st Division, Gen. Worth.	1st Brigade, Col. Garland.	2d Regiment Artillery. 3d do. do. 4th do. Infantry. Duncan's Field Battery.
	2d Brigade, Col. Clarke.	5th Infantry. 6th do. 8th do.
2d Division, Gen. Twiggs.	1st Brigade, Gen. Smith.	Rifle Regiment. 1st Artillery. 3d Infantry. Taylor's Battery.
	2d Brigade, Col. Riley.	4th Artillery. 1st Infantry. 7th do.

[1] Scott's Official Report, No. 34.

3d Division, Gen. Pillow.	1st Brigade, Gen. Cadwallader.	Voltigeurs. 11th Infantry. 14th do.
	2d Brigade, Gen. Pierce.	9th Infantry. 12th do. 15th do.
4th Division, Gen. Quitman.	1st Brigade, Gen. Shields.	S. Carolina Volunteers. N. York Volunteers.
	2d Brigade..	2d Penn. do. Detachment of U. S. Mar.

This organization apparently gives twenty regiments, and parts of five others. Had these regiments been full, up to their legal number, they would have contained twenty thousand men, a regiment, when completely organized, having a thousand. The whole army, however, contained but little more than half that number. The regiments, therefore, averaged but five hundred, and, in fact, some of them had but three hundred.

In order that the different corps should not be thrown together, and that the troops might move easily, the divisions took up their line of march on different days, but in such a manner that they might reinforce each other at four hours' notice. As it was known that there was no large Mexican army immediately in front, no evil could arise from this mode of march.

Accordingly on the 7th the second division, under General Twiggs, commenced its march, preceded by the brigade of cavalry under Harney. On the 8th, Quitman's division of volunteers moved; on the 9th the first division, under Worth; on the 10th the third division, under Pillow.[1] General Scott, the commander, joined and continued with the leading division.

---

[1] Scott's Official Report, No. 31, August 19th, 1847.

The army was now under full way, marching on to that singular capital of that singular nation, whose ancient and whose modern civilization has made a phenomenon in the history of society. The fragments of mutation and revolution lay scattered in its path—all was new and strange; yet, unmoved by these associations, and undiverted by these novelties, it marched steadily on to fulfil what was apparently the decree of destiny.

The road on which the troops marched was the great stage-travelled route from Vera Cruz to Mexico, through Puebla. The route travelled by Cortez, in his conquest, after diverging to the right a little south of Perote, here crossed the modern road and passed to the left through Cholula, and round the base of Popocatapetl, and finally rejoined the present road, near Lake Chalco. Cortez, no doubt, pursued the common way at that time, especially as Cholula was then a magnificent city. The modern road has been made to suit the modern relations of society and the new growth of towns. Nearly at right angles to the road from Vera Cruz, and west of the range of the Cordilleras, lies the road from Mexico to Acapulco on the Pacific. Near the city of Mexico, are the lakes of Chalco and Xachimilco. On this road to Acapulco is the village of San Augustine, at which the American army ultimately arrived, previous to the battles of Mexico.

On the morning of the 7th, Twiggs' division passed out of Puebla, and took its way through a beautiful, rolling country, where gardens supplied the city with fruits and vegetables. The road was ascending, and crossed, before it entered the city of Mexico, the Anahuac range of the Cordilleras, the most magnificent portion of that chain of mountains which extends from Cape Horn to the Artics—and from whose sky-crested summits the eye of fancy might extend its uninterrupted vision from the Atlantic to the Pacific, and call up, in bright and long array, the nations, the arts, and the triumphs of victorious science, to be spread over all this continent, in the ages of the deep and distant future! Many miles to the left arose the snow-topped Popocatapetl, whose venerable summit was eighteen thousand feet in the air; three thousand feet above the point where ice and snow dwell in perpetual congelation! A little further, arose the twin summit of Iztac-cithuatl, whose icy top looks over the earth in the same cold and isolated glory. Thirty miles from the road, as these were, yet in the clear atmosphere of this elevated plain they seemed near by, and their snows chilled the air. Thus amidst the ruins of Cholula and Tlascala, on either side, and in full view of these volcanic monuments to the grandeur of nature, the army marched on. The road gradually ascended through mountain scenery, which seemed to befit rather the north of New England then the region of the tropics. Thick woods would now and then cover the hills, while here and there little lakes were interspersed in deep valleys. The thirst of the soldier was relieved by the coldness of their waters, and his weariness was almost forgotten in the beauty and sublimity of surrounding nature. At length, on the third day, they reached the pass of Rio Frio. They left Puebla, seven thousand two hundred feet above the ocean, and were now ten thousand one hundred and twenty; having gradually ascended three thousand feet in forty-eight miles, and arrived in the midst of the Anahuac range of the Cordilleras, at a point forty-five miles distant from the city of Mexico.[1] Rio Frio, says an officer, is "a little stream pouring down from the Snow mountains, of icy coldness and crystal purity."[2] The mountains from which it runs are composed of porphyritic rocks, and their highest summits, like that of Popocatapetl, are ancient volcanoes.

At this point the army had anticipated resistance, and the position was favorable to defence. Being in the midst of the mountains, they here closed down on both sides of the road, so as completely to overhang and enfilade it. Signs of preparation were, indeed, found in temporary parapets, and timber felled. The intention, however, of defending this point had been abandoned. It was supposed that General Valencia, who commanded the division of the north, was stationed here. If so, he had retreated towards the capital.

A march of a few miles further, and the army passed over the highest crest of the mountains; and one of the most splendid scenes of the world opened upon the eyes of the weary soldiers.

It is thus described by an officer of the Rifles.[3]

"When all were pretty nearly worn out, a sudden turn in the road brought to our view a sight which none can ever forget. The whole vast plain of Mexico was before us. The coldness of the air, which was most sensibly felt at this great height—our fatigue and danger, were forgotten, and our eyes were the only sense that thought of enjoyment. Mexico, with its lofty steeples

---

[1] Stealey's Map of the Roads from Vera Cruz to Mexico.

[2] Letter to the New York Courier, dated August 31st.

[3] Letter to the New York Courier

and its checkered domes—its bright reality, and its former fame—its modern splendor, and its ancient magnificence, was before us; while around on every side its thousand lakes seemed like silver stars on a velvet mantle."

With this description we may compare another by an English officer, who seems to have been equally enraptured with the same view. "From an eminence, (says Captain Lyon,) we came suddenly in sight of the great valley of Mexico, with its beautiful city appearing in the centre, surrounded by diverging shady paséos, bright fields, and picturesque haciendas. The great lake Tezcuco lay immediately beyond it, shaded by a low floating cloud of exhalations from its surface, which hid from our view the bases of the volcanoes of Popocatapetl and Iztac-cithuatl—while their snowy summits, brightly glowing beneath the direct rays of the sun, which but partially illumined the plains, gave a delightfully novel appearance to the whole scene before me. I was, however, at this distance, disappointed as to the size of Mexico; but its lively whiteness and freedom from smoke—the magnitude of the churches, and the extreme regularity of its structure, gave it an appearance which can never be seen in a European city, and declare it unique—perhaps unequalled in its kind."[1]

Thus suddenly did the army burst upon this extraordinary view—a view as remarkable for its historical associations, as for the grandeur of its natural elements,—a scene too, which must forever connect this army with

---

[1] Captain Lyon's Journal of a Residence and Tour in the Republic of Mexico

the memory of the past, and the developments of the future.

There must have been some, also, in that martial array, who turned their thoughts from the scenes of war, to contemplate here some of the most singular features of the natural world. The valley of Mexico is one of the most extraordinary regions of the earth. It is a basin enclosed by a wall of porphyritic mountains. Its length, north and south, is about sixty miles, and its breadth (east and west) about forty miles.[1] It is really formed by a separation (south of the city of Mexico) of the great chain of the Cordilleras into two chains—one bending east and the other west, which again unite north of the city. The result of this conformation is to leave a basin, surrounded by the walls of the mountain. In this basin, "all the water furnished by the surrounding Cordilleras is collected. No stream issues from it excepting the brook of Tequisquiac, which joins the Rio de Tula. The lakes rise by stages, in proportion to their distance from its centre, or in other words, from the site of the capital Next to the lake of Tezcuco, Mexico is the least elevated point of the valley; the Plaza Mayor, or Great Square, being only one foot and one inch higher than the mean level of this lake, which is eleven and three-fourths feet lower than that of San Christobal. Zumpongo, which is the most northern, is $29\frac{211}{1000}$ inches higher than the surface of Tezcuco; while that of Chalco, at the southern extremity, is only $3\frac{632}{1000}$ feet more elevated then the Great Square of Mexico."[2]

---

[1] See Stealey's Maps of the Roads from Vera Cruz to Mexico.

[2] Humboldt's New Spain.

In consequence of this peculiarity, the city has, for a long series of ages, been exposed to inundations. Five immense floods have occurred since the Spanish invasion. Immense works have been constructed at different times to avoid this danger. One of these is the great cut, planned by Enrico Martinez, which connects the Rio de Suautitlon with the Rio Tula, and thus carries off the lake of Zumpongo.[1] Around the same lake are stone dikes. In the south, dikes and sluices have been formed round Lakes Chalco and Xochimilco, by which they are prevented from overflowing. By means like these, the city of Mexico is prevented from inundation, and is no longer, as it seems to have been in the time of Cortez, an island in a lake. The character of the country remains unchanged—and it is yet a marshy valley, in a basin of the Cordilleras, spotted with lakes and filled with volcanic remains. On some of the causeways, there is still a continuous body of water for miles from the city—while on others, the ground is marshy, but sometimes cultivated.

On the 10th, the division of Twiggs encamped at the base of the mountain,[2] and at this, the enemy's scouts began to be seen on all sides. On the 11th, this division reached Ayotla, only fifteen miles by the National Road from Mexico, and waited for the other divisions to come up.

At this point, a survey of the valley of Mexico showed

---

[1] This was thought, by Humboldt, to be one of the most gigantic hydraulic operations executed by man. Its length is 67,537 feet, the greatest depth 197, and its greatest breadth 361.

[2] Letter to the New York Courier.

the lake of Tezcuco directly in front of the road; and at the lower end, and about half way to Mexico, (seven miles,) on the left of the road, is El Penon, a fortified mountain. Directly west of that, at the upper end of Lake Xochimilco, and about five miles south of Mexico, is Mexicalcingo, another fortified point. Directly south and west of Ayotla, lies the lake of Chalco, and the lake of Xochimilco. Entirely west of these again, and running from the city of Mexico, nearly at right angles with the National Road, lies the road to Acapulco, leading west from Mexico to the Pacific. On this last road lies San Augustine, the general depot of the army in its subsequent operations. Between San Augustine and the city of Mexico, and on or near the Acapulco road, lie in succession, San Antonia, Contreras, and Churubusco, points where successive engagements took place. CONTRERAS is about four miles nearly northwest of San Augustine, on a road leading through San Angel to the Tacubaya causeway. CHURUBUSCO is on the Acapulco road, near a canal, at the crossing of which was a *tête du pont*, (bridge-head.)

A rapid *coup d'œil* (birds-eye view) of the topography of the valley, and the position of the army on the 13th of August, will show Twiggs's division at Ayotla, east of Lake Chalco; Worth's division near the village of Chalco, at the south end of the lake, and the divisions of Pillow and Quitman intermediate. In front, the great lake of Tezcuco, and on the left, Lake Chalco. The city of Mexico lay on the side of Lake Tezcuco, and fifteen miles, by the road from Ayotla, approached through the lakes and marshes by great causeways.

An attentive examination shows, that on the south and

west, there are three great roads which respectively enter Mexico by causeways. The *first*, is the Vera Cruz or National Road, on which the army now was, and which passed by El Penon, immediately in front, and for miles on a narrow causeway, built on the shoals of the lake. The *second* was the Acapulco road, which lay directly across Lake Chalco, from where the army now was, and proceeded through San Augustine and San Antonia, by a causeway to the city. The *third* was the Toluca road, passing into Mexico by the Tacubaya causeway, still further to the west.

The problem now presented to the commander-in-chief was, by which of these roads shall the army attempt its passage into the city? The solution of this question required a close *reconnaissance*, and an accurate survey, if possible, of the position and defences of the enemy.

On the 12th of August, the Rifle regiment, with three companies of cavalry, were pushed forward to reconnoitre *El Penon*.[1] This work was successfully performed, and the work pronounced impracticable, without immense loss, which the commander of the army thought unnecessary to the object. The reconnoitring party (rifles and dragoons) continued their search to the left, in order to find a way of easier approach to the city. At about five miles from Mexico, they were arrested by coming suddenly upon five strong batteries commanding the road. This was the post of Mexicalcingo, before described, at the head of Lake Xochimilco. The party (composed of about four hundred men) soon counter-

---

[1] Letter of an officer to the New York Courier.

marched, and found El Penon, with its bristling batteries, immediately between them and the camp of General Twiggs. For some unknown reason, they were not attacked; and after a rapid march, arrived in camp about midnight. General Scott pronounced this "the boldest reconnaissance of the war."

El Penon, which had been thus reconnoitred, is a rocky hill, which "completely enfilades and commands the National Road, and had been fortified and repaired with the greatest care by Santa Anna. One side was inaccessible by nature, the rest had been made so by art. Batteries, in all mounting fifty-one guns of different calibres, had been placed on its sides, and a deep ditch, twenty-four feet wide and ten feet deep, had been cut, connecting the parts already surrounded by marshes."[1] From the Penon to the city, was a causeway, surrounded by water. This position could not be turned, and therefore must be carried by assault. Against this, General Scott decided on grounds of humanity.

In his report of the 19th of August, 1847, he thus writes:

"This mound, close to the National Road, commands the principal approach to the city from the east. No doubt it might have been carried, but at a great and disproportionate loss, and I was anxious to spare the lives of this gallant army for a general battle, which I knew we had to win before capturing the city, or obtaining the great object of the campaign—a just and honorable peace."

---

[1] Letter to the New York Courier.

Of the pass, by Mexicalcingo, the general writes, and thus discloses the plan which was ultimately adopted.

"It might have been easy (masking the Penon) to force the passage; but on the other side of the bridge we should have found ourselves, four miles from this road, on a narrow causeway, flanked to the right and left by water, or boggy grounds. These difficulties closely viewed, threw me back upon the project long entertained, of turning the strong eastern defences of the city, by passing around south of Lakes Chalco and Xochimilco, at the foot of the hills and mountains, so as to reach San Augustine, and hence to manœuvre on hard, though much broken ground, to the south and southwest of the capital, which had been more or less under our view since the 10th inst."[1]

El Penon, being on the common and only good road from Puebla to Mexico, and being likewise an almost impregnable position, General Santa Anna had judged correctly and wisely in placing there his principal fortification. The fortress of Mexicalcingo, being likewise a strong one, and, if taken, leaving the American army on a narrow causeway, easily defensible, the Mexican general had apparently provided for every possible passage between the Lake Chalco and the Lake Tezcuco. This was the only way in which there was a regular and tolerable road from Puebla to Mexico. On this the American army had advanced, and the vanguard had actually reached Ayotla, several miles in front of the south end of Chalco. The measures of the Mexican general were,

---

[1] General Scott's Official Report, No. 31, dated August 19th.

therefore, judiciously taken, and at this time promised, if any defence could avail, to be successful.

The real question in military science at this time was, could the Lake Chalco be turned? If it could, did the new route present a better or safer way? The reconnaissances made, and the information of scouts, determined the fact that a passage existed round the south end of Lake Chalco which might be made practicable, and by which the army would be brought on to the Acapulco road, and advance to the city on a route less defended, and affording greater advantages in fighting. This route, if practicable, Scott had contemplated taking, and now at once put the army in motion for that purpose.

The order of march was reversed, and Worth's division, which was in the rear at Chalco, was now in advance, marching round the south end of Lake Chalco, and cutting their way to San Augustine. On the 15th the several divisions took up their line of march, and Worth's corps proceeded steadily on to the fortified position of San Antonia. "The road lay along the base of a high range of mountains, at times crossing rocky spurs of the mountains, or along the margin of the lake, on very narrow causeways very much cut up. The hills on the left were often precipitous, and a few sharp-shooters might have annoyed us exceedingly by their fire, and a few enterprising men might have blocked up the road completely by rolling down rocks, and yet they attempted it but once; a few shot soon dislodged them, and two or three hours' work cleared the road."[1]

On the 17th the head of General Worth's division

---

[1] Letter from an officer, published in the Washington Union.

reached San Augustine, and in a few hours after the other divisions were within striking distance. The march round the lake to San Augustine was twenty-seven miles, by a route deemed by the Mexicans impracticable; and on the 18th all the several corps were in position in the neighborhood of that post.[1]

Twiggs's division left Ayotla on the 16th with the train, the brigade of General Smith forming the rearguard. As the train was passing the little village of *Buena Vista* a Mexican division appeared in sight, attempting to cross the road and cut the train off. Here a skirmish ensued, which is thus described by an officer:

"On our left were large fields of half-grown barley, through which was seen advancing, in splendid order, the enemy's column. It was the most splendid sight I had ever seen. The yellow cloaks, red caps and jackets of the lancers, and the bright blue and white uniforms of the infantry, were most beautifully contrasted with the green of the barley-field. Our line of battle was soon formed, and we deployed through the grain to turn their left and cut them off from the mountains. A few shots, however, from the battery, soon showed them that they were observed, and countermarching in haste, they left their dead on the field. Thus ended our fight at Buena Vista. That night we stayed at Chalco."[2]

The train continued to move on, by roads over which it was almost impossible to drag the wagons. On the 18th it arrived in sight of the main army, which had now taken possession of San Augustine.

---

[1] Scott's Official Report, dated the 19th.

[2] Letter from an officer, in the New York Courier.

The army was now concentrated, the different divisions in sight of one another, and the arrangements made for final operations. On the 13th it was on the Puebla road on the east side of Lake Chalco, advancing on El Penon. On the 18th it was on the Acapulco road, near San Augustine, nine miles from the city of Mexico. The change was made in good order, and the ground to operate on was far better, and the defences in front less. The city of the Spanish-Aztecs was now within the grasp of the arms of the United States, predestined, in the convictions of the people, to be invincible wherever they should be carried. A conviction like this, existing in ages past, alike in the minds of Roman, Mohammedan, and Puritan, often makes the destiny which it affirms and courts. Asserted in the cause of liberty and justice, it would subdue a world to the civilization of Christianity. In any other cause, its predestined glory may fade before a darker fate.

CHAPTER XII.

Mexican Line of Defence.—Position of the American and Mexican Armies.—Action of the 19th.—Position in the Hamlet of Contreras.—Position of General Scott.—Arrangements for the Battle.—Distribution of the American and Mexican Forces.—Battle of Contreras.—Rout of the Mexicans.—Surrender of Mexican Generals.—Recapture of the Buena Vista Guns.—Scott's Arrangements.—Evacuation of San Antonia.—Storm of the Tête du Pont.—Battle of Churubusco.—Defeat of the Mexicans.—Loss.—Truce.

The Mexican plan of defence for the city of Mexico seems to have contemplated two lines of defence—an exterior and interior one. The exterior was composed of a line of forts and fortified eminences. The strongest was El Penon, on the National Road, completely commanding it, near the edge of Lake Tezcuco. This fortress, as we have already stated, was pronounced impracticable without immense loss. It contained fifty-one guns, disposed in several different batteries, with infantry breastworks, and the whole surrounded by a deep ditch connecting the marshes and waters about it. The next fort of this class was at Mexicalcingo, at the upper end of Lake Xochimilco, and commanding a narrow causeway to the city. This, also, was defended with batteries and infantry breastworks. The next position was the Bridge of Churubusco, a *tête du pont* at the crossing of a canal, armed also with cannon, on the Acapulco road. The next, but to the west, and front of this, was the Hill of Contreras, thoroughly armed with batteries and breast-

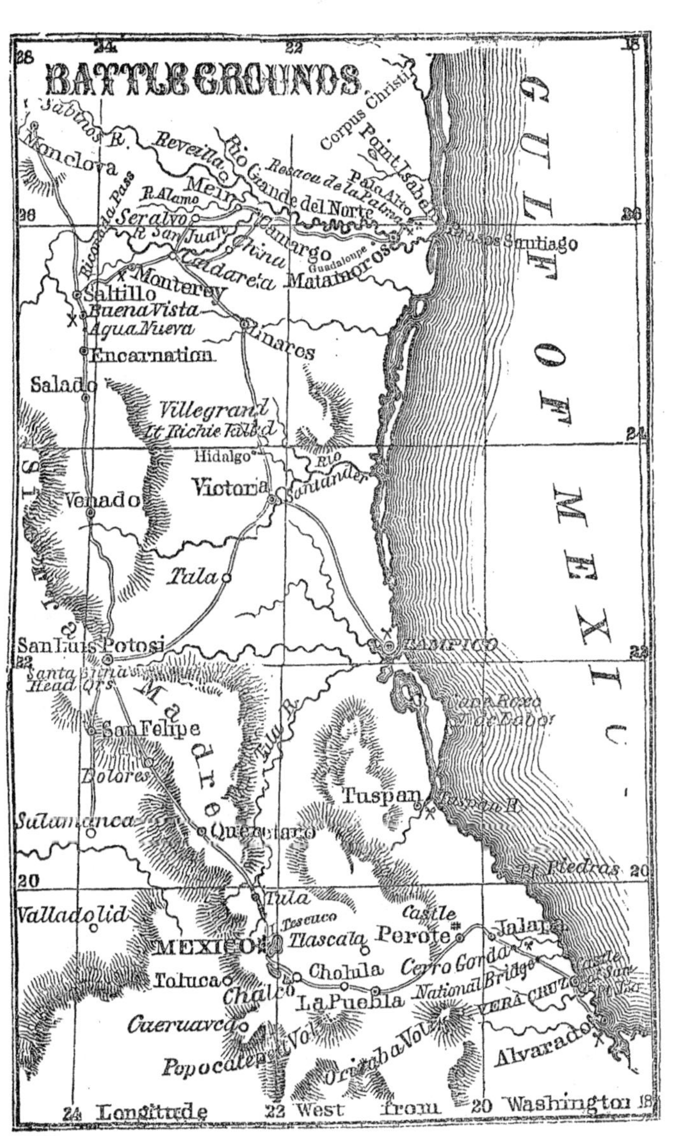

BATTLE GROUNDS
GULF OF MEXICO
Corpus Christi
Point Isabel
Palo Alto
Resaca de la Palma
Rio Grande del Norte
Brazos Santiago
Sabinos R.
Monclova
Reveilla
Mier
R. Alamo
Seralvo
R. San Juan
Camargo
China
Guadalupe
Matamoros
Monterey
Cadareita
Saltillo
Buena Vista
Agua Nueva
Linares
Encarnation
Salado
Villegrand
Lt. Richie Killed
Hidalgo
Rio
Victoria
Santander
Venado
Tala
San Luis Potosi
Tampico
Santa Anna's Head Qrs
Madre
San Felipe
Dolores
Tuspan
Tuspan R.
Salamanca
Queretaro
Piedras
Tula
Valladolid
Tescuco
Castle
Tlascala
Perote
Jalapa
MEXICO
Cholula
Cerro Gordo
Toluca
Chalco
La Puebla
National Bridge
Vera Cruz
Alvarado
Popocatepetl Vol.
Orizaba Vol.
24 Longitude
22 West
from
20 Washington

works. In the route, and still nearer to the city, was the HILL OF CHAPULTEPEC, on which was the Military College. This was at the point where the mountains approached the city. It was a strong position and well armed.[1] It is plain, from an examination of the map, that these positions really commanded all the practicable passes to the city on the whole semicircle, extending round from Lake Tezcuco in the east to where the mountains come near the city on the west. These fortifications were armed with near one hundred pieces of cannon, while the ground between them was either marshy, or covered with volcanic remains, sharp and abrupt, rendering it almost impassable even for footmen. Behind this line of exterior defences General Valencia, with 6,000 of the best troops of the Mexican army, was to manœuvre, and reinforce any point which might be exposed to attack.

The *interior line* seems to have been only the forts, and canals or ditches of the city itself. These, however, were by no means weak. The city was approached only by causeways. Canals and ditches surrounded it in various directions, and at the gateways were *garitas*, or small forts, constructed at the angles of the streets or entrances of the causeways, eight in number.[2] These defences of the city were also mounted with a large number of cannon. This interior line, however, was evidently weaker than the exterior one. These various defences were well calculated to protect the city against any thing less than a large army and protracted siege, had the energy

---

[1] This statement corresponds in substance with one made by Captain Lee of the engineers.

[2] See Scott's Official Report.

of the men, or the ability of their officers, corresponded with the natural strength of the positions. This, however, was not the case. Whether it be a superior strength, innate in the natural constitutions of the inhabitants of the northern temperate zone, or whether it be what is more than equivalent to strength, a higher and better education, it is certain that the arms of England and the United States have exhibited a great superiority over those of more southern nations—a superiority, whose final result on the dominion and civilization of the world is yet to be made known by the events of futurity.

On the 18th of August, the position of the armies, at night, was in the order following, viz.: Worth's division had, during the day, advanced from San Augustine in the direction of San Antonia, whose batteries were brought to bear on his troops, and the first shot killed Captain Thornton, a brave but unfortunate officer of the 2d dragoons.[1] The cavalry had been thrown in front to reconnoitre. The village proved to be strongly fortified, and a bold *reconnaissance* made by Captain Mason of the engineers, accompanied by Lieutenants Stevens and Tower, determined that this point could only be approached by the front, over a narrow causeway of great length, flanked with wet ditches of great depth.[2] Worth was ordered not to attack, but to threaten and mask the place. On the left of the road here, extending west, was an immense field of volcanic rocks and lava, called *pedregal*, and on the east it was wet and boggy.[3] This *pedregal* was

---

[1] Scott's Official Report.

[2] Official Report.

[3] Letter of an officer in the Washington Union.

thrown up in sharp rocks and broken pieces, in such a manner, that the Mexican officers supposed it to be impassable. It extended to the mountains, five miles to the left. That night Worth made the headquarters of his division at a *hacienda* on the road, near Antonia, and within reach of the enemy's guns.

On the same night the division of Twiggs slept in a little village, in sight of Worth's corps.[1] The divisions of Pillow and Quitman were near.

On the same evening (the 18th) General Valencia, whose division had previously been held liable to march to any point, and whose troops were called "the flower" of the Mexican army, occupied the fortified intrenchments at the heights of Contreras, about five miles to the northwest of San Augustine.[2] At the same time (evening of the 18th) General Rincon took command at Churubusco, whose fortifications were not then completed, but to finish which he immediately addressed himself.[3] The garrison of that post appears to have been composed, according to the official report, of the battalions of national guards, called *Independencia* and *Bravo*, which were subsequently reinforced (19th and 20th) by different batteries of artillery.

At San Antonia was posted another Mexican division, reinforced on the morning of the 19th, by the battalions of *Hidalgo* and *Victoria*. In the neighborhood of Contreras and San Angel were other divisions of the enemy under Santa Anna.

---

[1] Letter in the New York Courier and Enquirer.

[2] Official Report of General Salas.

[3] Official Report of General Rincon.

This, then, was the situation of the two armies on the night of the 18th August. General Scott's headquarters were at San Augustine. The pass of San Antonia, in front, being strong and on a narrow causeway, the plan of attack adopted seems to have been this—to *turn* Antonia by taking the fort at Contreras, and thus be able to march round San Antonia; or rather, to gain Coyhoacan on the San Angel, in the rear of San Antonia, and which was also but one mile from Churubusco. To do this, however, required that a new road should be cut for artillery from San Augustine to Contreras, and that, when there, that position, strongly defended by artillery, should be stormed and taken. This was the plan now devised by the American general, and to be immediately executed by the army.

On the morning of the 19th, all was animation in both armies. General Valencia was strongly posted at Contreras; Rincon was busy increasing the fortifications of Churubusco; Santa Anna was reinforcing both Antonia and Contreras, with bodies of troops drawn from the city; and General Scott, having made a new *reconnaissance* to the left by Captain Lee, with Lieutenants Beauregard and Tower,[1] now detached Pillow's division on the contemplated route to make a practicable road for heavy artillery.[2]

Captain Lee of the engineers, having discovered a corps of observation in the direction taken by Pillow's division, Twiggs was advanced in front to cover the party cutting the road.[3] This last division had now arrived at

[1] Scott's Official Report, (No. 31,) 19th August, 1847.

[2] Official Report. [3] Idem.

the village of San Juan, and were prepared for the severe labor of the next two days. The men were ordered to put their blankets on their shoulders, their knapsacks in their wagons, and two days' bread and beef in their haversacks. At one P. M., they left San Juan, and proceeded forward, dragging with them Magruder's battery and the mountain howitzers.[1] At two P. M., General Smith's brigade had arrived at the crest of a hill, from which Valencia, in his intrenchments, was plainly visible, and in the distance reinforcements marching to his assistance. These intrenchments of Valencia, at the hill of Contreras, had twenty-two pieces of artillery (mostly heavy) mounted in a battery commanding the difficult, broken, rocky ground, on which the American troops had to manœuvre. With this position the city of Mexico was connected, by an excellent road beyond the volcanic field, and by which it received, from time to time, great bodies of cavalry.[2]

At four P. M., General Scott took position on one of the eminences in front of Contreras, and found the brigades of P. F. Smith and Riley, (Twiggs' division,) supported by those of Pierce and Cadwallader, (Pillow's division,) picking their way over the broken ground in the enemy's front, and extending themselves towards the road which leads to the city. With great difficulty Captain Magruder's battery of twelve and six pounders, and Lieut. Callender's battery of mountain howitzers and rockets, had been advanced to within range of the intrenchments.[3] "The

---

[1] Letter of an officer in the New York Courier

[2] Scott's Official Report.

[3] Official Report

ground," says an officer, "was the worst possible for artillery; covered with rocks, large and small, prickly-pear and cactus; intersected by ditches filled with water, and lined with maguey plant, itself imperviable to cavalry; and with patches of corn, which concealed the enemy's skirmishers while it impeded our passage. The artillery advanced but slowly, under a most murderous fire of grape, canister, and round shot, until it got into position."[1]

Our artillerymen could get but *three* pieces in battery, while the enemy had *twenty-two*, which, being mostly heavy, rendered our fire nugatory. "For two hours," says the same officer, "our troops stood the storm of iron and lead which hailed upon them, unmoved. At every discharge they laid flat down to avoid the storm, and then sprung up to serve the guns. At the end of that time, two of the guns were dismounted, and we (the rifles) badly hurt; thirteen of the horses were killed and disabled, and fifteen of the cannoniers killed and wounded. The troops were then recalled."

In the mean time the Mexican lancers had been repeatedly repulsed. In another part of the field Riley's brigade sustained the enemy's fire, and were engaged in skirmishing. This action lasted for about three hours, during which time our troops maintained themselves under a heavy and severe fire, and successfully resisted the charges of large columns of cavalry.

The day of the 19th, however, closed without any decisive results. The infantry, unsustained by either cav-

---

[1] Letter of an officer in the New York Courier

alry or artillery, could not charge in column without being mowed down by the Mexican batteries, nor in line, without being successfully assailed by the Mexican cavalry.[1] To cut off the junction of further reinforcements from the capital (which till now arrived at will) the general-in-chief determined to occupy the hamlet and church of Contreras, on the road leading from the capital to Valencia's camp. Cadwallader's brigade, already advanced in that direction, had taken position, and needed assistance. The 14th regiment of infantry, Colonel Morgan, was then ordered by Scott to occupy the hamlet, and a few minutes later they were followed by the New York and South Carolina volunteers, composing the brigade of General Shields. These troops made their way through a dense forest to the left of the road at Contreras, (east side,) and in the night took post in the hamlet on the road. In the mean time the brigades of Smith and Riley had advanced still further, and taken post in rear and flank of the enemy's post at Contreras.

It was determined by Scott to make a diversion in the morning, or earlier, if practicable, in front of Fort Contreras, while the brigades of Smith and Riley should attack, and Shields should cut off the advance of reinforcements, or the retreat of the defeated through the hamlet on the road. This purpose was carried out.

General Persifer F. Smith of Twiggs' division was first on the ground, and had the merit of making the immediate dispositions for the battle of the following morning. They were made with skill and judgment, drawing from

---

[1] Scott's Official Report.

the commander-in-chief the warmest praise, and from the army universal admiration. The close of the 19th was, to the troops immediately engaged, neither pleasant nor inspiring. They closed a severe action without decisive results. The rifle regiment, with the 1st artillery and 3d infantry, (engaged in front with the enemy,) marched to their new positions through chapporal and cactus, tired, hungry, and sorrowful.[1] In the evening they marched into the little hamlet, and there spent the night, with the brigade of Riley in the same road. Shields' brigade was in an orchard near by, and Cadwallader nearer the enemy. The night was cold, wet, and dreary. An officer of the rifles thus describes it.[2]

"As we were within reach of their batteries, which could enfilade the road in which we lay, we built a stone breastwork at either end to conceal ourselves from their view and grape. There we were, completely surrounded by the enemy, cut off from our communications, ignorant of the ground, without artillery, weary, dispirited, and dejected—we were a disheartened set. With Santa Anna and Salas' promise of 'no quarter,' a force of four to one against us, and one half defeated already, no succor from Puebla and no news from Scott,[3] all seemed dark. Suddenly the words came whispered along, '*We storm at midnight!*' Now we were ourselves again.

"But what a horrible night! There we lay—too tired to eat, too wet to sleep—in the middle of that muddy

---

[1] Letter from an officer in the New York Courier.

[2] From the same.

[3] Scott was, till after dark, in a position opposite the enemy's centre. He then retired to San Augustine and wrote the despatch of the day.

road, officers and men side by side, with a heavy rain pouring down upon us—the officers without blankets or overcoats, (they had lost them in coming across,) and the men worn out with fatigue. About midnight, the rain was so heavy that the streams in the road flooded us; and there we stood, crowded together, drenched and benumbed, waiting till daylight."

The darkness and heavy rain impeded the troops, and rendered the transmission of orders[1] so difficult, that the attack on the enemy which had been planned for the dawn of day did not commence till a later hour. About four o'clock the troops of Riley and Smith, which had occupied the hamlet and road during the night, defiled into their position in rear of the enemy, by a ravine covered by orchards and corn-fields. The nature of the ground facilitated this operation. The batteries and intrenched camp of Valencia were on the side of a hill, towards the east or southeast, so as to command the road, it being the great object to defend the roads which led to the city. The volcanic and rocky formation here made several little eminences, with ravines between. In this instance there were other eminences in the rear still higher. The brigade of Riley passed through an orchard into the ravine behind Valencia, so as to be out of sight of Valencia's corps, and yet occupy a position near to him, in his rear. The brigade of Smith followed. That of Cadwallader had already taken position in rear of these, as a support, while Shields' was held in reserve—taking the place of Smith's men, in

---

[1] Scott had sent seven officers out for information that evening, of which not one got through. Captain Lee, alone, with a message from Shields, was able to get through.

the village of Contreras, and undertaking to hold that against the approach of the Mexican main army from the city,[1] or, in case Valencia was defeated, to cut off his retreat to the city. He was accompanied also by the 13th regiment under Colonel Morgan. In the mean time, a diversion (at General Smith's request) had been intended, by the advance in front of one of Worth's brigades and one of Quitman's, leaving San Augustine (the general depot) to be garrisoned by Harney's dragoons. This movement, however, occurred too late to affect the engagement.[2]

These movements were made, and the action ready to begin, at about six A. M. It appears that the march of the American troops in the night, and preparatory to the engagement, was altogether unknown to the Mexicans, whose attention was chiefly directed to an attack in front. The action of the afternoon of the 19th, in which the Americans had made no impression, inspired them with an idea that they might be victorious; and as the evening had come on leaving the Americans in front, they had the belief that the attack would be in front or along the line of the road. Here we may remark, that the idea of rapid night movements, with a view to turn positions or make surprises by skill and energy, seems not to be at all familiar to the Mexican generals. Had it been, why did they not discover, and endeavor to prevent the execution and use of the new road made round the heights of Cerro Gordo? Why did they not throw their troops into, and defend the narrow pass, between mountain and water,

---

[1] See Official Report.

[2] See Scott's Official Report.

round the south end of Lake Chalco? And why, now, with twenty thousand men in sight, did they not watch and defend the space between Valencia's batteries, and the road and hamlet occupied on the night of the 19th by the brigades of Riley and Smith? *They did not*, and lost the battle (stratagetically considered) on that account.

Let us now review the exact position of the two armies on the morning of the 20th—and which, all other things being equal, decided their fate—as to the position of Contreras. First, we observe, that the road leading by the heights of Contreras, goes to Mexico through San Angel. At the last place a road branches off, rather southeast, by Coyhoacan, to the San Antonia road at Churubusco. At the last place, and very near the junction of the roads, the San Antonia road crosses a little stream, or canal, called Churubusco River. At this point, covering the crossing, is a regular fortification, called *Tête du Pont*, or Bridge-head. This is connected with a church or convent, in the hamlet of Churubusco, by defences. Churubusco is approached, then, on the south and west, by two roads only; one from San Angel, through Coyhoacan; the other from San Antonia. Now the reader will mark that the Mexican positions were these: 1*st*. Valencia, with the division of the north, composed of about six thousand men, occupied the batteries and hill-side on the height of Contreras. This was a battery mounted with heavy pieces. The object of this defence was to command the road, which was a good one, from here to Mexico. 2*d*. At about two miles from this work, and parallel with the same road, lay the main body of the Mexican army, under Santa Anna, supposed to be about twelve thousand men. A reference to the map of the ground will show that this was a position well adapted to reinforce either Contreras upon one road, or Churubusco on the other. 3*d*. General Rincon, with the regiments of Bravo and Independencia, occupied the church and *tête du pont*, at Churubusco.[1] 4*th*. San Antonia, which had first arrested the march of Worth's division in this direction, was likewise garrisoned and fortified. In all these positions, taken in the aggregate, the Mexican forces amounted to about twenty-five thousand men. All of them were strong positions when skilfully and energetically defended. It is very evident, however, that if Contreras were taken, San Antonia would be turned and rendered useless. Churubusco then might be attacked without touching Antonia. The enemy must then concentrate his defence at the *tête du pont* of Churubusco. This actually took place.

The American positions we have already detailed. The object of Scott was first to force the fortifications of Contreras, and thus command the road through San Angel, and then to carry Churubusco, when the main road would be open to the city of Mexico. For this purpose, the brigades under the command of General P. F. Smith were detached to surround, if possible, the height of Contreras; Shields to support and hold the road; Worth to check Antonia and divert in front; while Quitman garrisoned the depot of San Augustine. The immediate arrangements and command at Contreras devolved upon General Smith, who most ably carried out the views of the commander-in-chief. The nature of the ground and

---

[1] General Rincon's Official Report.

the negligence of the Mexicans favored our troops in taking their respective places. We have seen that the brigades of Riley, Cadwallader, and Smith, each took their position in rear of the enemy, with only the crest of a hill between. Shields' position in the hamlet was such, that he was able on one hand to cut off or check reinforcements, and on the other to intercept the retreat of Valencia. In fact, the Americans had *cut the line* of the Mexican defence, and were thus able to attack their posts and divisions in detail. This was done.

At six A. M. the arrangements for battle were all made. The place and course of Riley's brigade was given by Lieutenant Tower, of the engineers. In the same manner, that of Cadwallader was pointed out by Lieutenants Beauregard and Brooks; while Captain Lee directed the course of the column under Colonel Ransom.[1] All these officers had reconnoitred the enemy's camp and forces.

When the word was given, our men sprung up in rear and on both flanks of the astonished Mexicans, rushed over the crest of the hill, and dashed pell-mell into the intrenchments! Nothing could resist them: the batteries were taken; the army of Valencia driven out in utter rout; and its flying remnants pursued on the road to Mexico! So admirable were the dispositions, and so impulsively energetic, that the battle was ended almost as soon as begun. The actual conflict lasted but *seventeen minutes!* The pursuit was for hours. The results were gigantic.

Of the scene during the battle, and the fierce ardor

---

[1] Scott's Official Report, (No. 32.)

which impelled the American[1] troops, we take a description from the same graphic writer whom we have before quoted. "At last, just at daylight, General SMITH slowly walking up, asked if all was ready. A look answered him. '*Men, forward!*' and we *did* 'forward.' Springing up at once, Riley's brigade opened, when the crack of a hundred rifles started the Mexicans from their astonishment, and they opened their fire. Useless fire—for we were so close that they overshot us, and before they could turn their pieces on us we were on them. Then such cheers arose as you never heard. The men rushed forward like demons, yelling and firing the while. The carnage was frightful, and though they fired sharply, it was of no use. The earthen parapet was cleared in an instant, and the blows of the stocks could be plainly heard, mingled with the yells and groans around. Just before the charge was made, a large body of lancers came winding up the road, looking most splendidly in their brilliant uniforms. They never got to the work, but turned and fled.[2] In an instant all was one mass of confusion, each

---

[1] The Mexicans uniformly, in their reports and letters, speak of the people of the United States of the north, as "Americans," although they are themselves just as much "Americans." This settles the question, whether the people of the United States have a *name*.

[2] This dastardly conduct of the Mexican cavalry is thus spoken of in the Official Report of General Salas, which corresponds in this respect with the above account:

"As soon as I observed the dispersion of our forces, I endeavored to check it. Crying 'Victory to Mexico!' and sounding the signal of attack, I succeeded in rallying our troops, and ordered General Anastasia Torrejon to make a charge with his cavalry; but this chief, far from obeying my orders, fled like a coward, and the cavalry following his example,

trying to be foremost in the flight. The road was literally blocked up, and while many perished by their own guns, it was almost impossible to fire on the mass from the danger of killing our own men. Some fled up the ravine on the left, or on the right, and many of these were slain by turning their own guns on them. Towards the city, the rifles and 2d infantry led off the pursuit. Seeing that a large crowd of fugitives were jammed up in a pass in the road, some of the men ran through the corn-field, and by thus heading them off and firing down upon them, about thirty men took over five hundred prisoners, nearly a hundred of them officers."[1]

In the mean time, the enemy (who previous to the assault were ignorant of the American forces in the ravine) had commenced a heavy fire on Shields' brigade in the hamlet. This, however, ceased when the charge was made by Riley. Shields then ordered his brigade, composed of the New York and South Carolina regiments, into the road, to cut off the retreat of such of Valencia's corps as passed that way. In this they succeeded. Large parties of the enemy were met by the fire of these regiments, and either scattered through the fields or made prisoners. At this point on the road three hundred and sixty-five were taken, of whom twenty-five were officers, and among the latter was General Nicholas Mendoza.[2]

The victory of CONTRERAS[3] was brilliant and decisive

---

trampled down the infantry in their flight, and completed our defeat."—SALAS' *Official Report*, August 28th, 1847.

[1] Letter of an officer in the New York Courier.

[2] Official Report of General Shields.

[3] Official Report of General Scott.

The aggregate loss of the enemy was seven hundred killed, about one thousand wounded, eight hundred and thirteen prisoners, of whom eighty-eight were officers, (including four generals,) twenty-two pieces of brass cannon, seven hundred pack-mules, and an immense number of small-arms, shot, shells, and ammunition. But the most important loss, to an experienced military eye, was that of one of the strong positions by which the roads to Mexico were commanded, and in consequence of which San Antonia was turned, and Churubusco attacked in flank. It was only two miles from the point where Shields captured Mendoza to San Angel, and but three miles (by good roads) from the last point (by Coyhoacan) to Churubusco. On these roads the American troops rushed in pursuit of the flying enemy, till they united with Worth's corps in the storm of the church and *tête du pont* at the last place.

Among the generals taken, were SALAS, MENDOZA, GARCIA, and GUADALUPE. The two former appear to have been men of talent, while of General Valencia, their commander, nothing was then heard; and he seems to have been either wanting in skill and courage, or to have been so overwhelmed with his misfortune, as to be unwilling to make his appearance.[1] By a private correspondence[2] between him and Santa Anna, it seems that the latter had directed him, on the 17th or 18th, (previous to the arrival of the army in front of the fortifications,) to abandon his post at San Angel, (probably the fortification,)

---

[1] Official Report of General Salas.

[2] Private intercepted correspondence between Valencia and Santa Anna, dated the 18th and 19th of August.

which Valencia, on the 18th, gave reasons why he should not obey; and on the 19th Santa Anna yields, but doubts the propriety of Valencia maintaining his post. Both appear to have been wrong in a military point of view. The heights of Contreras were a proper point to defend, but batteries should have been placed on two or three other eminences; and, above all, the commander should never have allowed a storming party to get into a ravine, within gunshot, without being known. Such a fact argues gross negligence.

One of the striking events of the day, was the recapture of the identical pieces of artillery taken at Buena Vista by the Mexicans. This circumstance is thus related by the commander-in-chief:[1]

"One of the most pleasing incidents of the victory is the recapture, in the works, by Captain Drum, 4th artillery, under Major Gardner, of the two brass six-pounders, taken from another company of the same regiment, though without the loss of honor, at the glorious battle of Buena Vista, about which guns the whole regiment had mourned for so many months. Coming up, a little later, I had the happiness to join in the protracted cheers of the gallant 4th, on the joyous event; and, indeed, the whole army sympathizes in its just pride and exultation."[2]

---

[1] General Scott's Official Report.

[2] In connection with this circumstance, it is proper to say that Captain O'Brien, who commanded the battery to which these guns were attached at Buena Vista, requested a court of inquiry, which was held in March, 1847 The court found the fact, that he was the last man who left the pieces, the others having been all killed and wounded. Their opinion was thus given:

The strength of the two armies in this engagement, may be thus stated. Including the brigade of Shields, placed in the hamlet, and which we have shown to have done most effective service, the American troops amounted to about four thousand five hundred; while the corps of Valencia and Mendoza were seven thousand, and at least twelve thousand were on the same road. If we deduct Shields' brigade, as keeping in check the main body of Mexicans, it is probable the actual battle was fought by three thousand five hundred on our side, against seven thousand Mexicans in fortified intrenchments. The discrepancy in numbers was not so great as in some other actions; but, on the other hand, the military dispositions were admirable, and the battle was won before it was fought.

We must now follow the army in its bloody march through and over the intrenchments of Churubusco. At 8 A. M., or two hours from its commencement, the fight of Contreras may be said to have been completed; the

---

OPINION.

"The court is unanimously of the opinion that the conduct of Captain O'Brien, during the whole time, was bold and intrepid, and deserving of the highest commendation. The firm stand made by him in the afternoon, by which he sacrificed his whole section, contributed largely to the success of the day, if it did not save us from disaster."

II. The proceedings of the court, in the above case, having been submitted to and examined by the commanding general, are by him fully approved.

III. The court of inquiry, of which Brevet Colonel W. G. Belknap, 8th infantry, is president, is hereby dissolved.

By order of Maj. Gen. Taylor.

(Signed) W. W. S. BLISS, Asst. Adjt. Gen

greater part of the time being occupied in pursuit of the broken and scattered remnants of Valencia's division—Valencia himself having disappeared.

Churubusco is really about four miles from the heights of Contreras, in a direct line east; but the road goes northeast to San Angel, and then forks southeast, so that the distance by the road is about six miles. This point was defended by General Rincon, (as we have before said,) with the regiments of Independencia and Bravo—reinforced largely on the morning of the 20th.[1] The retreating bodies of men, who had occupied Antonia, and the fragments left from Contreras, were concentrated in and about Churubusco, where they arrived but little before the advancing and attacking regiments of Scott. That morning, the commander of artillery, Don Martin Correra, arrived, bringing six pieces of cannon, which were placed in battery on the road to Coyhoacan, and in the centre of a field-work, erected around the hacienda, which was at the commencement of the causeway leading to the western gate of the city, and had to be passed before getting on the road. This hacienda consisted of an enclosure of stone walls—inside of which, was a stone building higher than these walls; and above all, a stone church, higher than the rest. The outside walls were pierced with two ranges of embrasures, and high enough to command the surrounding country, and fire plungingly upon those approaching to the assault.[2] The church and the hacienda were surrounded by this outside field-work. About

---

[1] General Rincon's Official Despatch, dated August 26th.

[2] Letter of an officer, in the New York Courier.

three hundred yards in the rear, and a little to the east, was the *tête du pont*, at the intersection of the causeway, or principal road with a canal or river. By passing along the causeway, the church and field-work would be left a little on the west side, and the troops would be first arrested by the tête du pont. This was the case with Worth's division.

On the morning of the 20th, about 8 A. M., when it was fully ascertained that the enemy (now defeated at *Contreras*) was in full retreat towards the great causeway road from San Antonia to Mexico, the two brigades (one of Worth's and one of Quitman's) which had been ordered to make a diversion in front of Contreras, were ordered back to their respective divisions. Quitman was directed with his remaining brigade (Shields' being now under the direction of General Twiggs, on the road from San Angel) to garrison San Augustine, the general depot of the army, and the loss of which could not be risked.[1] The division of Worth was ordered to proceed to the attack of San Antonia, and when that was carried, to march on and rejoin the other divisions in the attack of the defences of Churubusco. Accordingly, the brigades of Clarke and Garland (Worth's) proceeded to the attack of Antonia. This post, left unsupported by the line of troops, now driven from Contreras, and with comparatively open ground about it, could be turned. Accordingly, Colonel Clarke's brigade, conducted by Captain Mason of the engineers, and Lieutenant Hardcastle of the topographical corps, turned the enemy's right, by a sweep to the left, and came out on the high road

[1] Scott's Official Report, No. 32, August 28th.

to Mexico. In the mean time, the garrison had retreated, and were now cut in the centre by the advancing column of Clarke. One-half were driven off towards the east, and the other part on the causeway towards Churubusco. The brigade of Garland advancing in front, now occupied the evacuated hamlet—capturing the artillery in its batteries. These brigades were soon united, and rushed on in hot pursuit.[1]

The grand movement of the day now commenced—the march of the united army (Quitman's 2d brigade excepted) on the fortified post of Churubusco. This was made in two columns—the division of Worth from San Antonia in front, and the divisions of Twiggs and Pillow, with the brigade of Shields from Coyhoacan; to which point they had pursued the remains of the Mexican army,—routed at Contreras, and followed through San Angel. This naturally resolved the battle into *two* distinct actions on the same field, and so clearly connected as to be within half cannon-shot at the centres of contest. These were respectively, the tête du pont, attacked by the first column under Worth, and the fortified church and hacienda, attacked by the column of Twiggs and Pillow. Let us first follow Worth's attack.

It had got to be about 1 P. M., when the different divisions from the south and west were united, not in line, (nor together,) but within the same circuit of attack.[2] At the same time, the garrisons of Churubusco, (strongly reinforced,) the brigade of Perez, at Portalis, the broken corps from San Angel, and the principal divisions of

---

[1] Scott's Official Report.

[2] Letter in the New York Courier

Santa Anna's army were all prepared for battle, having concentrated in and about Churubusco. The division of Twiggs had commenced the attack on the fortified church about an hour, amidst an incessant roll of fire, when Worth, with Cadwallader's brigade, (Pillow's division,) commenced manœuvring on the tête du pont. The other fortification attacked by Twiggs, was just half-gunshot to the left, and but for the attack on it, would have poured a destructive fire on Worth. Both were attacked simultaneously—and thus the fire of Pablo de Churubusco was in a measure diverted. The brigade of Colonel Garland, with Smith's light battalion, moved along a little to the right of the road, directly up to the tête du pont. They advanced under the fire of a long line of infantry. Clarke's brigade marched at the same time, directly on the road; and this again was supported by the 11th and 14th regiments, (Cadwallader's,) and the whole moved steadily up under a tremendous discharge of both small-arms and cannon. Most of these corps, advancing perpendicularly, suffered greatly from the fire of batteries at the bridge-head.[1] At length, the line in front of Garland's column gave way, and made a rapid retreat to Mexico. The tête du pont was reached by Clarke's—its deep ditch was crossed by the 5th and 8th infantry—the parapets stormed—and one of the most formidable defences of Mexico crowned by its capture, the third action of the memorable 20th of August.

In the meanwhile, a yet more active, bloody, and eventful action took place to the left of Worth's line, in the attack on what may be called the Citadel of Churu

---

[1] Scott's Official Report.

busco, the fortification at the hacienda, before described. Scott, who on the 19th had been posted on an eminence in front of Contreras, and on that night gave directions for the early storm of Contreras—had this morning given (amidst the trophies of the field) his orders for the forward movement of Worth, and now (in the forenoon) joined General Pillow's division in its march to Coyhoacan. Here, just one mile west of Churubusco, at a point made convenient by several cross-roads, he made the arrangements for the day. Cadwallader's brigade was detached (as we have seen) to reinforce Worth at Antonia. Twiggs's division was ordered (except the rifles) to attack the citadel, San Pablo, in front. Pierce's brigade first, and soon after Shields', were directed to take a road which led to the rear of Churubusco, to divert the troops under Santa Anna, and threaten his right and rear; with a view also, should the attack in front succeed, to cut off the retreat of the Mexican forces to the city. General Shields commanded this corps, which was directed in its course by Captain Lee, of the engineers.[1] These dispositions were rapidly made, and as quickly executed. The troops moved regularly and gallantly into their places, and the battle of Churubusco was commenced, which, for three hours was vigorously maintained amidst the raging of all the elements, which mingle their terrible voices and their crimson banners on the battle-field. The veteran regiments of Smith and Riley quailed not amidst the whirlwind of fire, and the storm of balls which rolled from the well-directed guns of San Pablo in front; while far to the left, the gallant

[1] Scott's Official Report

volunteers of Carolina and New York, were rapidly filling their untimely, though glorious graves! Here, the Mexican general, Rincon, ably defended his post. There, the masses of Santa Anna poured themselves on the division of Shields! A lurid canopy of sulphurous smoke rose over the heads of the combatants, and, far over the ancient plains of Mexico, rolled the roar of cannon and the crash of arms—that awful music, which makes the song of battle, the prelude of death, and the voice of angry nations. One might imagine the fierce spirit of Guatimozin hovering exultant over the plain, where the Celt and the Saxon, the enemies of his race, poured out in mortal conflict, (as if in just retribution,) their blood and their lives, over the graves of his fathers.

In the centre of the batteries of San Pablo was placed the company of St. Patrick's, formed out of deserters from the American army.[1] These men fought desperately and skilfully, causing the deaths of many of the assailants, and delaying the capture of the post. An officer of the rifles thus describes the scene:[2] "The firing was most tremendous; in fact, one continued roll while the combat lasted. The enemy, from their elevated position, could readily see our men, who were unable to get a clear view from their position. Three of the pieces were manned by the '*deserters*,' a body of about one hundred who had deserted from the ranks of our army during the war. They were enrolled in two companies, commanded by a deserter,[3]

---

[1] Report of General Rincon, who says that the battalion of Bravo and the companies of St. Patrick were stationed in the front batteries.

[2] Letter in the New York Courier.

[3] This man's name is Thomas Riley, a deserter from the 3d infantry

and w re better uniformed and disciplined than the rest of the army. These men fought most desperately; and are said t only to have shot down several of our officers whom they knew, but to have pulled down the white flag of surrender no less than three times."

It was now two hours and a half from the commencement of the battle by the division of Twiggs, when the *ête du pont* gave way before the storming parties of Worth. The enemy were driven out at the point of the bayonet, and the larger part of Worth's and Pillow's divisions crossed the bridge and followed in vigorous pursuit. Captain Larkin Smith and Lieutenant Snelling of the 8th infantry, however, seized upon a field-piece and fired upon the church, or citadel. The furious battle at that point still continued; but in half an hour more—just three hours from the commencement—the citadel (San Pablo) was entered, sword in hand, by two companies of the 3d infantry under Captains Alexander and J. M. Smith, with Lieutenant Shepler. At the same moment the white flag had been exhibited, and Captain Alexander received the surrender, and hoisted on the balcony the flags of the gallant 3d infantry. A *fourth* time, in one day, had the eagle of victory perched upon her favorite standard. The bold bird of war seemed to rejoice with exultant flight in the career of the conquering Saxon!

But the dead and the dying were not yet to be left to the stillness of advancing night. Far to the left the tide of war still rolled its angry waves. The brigades of Pierce and Shields, supported by the rifles, had encountered, to the rear of the works of Churubusco, four thousand Mexican infantry supported by three thousand cavalry. Hotly and furiously did the battle rage in this quarter. Regiment after regiment, the 9th, 12th, 15th infantry, with Ransom, Wood, and Morgan, came up to the charge. Here were covered with glory and with blood the chivalry of Carolina, the bold soldiers of New York! Here Pierce, fainting with pain, was taken from the field; here the brave Butler fell; and here, a *fifth* time on the same extraordinary day, the banner of the Anglo-American waved over troops triumphantly victorious! The Spanish-Aztecs retreated from the bloody scene of their defeat, leaving hundreds of their bravest prisoners, and hundreds more to mingle their dust with the undistinguished dead, to be remembered no more. Over the dead and over the long causeway the fugitives are pursued by the gallant dragoons, and it was not till at the very gates of Mexico that the impulsive Captain Kearney reined in his horse.[1]

In the citadel (church) of Churubusco the brave Generals Rincon and Anaya,[2] (provisional president,) with hundreds of others, were taken prisoners. Thus had the army of Scott at Contreras, Antonia, the Tête du Pont, Churubusco, and in the field, five times in one glorious day, defeated the enemy in sight of the capital of Mexico, in that wonderful valley where, three hundred years before, Cortez had overwhelmed the Aztecs with the invincibles of Spain. History, the Kaleidescope of humanity, is again exhibiting strange and various and mysterious events. The northman had come from the dark forests of the Danube and the Elbe to overwhelm

---

[1] Orders had been dispatched to recall the dragoons, but they did not receive them; and Kearney lost his arm, and stopped only at the gates of Mexico.

[2] General Anaya has since been elected president.

the Roman in the English isles; again he embarks on the waters of the Atlantic and penetrates the woods of the western continent, builds republics, renews the glory of civilization, and now sends the chariots of war to overwhelm in conquest the descendants of those very invincibles whom Cortez had victoriously led from the Gulf of Mexico to the palace of the Montezumas. Is there no ministry of retribution in this—no angel of fate unfolding the cycles of providence?

Scott, now at Churubusco, turns with a glad spirit and grateful heart to the troops, and rejoices with them in the martial glory of their country. The old soldiers seize his hand; there is silence, and the old commander pours forth "in eloquent and patriotic words the commendation of their gallant conduct."[1]

An officer, who was present, says: "During this thrilling scene, I looked up to a balcony of the church that had been so bravely defended. It was filled by Mexican prisoners. Among them General Rincon, a venerable old soldier, was leaning forward, his countenance glowing and his eyes sparkling with every manifestation of delight. I verily believe that the old veteran, with the spirit of a true soldier, upon beholding a victorious general so greeted by the brave men he had just led to victory, forgot for a moment his own position, that he was defeated and a prisoner; and saw and thought only of the enthusiasm by which he was surrounded."[2]

First. Let us now examine the *results* of this great day in American military annals. Let us review in brief

---

[1] Letter in the Journal of Commerce.

[2] Letter in the Journal of Commerce.

the actions of the day and the defences overcome. *1st*. There were, as we have said, five distinct actions, although the last three were fought as parts of one great battle. There were, 1, The storm of Contreras; 2, The capture of Antonia; 3, The storm of the tête du pont; 4, The battle and assault of the church and outworks of Churubusco; 5, The action in the rear of Churubusco with the right wing of Santa Anna's corps. These last three were parts of one drama, but distinct in the skill, the action, and the relative effects. The tête du pont was about four hundred yards from the fortified church of Churubusco; and the field in which Pierce and Shields were engaged, nearly a mile in rear of both. There is no doubt the fierce attack on the church (citadel) aided the divisions of Worth in their assault on the tête du pont; and there is no doubt, either, that the fall of the latter determined, in a great measure, the fall of the former.

2d. The next point of interest is the relative proportions of either army in numbers and position. It must be remembered here, that the American army were in the heart of an enemy's country, and were *assailing fortified positions*. These facts may be fairly said to have doubled the real strength of the Mexican army. At *Contreras* the relative numbers, *actually in fight*, were—Americans, three thousand five hundred—Mexicans, seven thousand: in field, *supporting*, all counted, four thousand five hundred Americans—nineteen thousand Mexicans: at *Churubusco*, in all parts of the field, nine thousand Americans—thirty thousand Mexicans. There is no doubt that the actual garrison of the fortified church, under General Rincon, was comparatively small, and that those who defended the mere batteries of the tête du pont were not very numerous; but behind these, and especially behind the tête du pont, were long lines of infantry and cavalry, amounting, taken in all, to nearly thirty thousand.

3*d*. The third point is the strength of the batteries and defences. The following is a statement of these:[1]

	BATTERIES.	GUNS.	INFANTRY BREASTWORKS.
Contreras	1	22	0
San Antonia	7	24	2
Churubusco	2	15	0
Total	10	61	2

At the tête du pont of Churubusco, a canal, or river, passed behind, over which was a bridge. This was the field-defence of Santa Anna's army, which lay behind; and certainly any one who will examine the positions and defences of the Mexicans at Churubusco must pronounce them very strong, well chosen, and well defended, in regard to the fortified points.

Second. What were the results in respect to the enemy? These positions, which commanded the main roads to Mexico in that direction, were all taken; the causeways were laid open to the very gates of the city; and the vast *materiel* arrayed for its defence destroyed or captured.

At the end of this great day in war, Scott, while the troops were yet pursuing, proceeded on to Tacubaya; but on the way was met with propositions for peace. After

[1] Taken from a statement made by Captain Lee.

making his reply, he proceeded to Tacubaya, near the strong castle of Chapultepec. The guns from the castle were silent, and the headquarters of the American army were soon safely established in the palace of the archbishop, a huge pile of buildings, surrounded with beautiful gardens. Before him, in full view, rose the domes and spires of the famed city, environed by beautiful lakes, and the richest natural scenery. He was at the gates of the "Halls of the Montezumas," with an army flushed with victory, and impatient to be led to the assault. But neither the glory of military renown, nor the rich treasures which have been dug from the mines of Mexico, could dazzle the eye of the patriot soldier, or swerve him from the obligations to humanity.

Before the carnage of another battle, he must make one final effort to stay the iron arm of destruction, and reclaim warring nations to the paths of peace. Hence his beautiful letter, expressing the Christian sentiment, "Enough blood has been shed in this unnatural war." When the echoes of the cannon shall have died away, and the clangor of arms shall have ceased—when the steeled warrior shall have gone to his rest, and the conqueror and the vanquished shall lie down together—Christianity will weave her unfading chaplet for the soldier who has ever been true to her highest obligations and benign requirements.[1]

---

[1] The following are the results of the battles of the 20th :—

American loss—killed, wounded, and missing, 1,053.

Mexican loss—3,500 prisoners; 1,500 killed, wounded, and missing; 37 pieces artillery captured; small-arms, ammunition, and equipments for an army.

CHAPTER XIII.

Peace Negotiations.—President Polk's Commission.—Mexican Conditions.—American Ultimatum.—Failure of Negotiations.—Scott's Notice to Santa Anna.—Trial and Execution of the Deserters.—Description of Chapultepec.—Of Molino del Rey.—Mexican Defences.—March of Worth.—Strength of his Corps.—Battle of Molino del Rey.—Mexican Loss.—Evacuation of Molino del Rey.—Preparations for the Attack of Chapultepec.—Erection of Batteries.—Storm of Chapultepec.—Action of the 13th.—Capture of Mexico.—Entrance into the City.—Scott's Address to the Soldiers.—Insurrection of the Leperos.—Appearance of the City.

In the last chapter we recorded the memorable events of the 20th of August, 1847, in the valley of Mexico,—events unequalled in their extraordinary character and their dramatic interest by any preceding part of the military history of America. Kearney had hardly been recalled from his adventurous charge to the gates of Mexico, when the shades of evening gathered round the bloody field of Churubusco. The battle had passed, and the vale lay as silent as the lonely bodies of the slain. Passed away are all the rolling thunders of the red artillery, and quenched their fires as the silent and quenched volcanoes of the snow-crowned Popocatapetl, rearing its cold head upon the distant horizon. Nature sleeps, and the dead sleep, and the weary soldier sleeps, while the sentry and the stars keep watch together. But though the fires of volcanoes may sleep, and the artillery may cease to flash, the events of time and providence will never sleep.

HISTORY MOVES ON. Its recording pen never ceases to write while man is an actor in the drama of providence, and humanity continues to develop its mighty and mysterious powers.

On the morning of the 21st, Scott, *en route* to Coyhoacan, was met by commissioners from Santa Anna, proposing an armistice. The time was not then agreed to, but Scott told them he should sleep that night at Tacubaya. The commissioners then told him that if he would delay his march a few hours, they would send an order to the fortress of Chapultepec not to fire on him! The general, however, did not delay his march, but entered Tacubaya early in the afternoon, attended by the dragoons alone; Worth's division did not arrive till late in the evening.[1] That night Scott occupied the Archiepiscopal Palace of Mexico. At this time it is unquestionably true that the American general might have entered the plaza of Mexico, or have demolished its splendid edifices by the fire of his bombs. He did not; but, in conformity with the dictates of humanity, on the following morning received the propositions of the Mexican commissioners for a truce. This he arranged on his own terms, when the negotiations commenced.

To understand this negotiation, we must recur to the events in the order of time. In the first place, we must note the commission of President Polk to Mr. N. P. Trist. It seems that on the 15th day of April, 1847, the President gave a formal commission to Mr. Trist, in which he states that he has "invested him, in the fullest and most complete manner, with ample power and authority, in the

---

[1] Letter in the Journal of Commerce.

name of the United States, to meet and confer with any person or persons, who shall have similar authority from the republic of Mexico, and between them to negotiate and conclude an arrangement of the differences which exist between the two countries—a treaty of peace, amity, and lasting boundaries."[1] The President had no power by the Constitution, to constitute a mission to a foreign country, nor would he have power to make a treaty without the advice and consent of the Senate. Mr. Trist, then, notwithstanding his commission, was in fact the mere agent of the President, and no more. Accordingly, he carried out with him from the department of state a "project of a treaty" to be presented to the Mexican government.[2] The inference from this transaction is, that the cabinet at Washington supposed that the Mexican people were anxious for peace, and there was nothing for the President of the United States to do but to say on what terms peace should be made. The opposite of this idea appears to have been the state of the Mexican mind, for they met the American agent with instructions to their commissioners that the treaty should be made on the basis that they had triumphed, and as if the war could be prosecuted by them with advantage.[3] In this spirit met the commissioners. Mr. Trist, the agent of President Polk, at two thousand miles from his principal, tied down to the letter and detail of a treaty drawn up by the Secretary of State, without the power to change it; and the Mexican

---

[1] See copy of Mr. Trist's commission.

[2] See official copy of the "Project of a Treaty.

[3] See conditions for the Mexican commissioners drawn up by Santa Anna, Pacheco, &c., &c.

commissioners meeting him, as if their country was intact, and their arms invulnerable to conquest.

On the 25th of August, Mr. Trist addressed a note to the Mexican Minister of Foreign Relations, informing him that he is ready to treat with commissioners on the part of Mexico. On the 26th, Mr. Pacheco replies, that he is engaged in appointing commissioners for that purpose, who would assemble the following evening at the village of Atzcopozalco, an intermediate point between the two armies.

The invitation and appointment Mr. Trist accepted in a note of the same date.

Among the commissioners appointed by the Mexican secretary was General Herrera, formerly president of the republic. This distinguished man promptly declined the appointment. The grounds on which he declined are worthy of note. He was president in 1845, when the mission of Slidell occurred. He was willing to hear Slidell state his terms; but that person, as we have already stated, had neither the patience nor temper to wait and watch events, but impetuously demanded that he should be immediately received. The downfall of Herrera immediately took place; and Herrera now says: "For the single act of being willing to listen to his propositions, my administration was calumniated in the most atrocious manner, this act alone causing the revolution which deprived me of the command; and to take part in the same question, at this day, would cause a renewal of the calumnies which then assailed me." Mr. Pacheco, however, insisted upon his acceptance, and he finally acted on the commission. The Mexican commission was composed of the following persons:

Don Jose Joaquin de Herrera, general of division
Don Bernardo Conto, general of brigade.
Don Ignacio Mora y Villamil, general.
Don Miguel Atristain,
Don Jose Miguel Arroyo, Secretary.

The great points of negotiation were the boundaries to be drawn between Mexico and the United States, one party insisting upon territory to be taken from the other. The boundaries in the "project" of Mr. Trist were chiefly these:

Article 4th of the "project" requires that the boundary line should commence in front of the mouth of the Rio Grande, and should follow the middle of that river to the southern boundary of New Mexico; thence west with the southern line of New Mexico to the western boundary; thence north with the river Gila till it empties into the Rio Colorado; thence down the Colorado and the gulf of Mexico to the Pacific.

Article 8th required the free right of way forever over the isthmus of Tehuantepec.

An examination of the map will show that our government demanded, 1*st*, The cession of the disputed territory between the Nueces and the Rio Grande; 2*d*, Of New Mexico; 3*d*, Of both Upper and Lower California.

The Mexican commissioners presented a counter-project, which contained the following definition of boundary:

1*st*, The dividing line between the two republics shall commence in the bay of Corpus Christi; thence to the mouth of the Nueces; thence with the middle of said stream to its source; thence west to the eastern boundary of New Mexico; thence north with that boundary to the 37th degree of latitude; thence west with that parallel tc the Pacific. 2*d*, That the government of Mexico would found no settlement or colony between the Nueces and the Rio Grande, leaving that country as an uninhabited frontier.

The map shows that this proposition grants to the United States the best part of California, while it proposes to leave the territory in dispute an uninhabited region. Barren by nature, it is not likely to invite inhabitants till the better parts of the continent are settled. In a subsequent oral discussion between Mr. Trist and the Mexican commissioners, it appears that the former was willing to abandon the claim to Lower California, and to refer the decision on the Nueces territory to the cabinet at Washington.[1] As between Mr. Trist and the Mexican commissioners, the failure of the negotiation turned wholly on the claim of the south part of New Mexico; for, above the 37th degree Mexico had conceded every thing, and Mr. Trist, in the name of the United States, was willing to concede Lower California. New Mexico had never been claimed by the United States at all, previous to this negotiation, nor had we any plausible claim to it except that which President Polk had formally disclaimed, —that of conquest.[2]

The formal report made by the Mexican commissioners to the secretary for foreign relations, the 7th of September, 1847, announced that the discussions had closed and

---

[1] The Mexican commissioners' statement to the secretary of foreign affairs, dated Sept. 7th, 1847.

[2] President Polk disclaimed conquest in his messages.

the negotiations failed. In the mean time, various documents had been issued by the Mexican authorities, which disclosed the fact that Mexico was not ready for peace. One was a protest of the representatives of the states of Mexico, Jalisco, and Zacatecas, signed by Valentin Gomez Farias and his colleague deputies, declaring that, under existing circumstances, "the city of Mexico would not allow the necessary freedom in its discussions and deliberations, if Congress should assemble in that city, and that it would not comport with the dignity of the republic that its representatives should deliberate there on this matter." They also declared that any arrangement in regard to external relations, "without the ratification of Congress," would be null and unconstitutional. They further affirm, that this step is taken with the express view to save the republic "from the ignominy which would inevitably attach to a treaty concluded and ratified under the guns of the enemy, and on the day succeeding unlooked-for reverses."[1] At the same time, the secretary of state issued a circular to the states of Puebla and Mexico, calling for a levy *en masse*, "in order that they may attack and harass the enemy with whatever weapons each may conveniently procure, whether good or bad, by fire and sword, and by every practicable means which it is possible to employ in the annihilating of an invading army." These and other declarations and documents, prove conclusively that, however fairly and sincerely General Herrera and his colleagues may have conducted the negotiations, yet, in fact, the Mexican population were indisposed to peace.

---

[1] There is no evidence that any considerable number of Mexicans have ever been for peace.

On the 6th of September, Scott had given General Santa Anna notice of certain breaches of the armistice. To this the Mexican chief replied with similar complaints. On the 7th, the failure of the negotiations became known, and General Scott took his measures for the recommencement of hostilities.

Before we proceed, however, to narrate events of new and extraordinary interest in the valley of Mexico, we must turn aside to witness another and a sadder tragedy —one in which no rays of glory light up the darkness of death, but the gloomy curtains of despair and shame are drawn round the unpitied and unhonored CRIMINAL. Desertion in the face of an enemy, and during the existence of actual war, has been, among all nations and in all time, punished with death. It is treason—disloyalty—in its worst, least excusable, and most dangerous form. Of this crime, were "the companies of St. Patrick"[1] palpably and undeniably guilty. They had fought in the ranks of the Mexican army, at the batteries of Churubusco; they had fought longest and hardest against those very colors which they had sworn to defend; they were deserters, and many of them were taken prisoners. Soon after the battles of the 20th, and while the negotiations were pending, *twenty-nine* of these men were tried by a general court-martial, of which Colonel Riley of the 2d infantry was president. The court found these men guilty, (two-thirds of the whole court concurring in each several case,) and sentenced each one of them to hang by the neck till dead. In a general order, dated the 8th of September, General Scott approved the sentence, with

[1] See the Report of General Rincon.

the exception of three, who had deserted previous to the commencement of the war, and two others, who were recommended to favor by the court; and four, in whose palliation there appeared some mitigating circumstances. The remainder were executed according to the sentence. *Sixteen* were executed at San Angel, on the 10th of September. *Six* of the whole number tried were deserters from the 3d infantry, *three* from the 5th infantry, *four* from the 7th infantry, *two* from the 2d infantry, *five* from the 3d artillery, *six* from the 4th artillery, *one* from the 1st artillery, and *two* from the 2d dragoons. General Scott, in examining the proceedings of the court, appears to have released every man from the penalty of death, in whose favor any reason or mitigation could be pleaded. Among the three whom he found were not legally subject to the penalty of death, because they had deserted previous to the commencement of the war, was the notorious Riley, the commander of the deserters' company. His sentence was commuted, so that he was lashed and branded. The lesson given by this terrible execution was undoubtedly a severe one, but one which war necessarily carries with it, and without which the discipline of the army could not be maintained.

On the 7th September, Scott, having determined to carry the city of Mexico by assault, accompanied by General Worth, made a *reconnaissance* of the formidable defences of the enemy immediately in front of Tacubaya, and commanding the principal causeway and the aqueduct supplying the city with water. This observation determined the general-in-chief to attack what may be called the defences of Chapultepec. These were several, collaterally supporting one another, and constituting on the whole a very strong *point d'appui* and support for the

Mexican army; the larger part (if not the whole) was now assembled at this point. We must now take a view of these defences to understand the actions which ensued. Early on the same morning, Captain Mason of the engineers made a close and daring *reconnaissance* of the enemy's line, round and on Chapultepec. The results of this investigation may be thus stated:

The little village of Tacubaya, at which General Scott's headquarters had been now established nearly three weeks, is about two miles and a half from the city of Mexico. About twelve hundred yards north of it, just *point-blank* range for twelve-pounders, is the hill and fortified buildings of Chapultepec. At this point, the causeway branches off to the east, being about two miles in length to the city. The Tacubaya road passed on till, in two miles more, it entered the San Cosme causeway. These causeways are the avenues to the city; and bombs and cannon of heavy calibre, placed on the hill of Chapultepec, *could command them, and the city itself.* The knowledge of this fact informs us, at once, why General Scott deemed it necessary to possess this castle, in order to take the city. Once possessed, the city must fall of course. Without it, the avenues to the city, and the city itself, would be exposed to the bombardment of the enemy's batteries.

Let us now examine in detail, the particular points of the defence.

CHAPULTEPEC is a porphyritic rock, called in the Aztec language, "Grasshopper's Hill." It rose from the former margin of the lake—was the resort of the Aztec princes, and is the real site of the much-sought Halls of the Montezumas. Here are the remains of gardens, groves, and grottoes—the lingering remnants of that magnificence which adorned the ancient city of Mexico. Here also, the Spanish viceroys selected their residence, as the most beautiful spot in the valley of Mexico. And here was now placed the Military college. The cadets of the institution were now among its defenders. The buildings on the top were well fortified, and the base of the hill was nearly surrounded by a thick stone-wall. On the north, east, and south, this hill was abrupt and stony. On the west only (from the city) it seemed to permit any approach. On this side, down the slope, was a heavy forest. On this side, the American commander determined to assault it; but here also, were formidable defences.

El Molino del Rey is just at the foot of this hill-slope—adjoins the grove of trees, and is a stone building of thick and high walls, with towers at the end. This was strongly garrisoned, and made a sort of depot, and was supposed to have been used as a foundry recently, though really built for mills, and called, "the King's Mill."

Casa de Mata is another massive, thick-walled stone building, standing about four hundred yards to the west of Molino del Rey, and in a straight line with that and the castle of Chapultepec. It is also at the foot of a gentle declivity or ridge, descending from the village of Tacubaya.

It follows then, from this topographical survey, that Chapultepec is a position commanding all the roads around, and that this position can be approached only on one side, on which is a grove of trees; and that at the foot of this slope, lie Molino del Rey and Casa de Mata, well defended, so that the first attack must necessarily be made on Molino del Rey, or Chapultepec could not be taken; and if not taken, there was no safe passage to the city. The first thing to be done then, was the storming of Molino del Rey.

Accordingly, after the reconnaissance of the 7th, General Scott ordered General Worth with the 1st division, reinforced by Cadwallader's brigade, and a detachment of dragoons and artillery, to attack and carry the lines and defences of the enemy at the foot of the hill; capture Molino del Rey; destroy the supposed *materiel* there; and then withdraw again to the village of Tacubaya.[1]

The position of the enemy was well selected to defend the naturally strong grounds they had assumed. His left rested upon and occupied the stone building, Molino del Rey; his right, in the same manner, rested upon the stone building called Casa de Mata. Midway between these was his field-battery, and on each side of it was his lines of infantry.[2] The Mexican account of the position of their army does not differ essentially from that given by our officers. It states, that the left wing of their army rested on Molino del Rey, close to the forest of Chapultepec; that this point was commanded by General Leon, who had the battalion of Mina, and the battalions of Union and La Patria of Oaxaca, the companies of Puebla, and a body from Queretaro, all composed of National Guards. The right wing rested on the Casa de Mata, and was composed of the brigade of General Perez, fifteen

---

[1] Official Despatch of General Worth, dated Sept. 10th, 1847.

[2] General Worth's Report.

hundred of the regular army.[1] Independent of these strongly-garrisoned fortresses, the Mexican army, to the number of at least ten thousand men, under the command of Santa Anna, were posted as above described, in a line with a field-battery between posts. The corps ordered by General Scott to the attack of this line was composed as follows :

1st division, (General Worth,) . .	about 2,000
Cadwallader's brigade, (11th, 14th, and Voltigeurs)	784
Three squadrons of dragoons and company of mounted riflemen, under Major Sumner, . .	270
Drum's battery, (three field-pieces,) Huger's battery, (two 24-pounders,) . .	100
Total corps of General Worth,[2] .	men 3,154

It must be recollected, however, that when this arrangement was made, no one in the American army knew the real strength of the fortified posts occupied by the Mexican army. Worth made the most judicious arrangements for the attack. The object in view was to break up, 1st, the enemy's lines of intrenchments, and, 2dly, to destroy the munitions in Molino del Rey, after which the troops were to retire. Those defences being completely under the guns of the castle of Chapultepec, it may be assumed that the commanding-general deemed it unnecessary to retain the troops in that exposed situation, when the ob-

[1] Extract from the *Boletin,* Mexican newspaper.
[2] General Worth's Report.

ject for which they had gone there had been accomplished.

Worth divided his corps into three columns, with a reserve, to act respectively against the wings and centre of the enemy. 1st. The right column (opposite the enemy's left, Molino del Rey) was composed of Garland's brigade, to look at and in time attack El Molino. This column was accompanied by Captain Drum, and two pieces of artillery. To attack with this column, and thus keep in check Chapultepec and its defences, Captain Huger's battery of 24-pounders was placed on the ridge descending from Tacubaya, and at about six hundred yards from El Molino. 2d. A storming party of five hundred picked men was placed to the left of this battery, under the command of Major Wright of the 8th infantry, to assail the enemy's centre, and capture his field-battery. 3d. The second brigade (now under the command of Colonel M'Intosh) was placed higher up the ridge, accompanied by Duncan's battery, to watch the enemy's left, support Major Wright, or assail, as circumstances might require. Cadwallader's brigade was held in reserve, in a position between the last column (M'Intosh's) and the battering guns, that they might support either column, as they might need. Sumner's dragoons were on the extreme left, guarding that flank. Such were the dispositions made by Worth[1] on the night of the 7th of September. At 3 o'clock on the morning of the 8th, the columns were put in motion, and at daylight they were all in their respective positions. At half-past 4 A. M., when things could be distinctly seen, the battle

[1] See Worth's Official Report.

began by the firing of Huger's battery (24-pounders) on Molino del Rey, which continued till that strong point was sensibly shaken.[1] At this time, the storming party under Major Wright rushed forward, under the guidance of Captain Mason of the engineers, and Lieut. Foster. They were received unexpectedly with a tremendous fire of artillery. They still dashed on, drove the artillery-men from their pieces, and had actually taken the battery, when the enemy, perceiving how small was the body of men by whom he was dispossessed, re-rallied, and the infantry of their whole line poured in a destructive fire. Here no less than *eleven* out of only fourteen officers were either killed or wounded! The column was driven back for a moment, and the Mexican troops regained possession of the disputed point. They are said to have killed nearly all the wounded left on the field.[2] The light battalion left to cover Huger's battery, and the right wing of Cadwallader's brigade, under Captain Kirby Smith, were now ordered forward. They came gallantly into action. The enemy's line was defeated. The contested point was carried, and the two wings of the enemy, Molino del Rey and Casa de Mata, were left isolated.

On our right the battle raged with equal fury and with equal success. Garland's brigade, sustained by Drum's artillery, assaulted the left of the enemy at Molino del Rey, and after a hot conflict drove him from that apparently impregnable position under the guns of Chapultepec. On the left of our army, at Casa de Mata, another fearful and bloody action was maintained. The brigade

---

[1] General Worth's Official Report.

[2] Letter from an officer in the New York Courier and Enquirer

of Colonel M'Intosh moved on, till by coming in front of Duncan's battery, that was for a time silent, and the advancing column assaulted Casa de Mata. Again the enemy's defences proved stronger than had been anticipated. Instead of field intrenchments, or an old house, it was a strong stone citadel, with bastions and ditches. Within musket range, a deadly fire of musketry was opened upon the advancing column. Still the column rushed on till it reached the very verge of the parapet! Again did the heroes of Mexico fall within sight of victory. M'Intosh, Scott, Waite, had now fallen, and the column fell back to the left of Duncan's battery, again to rally, and again to charge. Just as this attack was made, a heavy column of cavalry and infantry was seen defiling round the enemy's right upon our extreme left. Thousands of the Mexican lancers in bright uniform now came to crush apparently the small band who were storming Casa de Mata. Then it was that Duncan's battery, silent by the interposition of our storming column, moved rapidly to the extreme left, supported by the Voltigeurs, under Colonel Andrews. As the Mexican column came within range of canister-shot, the battery opened an effective fire, which soon scattered its columns. At the same moment, Major Sumner's cavalry, formed on the left, charged and completed the rout. The retreat of our assaulting infantry had again opened Casa de Mata to the fire of our artillery. It was opened upon it. The Mexican infantry was already defeated. Their cavalry was already in flight. A few shots more from our artillery, and Casa de Mata was abandoned. All was now done that was attempted. Molino del Rey was taken. Casa de Mata was taken. Fourteen thousand of the Mexican army,

CHARGE AT MOLINO DEL REY.

thus strongly posted, had been defeated by one-fourth their numbers. Fifty-two commissioned officers and eight hundred prisoners were captured. Great quantities of arms and ammunition were also taken.

Casa de Mata was blown up, and the ammunition and other *materiel* of war found in Molino del Rey destroyed. When this was accomplished, these places were evacuated by the orders of the commander-in-chief. It is evident to all intelligent minds that they could not be held unless Chapultepec had also been carried; for that, the corps under Worth were inadequate, and were not detached for that purpose. The testimony of General Worth, furnished in his official report, proves that after the most accurate and daring reconnaissance on the part of the engineers, and also by general officers, the impression was left on the minds of all those officers, that the defences of Molino del Rey, and especially of Casa de Mata, were less strong than they really proved to be. They were thought likewise to be more important and valuable to the Mexican army than they really were, as depositories of munitions. General Scott, therefore, had detached an ample force to carry outposts of such a kind as were anticipated, but insufficient to carry, without too much loss, the castle of Chapultepec. The movement was necessary, however, for another and a different reason from those which have been given. Chapultepec *must* be carried. To do this, the destruction of the defences at the foot of the hill, and covering the Mexican army, was essential to success. The strength of those defences, unknown and impossible to know, was the only cause of the extraordinary loss, which rendered this proportionably the bloodiest battle of the war. One-fourth of Worth's entire force were either killed or wounded! Noi were the Mexicans less sorely injured. Desperately did they fight. Leon, their bravest general; Balderez, the gallant colonel of the battalion of Mina; Huerta, Moteos, and other distinguished officers, were lost on that fatal field.

Such was the battle of MOLINO DEL REY; long to be remembered as the scene of extraordinary actions, and long grieved, as that which made the graves of brave and noble men.

On the afternoon of the 8th, the corps of Worth, having accomplished the purpose of the battle, retired to Tacubaya, and the commander-in-chief directed his inquiries to the defences of Mexico and the modes of overcoming them. On the 9th and 10th, reconnaissances were made in every practicable direction, especially by the engineers Lee, Beauregard, Stevens, and Tower, and also by the commander-in-chief. These reconnaissances were especially directed to the south and west. The San Antonia road (on which lay Antonia and Churubusco) came in on the south. This is the road, the reader will recollect, by which the army had advanced till after the battle of Churubusco. Then it diverged to the northwest, through Coyhoacan, San Angel, and Tacubaya. This road was, in fact, the great Acapulco road, passing southwest from the city of Mexico to the Pacific ocean, and which the army had reached by its bold and successful march round the Lake Chalco. The general-in-chief and engineer now sought, whether by this or any other route, they could most successfully approach and enter the city. The observations disclosed these facts, that there were 1*st*, Five great roads leading to the city of

Mexico, viz.:[1] the road to Vera Cruz, which the army had followed to Ayotla; the road to Acapulco, by which it advanced to Antonia and Churubusco; the road to Toluca, on which it now was, at Tacubaya; the road to Guadalupe, by which Santa Anna finally retreated; and the road to Tampico, which went northeast round Lake Tezcuco. 2*d*, These roads terminated in eight gates. *Three* of these gates were approached by causeways from the Acapulco road, viz.: the San Antonia, Perdido, and Piedad; *two* by the Toluca road, by Tacubaya, viz.: Chapultepec and San Cosme. Each of the other three roads had a gate also. These gateways were small forts mounting cannon, which, in time of peace, were used as a sort of custom-houses, the city being unapproachable from any other quarter than these causeways. They were now converted into a sort of bastions for the city, or enfilading forts. Around the greater part of the city, especially where these great roads approached, there was a great ditch, or canal, which it was almost impossible to bridge in face of the enemy's cannon and small-arms.

Let the reader now conceive the city and defences of Mexico, as we have described their features. A large, regular, solid-built city, at the very bottom of a large, oblong valley, surrounded by a lofty range of mountains. These mountains turn the water into the valley below, forming great lakes, occupying no small part of the entire surface of the valley. The city is partially drained from these inundating waters; but only partially so. Much the greatest part of the land between these lakes is, in the rainy season, a marsh, too wet and

---

[1] Stealey's map of the environs of Mexico.

boggy for wagons, or horses, or an army to pass. Over these bogs and wet grounds the great causeways are cut, and over them only can the city be approached. The entrances of these causeways are defended by the bastioned gateways: and finally, around the city is a canal, or ditch. It was now the wet season, and the ground was marshy and the lakes high. Such was the series of obstacles, natural and artificial, which, on the 9th of September, presented themselves to the experienced eye of General Scott. He saw himself with a small army, reduced by bloody battles and severe sickness, in the heart of the valley of Mexico. In front, a city of two hundred thousand inhabitants, an army of twenty-five thousand men, and defences, which in other hands would seem impregnable; and finally, with the line of his communication, connecting the army with the base of its supply, cut off! This position was one, which can only be equalled in military history by the conquest of Egypt by Bonaparte, when his retreat was cut off by the English victory of Aboukir Bay. The difference is, that Napoleon was foiled, but the American general was not. Mexico had no St. Jean d'Acre for the general who had conquered at Niagara, at San d'Ulloa, at Cerro Gordo, and Churubusco! He marched on, and marched victoriously through all the obstacles of nature and of art!

On the 11th of September, Scott had completed all his reconnaissances, made his arrangements, and now had determined on the final assault. The general determined to attack the western, or southwestern gates, by the Chapultepec causeway: but, to deceive the enemy, and economize our own soldiers, he arranged a masked movement against the southern gates, while the real one was on the other side. The point of attack was Chapultepec. The mask movement was made by the divisions of Quitman and Pillow, *in daylight*, on the 11th, marching from Coyhoacan to manœuvre and make false attacks on the San Antonia road, before the gates of the south side. In the same manner Twiggs, with Riley's brigade, and Taylor's and Steptoe's batteries, was left in front of the same gates to threaten and act according to circumstances. The former divisions (Pillow's and Quitman's) were to return *by night* to Tacubaya, while Twiggs still remained on the southern front; Smith's brigade was posted at San Angel; Worth's division remained with the general-in-chief, at Tacubaya. This was the position of the several corps on the afternoon of the 11th.[1] That night, the divisions of Pillow and Quitman moved up to Tacubaya, according to the orders of the general-in-chief, previously given; Twiggs, with his brigade and batteries alone remaining, to keep up the appearance of attack on the south side.

All things were now ready for the full development of the assault. The point *d'appui* for the enemy was the Castle of Chapultepec, and constituted the point of attack for the American army—commanding with its cannon, the Chapultepec and San Cosmo causeways. We have already described the hill of Chapultepec, a steep, bluff, rocky height, rising one hundred and fifty feet above the surrounding grounds, and defended by a strong castle of thick stone walls. The whole fortress or work of defence, is about nine hundred feet in length; and the *terre-plein* and main buildings, about six hundred feet.

The following account is given by an officer of the army

---

[1] Scott's Official Report, dated Sept. 18th, 1847, No. 34.

"The Castle is about ten feet high, and the whole structure, including the wings, bastions, parapets, redoubts, and batteries, is very strongly built, and of the most splendid architecture. A splendid dome decorates the top, rising in great majesty about twenty feet above the whole truly grand and magnificent pile, and near which is the front centre, supported by a stone arch, upon which is painted the coat-of-arms of the republic, where once floated the tri-colored banner, but is now decorated by the glorious stars and stripes of our own happy land. Two very strongly-built stone walls surround the whole; and at the west end, where we stormed the works, the outer walls are some ten feet apart, and twelve or fifteen feet high, over which we charged by the help of fascines. It was defended by heavy artillery, manned by the most learned and skilful gunners of their army, including some French artillerists of distinction. The infantry force consisted of the officers and students of the institution, and the national guards, and chosen men of war of the republic—the whole under the command of General Bravo, whom we made prisoner. The whole hill is spotted with forts and outposts, and stone and mud walls, which were filled with their picket or castle guard. A huge high stone-wall extends around the whole frowning craggy mount, and another along the southeast base, midway from the former and the castle. A well-paved road leads up in a triangular form to the main gate, entering the south *terre-plein;* and the whole works are ingeniously and beautifully ornamented with Spanish fastidiousness and skill."[1]

---

[1] Letter of Lieut. Sutton, of the 15th Infantry, in the *Union.*

This was now to be assaulted—and the next step was, on the night of the 11th, the erection of batteries which would command the fortress. The ground for these was traced out by Captains Huger and Lee, and they were thus placed:

Battery No. 1, mounted two eighteen-pounders, and one eight-inch mortar, and was commanded by Captain Drum. This battery was about six hundred yards from the castle, just to the left of the Tacubaya road.

Battery No. 2, mounted one twenty-four pounder, and one eight-inch mortar, and was commanded by Captain Hagner, of the Ordnance. This battery was placed to the front and to the left of Tacubaya, a little further from the castle.

Battery No. 3, mounted one eighteen-pounder, and one eight-inch mortar. This was placed half way between Tacubaya and Molino del Rey, and was commanded by Captain Brooks and Lieutenant Anderson, of the 2d artillery, alternately.

Battery No. 4, was placed near Molino del Rey—was commanded by Lieutenant Stone, of the Ordnance, and mounted one large mortar.

The object of these batteries was to cripple the defences of the castle, preparatory to an assault. Accordingly, the next morning, (the 12th,) these batteries being in position, commenced firing at daylight. The air was filled with blazing fuzes and whirling balls. Every ball went through the building, and every shell tore up the ramparts—while from the bastions and batteries of Chapultepec, the enemy rained down an incessant fire upon the assailants below. Such was the work of the 12th—closed only when daylight disap peared, and left the troops to darkness and to a short repose.

The divisions of Pillow and Quitman were in position on the night of the 11th, waiting for orders. Twiggs was still firing away at the southern gates, to divert and deceive the enemy. On the afternoon of the 12th, Smith's brigade (stationed at San Angel) was moved up to Piedad, a small village two miles from Chapultepec. General Scott had appointed the momentary cessation of fire from our batteries, as a signal of assault. This was to take place in two columns, commanded respectively by Generals Quitman and Pillow, each preceded by a storming party of two hundred and fifty select men; and the whole supported by Worth's division in reserve. The storming party for Pillow, was furnished from Worth's division, and commanded by Captain McKenzie, of the 2d artillery. The storming party of Quitman's column was furnished by Twiggs' division, and commanded by Captain Casey, of the 2d infantry.

At 8 A. M., on the morning of the 13th, the general-in chief sent word, by his aids, to Pillow and Quitman, that the concerted signal was about to be given.[1] The brigade of General Smith had left Piedad, at 6 A. M., and was now arrived on the ground. It was to act with the column of Quitman. The column of Pillow was to advance on the west side, that of Quitman on the southeast. The reserve under Worth was to turn the castle, and come into the road on the north, there either to assist in the assault or cut off the retreat of the enemy.

This entire plan was successfully carried out. Both

[1] General Scott's Official Report.

columns charged with alacrity at 9 A. M. of the 13th Pillow advanced through an open grove on the west, filled with sharpshooters. These were speedily dislodged, and the column emerged into an opening at the foot of the rocky acclivity. Here General Pillow was wounded, and the command devolved on General Cadwallader.[1] The broken acclivity was still to be ascended, and a redoubt half-way up to be carried. Bravely led by gallant officers, bravely did the men advance. Slowly, but surely did they advance; step by step the ground is gained. Now the first battery is taken! Now the soldiers march over mines![2] Now the match is lighted to fire them! The man is shot down, and the assailants are safe, from all but this terrible shower of balls! Now they reach the ditch, and the stone wall is beyond. The fascines[3] are applied—the ditch is bridged. The scaling ladders are applied to that massive wall, and they mount! they mount! The castle is carried, and now the flags of these brave regiments fly on its ramparts! The loud hurrah resounds through the ranks!

But what is doing by the column of the brave Quitman? Have they no part? As bravely, and as actively, and successfully did they storm the rock-built castle of Chapultepec.

---

[1] Official Report.

[2] General Scott, in his Official Report, says that men in attempting to fire the mines were shot down. General Bravo, who commanded, says that the engineer who had charge of them disappeared, and they could not be fired. Both statements are no doubt true.

[3] Fascines are bundles of withes, or sticks, tied round and filled up with earth, to fill up ditches.

Moving over a causeway from Tacubaya, flanked on either side by deep ditches, and cut in several places Quitman had little room to manœuvre, while in front was a strong body of the enemy, and two or three small pieces. All these obstacles were overcome, the enemy routed, and the volunteers of Quitman, of New York, of Pennsylvania, and of South Carolina, arrived in time to join the storming parties, as they scaled the walls of Chapultepec. Here, too, the "Rifles," so often distinguished, joined the assault, and shared in the bloodiest adventures of the day. An officer of that gallant corps thus describes the scene:

"After about an hour's hard firing, the enemy's fire began to slacken, and the word was given to charge. We rushed forward, and in three minutes we carried the first battery. The rifles entered the battery with the storming party, which was commanded by one of its captains. We followed the fugitives close up to the aqueduct, and, turning to the left, clambered up the steep path to the castle. The enemy were running down in crowds, and the slaughter was tremendous in the road and orchard. Our men were infuriated by the conduct of the Mexicans at Molino del Rey, and took but few prisoners. The castle was completely torn to pieces; nearly every part was riddled by our shot, while the pavements and fortifications were completely torn up by the shells. In it were crowds of prisoners of every rank and color; among whom were fifty general officers, and about a hundred cadets of the Mexican military academy. The latter were pretty little fellows, from ten to sixteen years of age. Several of them were killed fighting like demons, and indeed they showed an example of courage worthy of imitation by some of their superiors in rank."[1]

Thus was Chapultepec taken. Its rocky heights—its strong batteries—its military college—its mines—its succoring army—were all in vain. The heroes who had stormed the hill of Contreras, the intrenchments of Churubusco, and the King's Mill, failed not here. Chapultepec is taken, and the great causeways to Mexico are no longer defended by fortresses. The gates alone remain.

Just at this time the general-in-chief arrived at the castle, and took a *coup d'œil* view of the whole field, as it lay around the city of Mexico. His determination was instantly taken. On the right, the road passed on to the Belen gate; on the left, it passed to the San Cosmo causeway and gate. Worth had *turned* the castle during the conflict, passed round to the north centre of Chapultepec, and there attacked the right wing of the Mexican army on the road. Now he had already pursued the enemy, and was marching on the San Cosmo road. Quitman on the other hand was pursuing the enemy by the causeway to the Belen gate. Scott knew that the San Cosmo gate was easier taken than the Belen, and therefore ordered Cadwallader's brigade and other forces up to Worth, intending his to be the main attack. He garrisoned Chapultepec with the 15th regiment of infantry, and after sending guns and ammunition to both Worth and Quitman, and taking care of the ordnance and prisoners, he followed Worth's division on the San Cosmo road. This corps soon come to a suburb, just in front of the gate of San Cosmo, and there found the enemy again prepared

[1] Letter in the New York Courier and Enquirer.

for battle, behind ditches, and on the flat roofs of houses, making the village a fortification, and defending it inch by inch. The pioneers, with picks and crowbars, soon made their way through windows and houses, burrowing their way. The mountain howitzers began to play, and by 8 P. M. the positions were carried, and Worth quietly rested his troops in the suburbs of Mexico. A single gate, unable to make successful resistance now, alone raised its feeble barrier between the northman and the now humbled con querors of the Aztecs.

On the other causeway the scene was yet more remarkable. Quitman, reinforced with Smith's brigade, in the ardor of pursuit had carried an intermediate battery, and actually entered the Belen gate, after a hard battle. The capture of the Belen gate is thus described by an officer of the "Rifles."

"Again we commenced our slow and deadly march, as we gradually approached the *garita*, or gate of the city, the enemy retreating slowly before us. As soon as they crossed the gate a tremendous fire of artillery opened upon us on both sides of the aqueduct as well as from two flanking batteries on both sides the road. Here our loss was very great. Slowly creeping from arch to arch, we lost many men by the batteries in front, while the fire from flanking batteries coming through the arches killed many who were safe from that in front. About noon we got close up to the *garita*, and the enemy's fire being partly silenced by our artillery in the road, and thus being driven out of the cross-battery on the left, we once more gave the rifle yell, and charged the *garita*. Again we were first, and at twenty minutes past one, of the 13th of September, the regiment entered the city of Mexico

But our work was not yet ended. Directly in front was still another battery, with flanking batteries as before. Our regiment again went forward, and assisted by some others we occupied a house and some of the arches, and not only kept them off, but repelled four attempts at charges which they made. Meanwhile we had constructed a battery of sand-bags at the *garita,* and kept up a sharp fire in front. Towards dark those in front were recalled, and all retired behind the batteries. That night the battery was completed, and the men slept on their arms in the arches of the aqueduct."[1]

Thus closed the 13th of September in the valley of Mexico. The morning had found the armies of the North and the South in a yet undecided position. It is true that victory had constantly granted her favors to the army of Scott; but that army was small, and the columns of the enemy were numerous, and his defences strong. Chapultepec looked down from almost impregnable heights. The rays of the risen sun glanced from the plumes and swords and guns of twenty thousand men. Mexico poured out her throng to defend her gates and walls, and ditches and causeways raised their obstacles and embarrassments in the way of the American general. Night had now come, and all these arms, and fortresses, and soldiers, and obstacles had disappeared, as if charmed away by the magician's wand, before the triumphant energy of the northern soldier. The flag of the republic of the North waved in the evening breeze from the rock-built castle of Chapultepec, and now as the clouds of night gather in darkness round its summit, some famished dog may find

---

[1] Letter in the New York Courier and Enquirer.

his meal on the cold flesh of its brave but unfortunate defenders. The clouds will break away, and the stars beam out upon that lonely hill; but from those cold bodies no cloud will break, no stars beam out on earth for the loved hearts who wait and watch for them.[1] The victor rushes on! Batteries are taken, causeways passed, and his cannon thunder and batter at the gates of Mexico. Night has found him too, and the sentinel alone keeps watch round the wearied soldier of America, who sinks to rest with his garments yet rolled in blood. Neither the glorious drama of such a day, the grandeur of such a scene, nor the strange novelty of such events, can repel the weariness of fatigue, or prevent the necessity of repose. He sinks to rest as softly and calmly as the innocent child, and welcomes to his aching limbs and drowsy eyes,

"Tired Nature's sweet restorer, balmy sleep."

Daylight of the 14th of September had scarcely arrived, when the *Ayuntamiento* (city council) of Mexico waited upon General Scott, informed him that both the Mexican government and army had marched out of the city some hours before, and demanded terms of capitulation.[2] The general replied that the city was virtually in his power the night previous, and that the American army would come under no terms not *self-imposed.* About daylight he gave his orders to Worth and Quitman to advance and occupy the city. The corps of Quitman rushed forward,

---

[1] Intercepted Mexican letters show that many of the Mexican officers were anxiously awaited by sisters, wives, and mothers.

[2] Scott's Official Despatch.

and soon the colors of its regiments were planted on the far-famed palace of Mexico. Worth's division had been delayed at the Alameda; that the men who had entered the Belen gate the night before, might be first in the grand plaza. At 7 A. M., on the 14th of September, 1847, the flag of the American Union was hoisted on the walls of the national palace in the city of Mexico. Soon after this event, at 9 A. M., a "tremendous *hurrah* broke from the corner of the plaza, and in a few minutes were seen the towering plumes and commanding form of our gallant old hero, GENERAL SCOTT, escorted by the 2d dragoons. The heartfelt welcome that came from our little band was such as Montezumas' Halls had never heard, and must have deeply affected the general."[1]

Soon after this a firing was heard, and it appeared that the *Leperos*, or mob of the city, with some liberated convicts, had made an insurrection. A fire was opened on our men from the flat roofs of houses, from windows and corners of streets, by the vagabonds of the city, liberated convicts, and disbanded soldiers. This was not put down till twenty-four hours had passed, and till many were killed and wounded. The object was as much plunder, as hatred.[2]

We insert here the official report of the commander-in-chief, General Scott.

---

[1] Letter of an officer of the Rifles.

[2] Scott's Official Report.

HEADQUARTERS OF THE ARMY.
National Palace of Mexico, Sept. 18, 1847.

SIR:—At the end of another series of arduous and brilliant operations of more than forty-eight hours' continuance, this glorious army hoisted, on the morning of the 14th, the colors of the United States on the walls of this palace.

The victory of the 8th, at the Molino del Rey, was followed by daring reconnoissances on the part of our distinguished engineers—Capt. Lee, Lieuts. Beauregard, Stevens, and Tower,—Major Smith, senior, being sick, and Capt. Mason, third in rank, wounded. Their operations were directed principally to the south—towards the gates of the Piedad, San Angel, (Nino Perdido,) San Antonio, and the Paseo de la Viga.

This city stands on a slight swell of ground, near the centre of an irregular basin, and is girdled with a ditch in its greater extent—a navigable canal of great breadth and depth—very difficult to bridge in the presence of an enemy, and serving at once for drainage, custom-house purposes, and military defence; leaving eight entrances or gates, over arches—each of which we found defended by a system of strong works, that seemed to require nothing but some men and guns to be impregnable.

Outside and within the cross-fires of those gates, we found to the south other obstacles but little less formidable. All the approaches near the city are over elevated causeways, cut in many places (to oppose us), and flanked on both sides by ditches, also of unusual dimensions. The numerous cross-roads are flanked in like manner, having bridges at the intersections, recently broken. The meadows thus checkered, are, moreover, in many spots, under water or marshy; for, it will be remembered, we were in the midst of the wet season, though with less rain than usual, and we could not wait for the fall of the neighboring lakes and the consequent drainage of the wet grounds at the edge of the city—the lowest in the whole basin.

After a close personal survey of the southern gates, covered by Pillow's division and Riley's brigade of Twiggs'—with four times our numbers concentrated in our immediate front—I determined on the 11th to avoid that net-work of obstacles, and to seek, by a sudden diversion, to the southwest and west, less unfavorable approaches.

To economize the lives of our gallant officers and men, as well as to ensure success, it became indispensable that this resolution should be long masked from the enemy; and again, that the new movement, when discovered, should be mistaken for a feint, and the old as indicating our true and ultimate point of attack.

Accordingly, on the spot, the 11th, I ordered Quitman's division from Coyoacan, to join Pillow, by daylight, before the southern gates, and then that the two major-generals, with their divisions, should, by night, proceed (two miles) to join me at Tacubaya, where I was quartered with Worth's division. Twiggs, with Riley's brigade and Captains Taylor's and Steptoe's field batteries—the latter of 12-pounders—was left in front of those gates, to manœuvre, to threaten, or to make false attacks, in order to occupy and deceive the enemy. Twiggs' other brigade (Smith's) was left at supporting distance, in the rear, at San Angel, till the morning of the 13th, and also to support our general depot at Miscoac. The stratagem against the south was admirably executed throughout the 12th and down to the afternoon of the 13th, when it was too late for the enemy to recover from the effects of his delusion.

The first step in the new movement was to carry Chapultepec, a natural and isolated mound, of great elevation, strongly fortified at its base, on its acclivities, and heights. Besides a numerous garrison, here was the military college of the republic, with a large number of sub-lieutenants and other students. Those works were within direct gun-shot of the village of Tacubaya, and, until carried, we could not approach the city on the west, without making a circuit too wide and too hazardous.

In the course of the same night (that of the 11th) heavy batteries, within easy ranges, were established. No. 1, on our right, under the command of Capt. Drum, 4th artillery, (relieved late next day, for some hours, by Lieut. Andrews of the 3d,) and No. 2, commanded by Lieut. Hagner, ordnance—both supported by Quitman's division. Nos. 3 and 4 on the opposite side, supported by Pillow's division, were commanded, the former by Capt. Brooks and Lieut. S. S. Anderson, 2d artillery, alternately, and the latter by Lieut. Stone, ordnance. The batteries were traced by Capt. Huger and Capt. Lee, engineer, and constructed by them with the able assistance of the young officers of those corps and the artillery.

To prepare for an assault, it was foreseen that the play of the batteries might run into the second day; but recent captures had not only trebled our siege pieces, but also our ammunition; and we knew that we should greatly augment both by carrying the place. I was, therefore, in no haste in ordering an assault before the works were well crippled by our missiles.

The bombardment and cannonade, under the direction of Capt. Huger, were commenced early in the morning of the 12th. Before nightfall, which necessarily stopped our batteries, we had perceived that a good impression had been made on the castle and its outworks, and that a large body of the enemy had remained outside, towards the city, from an early hour to avoid our fire, and to be at hand on its cessation, in order to reinforce the garrison against an assault. The same outside force was discovered the next morning, after our batteries had reopened upon the castle, by which we again reduced its garrison to the minimum needed for the guns.

Pillow and Quitman had been in position since early in the night of the 11th. Major-general Worth was now ordered to hold his division in reserve, near the foundry, to support Pillow; and Brigadier-general Smith, of Twiggs' division, had just arrived with his brigade from Piedad, (2 miles,) to support Quitman. Twiggs' guns, before the southern gates, again reminded us, as the day before, that he, with Riley's brigade and Taylor's and Steptoe's batteries, was in activity, threatening the southern gates, and there holding a great part of the Mexican army on the defensive.

Worth's division furnished Pillow's attack with an assaulting party of some 250 volunteer officers and men, under Capt. McKenzie, of the 2d artillery; and Twiggs' division supplied a similar one, commanded by Capt. Casey, 2d infantry, to Quitman. Each of those little columns was furnished with scaling ladders.

The signal I had appointed for the attack was the momentary cessation of fire on the part of our heavy batteries. About 8 o'clock in the morning of the 13th, judging that the time had arrived by the effect of the missiles we had thrown, I sent an aid-de-camp to Pillow, and another to Quitman, with notice that the concerted signal was about to be given. Both columns now advanced with an alacrity that gave assurance of prompt success. The batteries, seizing opportunities, threw shots and shells upon the enemy over the heads of our men, with good effect, particularly at every attempt to reinforce the works from without to meet our assault.

Major-general Pillow's approach, on the west side, lay through an open grove, filled with sharp-shooters, who were speedily dislodged; when being up with the front of the attack, and emerging into open space, at the foot of a rocky acclivity, that gallant leader was struck down by an agonizing wound. The immediate command devolved on Brigadier-general Cadwallader, in the absence of the senior brigadier (Pierce) of the same division—an invalid since the events of August 19. On a previous call of Pillow, Worth had just sent him a reinforcement—Colonel Clarke's brigade.

The broken acclivity was still to be ascended, and a strong redoubt, midway, to be carried, before reaching the castle on the heights. The advance of our brave men, led by brave officers, though necessarily slow, was unwavering, over rocks, chasms, and mines, and under the hottest fire of cannon and musketry. The redoubt now yielded to resistless valor, and the shouts that followed announced to the castle the fate that impended. The enemy were steadily driven from shelter to shelter. The retreat allowed not time to fire a single mine, without the certainty of blowing up friend and foe. Those who at a distance attempted to apply matches to the long trains, were shot down by our men. There was death below, as well as above ground. At length the ditch and wall of the main work were reached; the scaling ladders were brought up and planted by the storming parties; some of the daring spirits first in the assault were cast down—killed or wounded; but a lodgment was soon made; streams of heroes followed; all opposition was overcome, and several of our regimental colors flung out from the upper walls, amidst long-continued shouts and cheers, which sent dismay into the capital. No scene could have been more animating or glorious.

Major-general Quitman, nobly supported by Brigadier-generals Shields and Smith, (P. F.,) his other officers and men, was up with the part assigned him. Simultaneously with the movement on the west, he had gallantly approached the southeast of the same works, over a causeway with cuts and batteries, and defended by an army strongly posted outside, to the east of the works. Those formidable obstacles Quitman had to face, with but little shelter for his troops or space for manœuvring. Deep ditches flanking the causeway, made it difficult to cross on either side into the adjoining meadows, and these again were intersected by other ditches. Smith and his brigade had been early thrown out to make a sweep to the right, in order to present a front against the enemy's line, (outside,) and to turn two intervening batteries near the foot of Chapultepec. This movement was also intended to support Quitman's storming parties, both on the causeway. The first of these, furnished by Twiggs' division, was commanded in succession by Captain Casey, 2d infantry, and Captain Paul, 7th infantry, after Casey had been severely wounded; and the second, originally under the gallant Major Twiggs, marine corps, killed, and then Captain Miller, 2d Pennsylvania volunteers. The storming party, now commanded by Captain Paul seconded by Captain Roberts, of the rifles, Lieutenant Stewart, and others of the same regiment, Smith's brigade, carried the two batteries in the road, took some guns, with many prisoners, and drove the enemy posted behind in support. The New York and South Carolina volunteers (Shields' brigade) and the 2d Pennsylvania volunteers, all on the left of Quitman's line, together with portions of his storming parties, crossed the meadows in front, under a heavy fire, and entered the outer enclosure of Chapultepec just in time to join in the final assault from the west.

Besides Major-generals Pillow and Quitman, Brigadier-generals Shields, Smith, and Cadwallader, the following are the officers and corps most distinguished in those brilliant operations: The voltigeur regiment in two detachments, commanded respectively by Colonel Andrews and Lieutenant-colonel Johnstone—the latter mostly in the lead, accompanied by Major Caldwell; Captains Barnard and Biddle, of the same regiment—the former the first to plant a regimental color, and the latter among the first in the assault; the storming party of Worth's division, under Captain McKenzie, 2d artillery, with Lieutenant Seldon, 8th infantry, early on the ladder and badly wounded; Lieutenant Armistead, 6th infantry, the first to leap into the ditch to plant a ladder; Lieutenants Rodgers of the 4th, and J. P. Smith of the 5th infantry—both mortally wounded; the 9th infantry, under Colonel Ransom, who was killed while gallantly leading that gallant regiment; the 15th infantry, under Lieutenant-colonel Howard and Major Woods, with Captain Chase, whose company gallantly carried the redoubt, midway up the acclivity; Colonel Clarke's brigade (Worth's division) consisting of the 5th, 8th, and part of the 6th regiments of infantry, commanded respectively by Captain Chapman, Major Montgomery, and Lieutenant Edward Johnson—the latter specially noticed, with Lieutenants Longstreet, (badly wounded, advancing, colors in hand,) Pickett, and Merchant, the last three of the 8th infantry; portions of the United States marines, New York, South Carolina, and 2d Pennsylvania volunteers, which, delayed with their division (Quitman's) by the hot engagement below, arrived just in time to participate in the assault of the heights—particularly a detachment under Lieutenant Reid, New York volunteers, consisting of a company of the same, with one of marines; and another detachment, a portion of the storming party, (Twiggs' division, serving with Quitman,) under Lieutenant Steele, 2d infantry, after the fall of Lieutenant Gantt, 7th infantry.

In this connection, it is but just to recall the decisive effect of the heavy batteries, Nos. 1, 2, 3, and 4, commanded by those excellent officers, Captain Drum, 4th artillery, assisted by Lieutenants Benjamin and Porter of his own company; Captain Brooks and Lieutenant Anderson, 2d artillery, assisted by Lieutenant Russell, 4th infantry, a volunteer; Lieutenants Hagner and Stone of the ordnance, and Lieutenant Andrews, 3d artillery; the whole superintended by Captain Huger, chief of ordnance with this army—an officer distinguished by every kind of merit. The mountain howitzer battery, under Lieutenant Reno, of the ordnance, deserves, also, to be particularly mentioned. Attached to the voltigeurs, it followed the movements of that regiment, and again won applause.

In adding to the list of individuals of conspicuous merit, I must limit myself to a few of the many names which might be enumerated: Captain Hooker, assistant adjutant-general, who won special applause, successively, in the staff of Pillow and Cadwallader; Lieutenant Lovell, 4th artillery, (wounded,) chief of Quitman's staff; Captain Page, assistant adjutant-general, (wounded,) and Lieutenant Hammond, 3d artillery, both of Shields' staff, and Lieutenant Van Dorn, (7th infantry,) aid-de-camp to Brigadier-general Smith.

Those operations all occurred on the west, southeast, and heights of Chapultepec. To the north and at the base of the mound, inaccessible on that side, the 11th infantry, under Lieut. Col. Hebert, the 14th, under Col. Trousdale, and Capt. Magruder's field battery, 1st artillery—one section advanced under Lieut. Jackson—all of Pillow's division—had, at the same time, some spirited affairs against superior numbers, driving the enemy from a battery in the road, and capturing a gun. In these, the officers and corps named gained merited praise. Colonel Trousdale, the commander, though twice wounded, continued on duty until the heights were carried.

Early in the morning of the 13th, I repeated the orders of

the night before to Major-general Worth, to be, with his division at hand, to support the movement of Major-general Pillow from our left. The latter seems soon to have called for that entire division, standing momentarily in reserve, and Worth sent him Col. Clarke's brigade. The call, if not unnecessary, was at least, from the circumstances, unknown to me at the time; for, soon observing that the very large body of the enemy, in the road in front of Major-general Quitman's right, was receiving reinforcements from the city—less than a mile and a half to the east—I sent instructions to Worth, on our opposite flank, to turn Chapultepec with his division, and to proceed, cautiously, by the road at its northern base, in order, if not met by very superior numbers, to threaten or to attack, in rear, that body of the enemy. The movement, it was also believed, could not fail to distract and to intimidate the enemy generally.

Worth promptly advanced with his remaining brigade—Colonel Garland's—Lieut. Col. C. F. Smith's light battalion, Lieut. Col. Duncan's field battery—all of his division—and three squadrons of dragoons, under Major Sumner, which I had just ordered up to join in the movement.

Having turned the forest on the west, and arriving opposite to the north centre of Chapultepec, Worth came up with the troops in the road, under Col. Trousdale, and aided, by a flank movement of a part of Garland's brigade, in taking the one gun breastwork, then under the fire of Lieut. Jackson's section of Capt. Magruder's field battery. Continuing to advance, this division passed Chapultepec, attacking the right of the enemy's line, resting on that road, about the moment of the general retreat consequent upon the capture of the formidable castle and its outworks.

Arriving some minutes later, and mounting to the top of the castle, the whole field, to the east, lay plainly under my view.

There are two routes from Chapultepec to the capital—the one on the right entering the same gate, Belen, with the road from the south, via Piedad; and the other obliquing to the left, to intersect the great western, or San Cosmo road, in a suburb outside of the gate of San Cosmo.

Each of these routes (an elevated causeway) presents a double roadway on the sides of an aqueduct of strong masonry and great height, resting on open arches and massive pillars, which together afford fine points both for attack and defence. The sideways of both aqueducts are, moreover, defended by many strong breastworks at the gates, and before reaching them. As we had expected, we found the four tracks unusually dry and solid for the season.

Worth and Quitman were prompt in pursuing the retreating enemy—the former by the San Cosmo aqueduct, and the latter along that of Belen. Each had now advanced some hundred yards.

Deeming it all-important to profit by our successes, and the consequent dismay of the enemy, which could not be otherwise than general, I hastened to despatch from Chapultepec—first Clark's brigade, and then Cadwallader's, to the support of Worth, and gave orders that the necessary heavy guns should follow. Pierce's brigade was, at the same time, sent to Quitman, and, in the course of the afternoon, I caused some additional siege pieces to be added to his train. Then, after designating the 15th infantry, under Lieut. Col. Howard—Morgan, the colonel, had been disabled by a wound at Churubusco—as the garrison of Chapultepec, and giving directions for the care of the prisoners of war, the captured ordnance and ordnance stores, I proceeded to join the advance of Worth, within the suburb, and beyond the turn at the junction of the aqueduct with the great highway from the west to the gate of San Cosmo.

At this junction of roads, we first passed one of those formidable systems of city defences, spoken of above, and it had not a gun!—a strong proof, 1. That the enemy had expected us to fail in the attack upon Chapultepec, even if we meant any thing more than a feint; 2. That, in either case, we designed, in his belief, to return and double our forces against the southern gates—a delusion kept up by the active demonstrations of Twiggs and the forces posted on that side; and, 3. That advancing rapidly from the reduction of Chapultepec, the enemy had not time to shift guns—our previous captures had left him, comparatively, but few—from the southern gates.

Within those disgarnished works, I found our troops engaged in a street fight against the enemy posted in gardens, at windows, and on house-tops—all flat, with parapets. Worth ordered forward the mountain howitzers of Cadwallader's brigade, preceded by skirmishers and pioneers, with pickaxes and crowbars, to force windows and doors, or to burrow through walls. The assailants were soon in an equality of position fatal to the enemy. By eight o'clock in the evening, Worth had carried two batteries in this suburb. According to my instructions, he here posted guards and sentinels, and placed his troops under shelter for the night. There was but one more obstacle—the San Cosmo gate, (custom-house,) between him and the great square in front of the cathedral and palace, the heart of the city; and that barrier it was known could not, by daylight, resist our siege guns thirty minutes.

I had gone back to the foot of Chapultepec, the point from which the two aqueducts begin to diverge, some hours earlier, in order to be near that new depot, and in easy communication with Quitman and Twiggs, as well as with Worth.

From this point I ordered all detachments and stragglers to their respective corps, then in advance; sent to Quitman additional siege guns, ammunition, intrenching tools; directed Twiggs' remaining brigade (Riley's) from Piedad, to support Worth, and Captain Steptoe's field-battery, also at Piedad, to rejoin Quitman's division.

I had been, from the first, well aware that the western or San Cosmo, was the less difficult route to the centre, and conquest of the capital, and therefore intended that Quitman should only manœuvre and threaten the Belen or southwestern gate, in order to favor the main attack by Worth, knowing that the strong defences at the Belen were directly under the guns of the much stronger fortress, called the Citadel, just within. Both of these defences of the enemy were also within easy supporting distance from the San Angel (or Nino Perdido) and San Antonio gates. Hence the greater support, in numbers, given to Worth's movement as the main attack.

These views I repeatedly, in the course of the day, communicated to Major-general Quitman; but being in hot pursuit—gallant himself, and ably supported by Brigadier-generals Shields and Smith, Shields badly wounded before Chapultepec, and refusing to retire, as well as by all the officers and men of the column—Quitman continued to press forward, under flank and direct fires, carried an intermediate battery of two guns, and then the gate, before two o'clock in the afternoon, but not without proportionate loss, increased by his steady maintenance of that position.

Here, of the heavy battery, (4th artillery,) Captain Drum and Lieutenant Benjamin were mortally wounded, and Lieutenant Porter, its third in rank, slightly. The loss of those two most distinguished officers the army will long mourn. Lieutenants J. B. Morange and William Canty, of the South Carolina volunteers, also of high merit, fell on the same occasion, besides many of our bravest non-commissioned officers and men, particularly in Captain Drum's veteran company. I cannot, in this place, give names or numbers; but full returns of the killed and wounded, of all corps, in their recent operations, will accompany this report.

Quitman within the city—adding several new defences to the position he had won, and sheltering his corps as well as practicable—now awaited the return of daylight under the guns of the formidable citadel, yet to be subdued.

About 4 o'clock next morning, (Sept. 14,) a deputation of the *ayuntamiento* (city council) waited upon me to report that the federal government and the army of Mexico had fled from the capital some three hours before; and to demand terms of capitulation in favor of the church, the citizens, and the municipal authorities. I promptly replied, that I would sign no capitulation; that the city had been virtually in our possession from the time of the lodgments effected by Worth and Quitman the day before; that I regretted the silent escape of the Mexican army; that I should levy upon the city a moderate contribution, for special purposes; and that the American army should come under no terms not self-imposed: such only as its own honor, the dignity of the United States, and the spirit of the age, should, in my opinion, imperiously demand and impose.

For the terms, so imposed, I refer the department to subsequent General Orders, Nos. 287 and 289, (paragraphs 7, 8, and 9 of the latter,) copies of which are herewith enclosed.

At the termination of the interview with the city deputation, I communicated, about daylight, orders to Worth and Quitman to advance slowly and cautiously (to guard against treachery) towards the heart of the city, and to occupy its stronger and more commanding points. Quitman proceeded to the great plaza or square, planted guards, and hoisted the colors of the United States on the national palace, containing the halls of Congress and executive departments of federal Mexico.

In this grateful service, Quitman might have been anticipated by Worth, but for my express orders, halting the latter at the head of the Alameda, (a green park,) within three squares of that goal of general ambition. The capital, however, was not taken by any one or two corps, but by the talent, the science, the gallantry, the prowess of this entire army. In the glorious conquest, all had contributed, early and powerfully, the killed, the wounded, and the fit for duty, at Vera Cruz, Cerro Gordo, Contreras, San Antonia, Churubusco, (three battles,) the Molino del Rey, and Chapultepec, as much as those who fought at the gates of Belen and San Cosmo.

Soon after we had entered, and were in the act of occupying the city, a fire was opened upon us from the flat roofs of the houses, from windows and corners of streets, by some two thousand convicts, liberated the night before by the flying government, joined by, perhaps, as many Mexican soldiers, who had disbanded themselves, and thrown off their uniforms. This unlawful war lasted more than twenty-four hours, in spite of the exertions of the municipal authorities, and was not put down till we had lost many men, including several officers, killed or wounded, and had punished the miscreants. Their objects were to gratify national hatred, and in the general alarm and confusion, to plunder the wealthy inhabitants, particularly the deserted houses. But families are now generally returning; business of every kind has been resumed, and the city is already tranquil and cheerful, under the admirable conduct (with exceptions very few and trifling) of our gallant troops.

This army has been more disgusted than surprised, that by some sinister process on the part of certain individuals at home, its numbers have been, generally, almost trebled in our public papers, beginning at Washington.

Leaving, as we all feared, inadequate garrisons at Vera

Cruz, Perote, and Puebla, with much larger hospitals; and being obliged, most reluctantly, from the same cause (general paucity of numbers) to abandon Jalapa, we marched (August 7–10) from Puebla with only 10,738 rank and file. This number includes the garrison of Jalapa, and the 2,429 men brought up by Brigadier-general Pierce, August 6.

At Contreras, Churubusco, &c., [August 20,] we had but 8,497 men engaged—after deducting the garrison of San Augustin, (our general depot,) the intermediate sick and the dead; at the Molino del Rey, (September 8,) but three brigades, with some cavalry and artillery—making in all 3,251 men—were in the battle; in the two days—September 12th and 13th—our whole operating force, after deducting, again, the recent killed, wounded, and sick, together with the garrison of Miscoac (the then general depot) and that of Tacubaya, was but 7,180; and, finally, after deducting the new garrison of Chapultepec, with the killed and wounded of the two days, we took possession, (September 14th,) of this great capital with less than 6,000 men. And I reassert, upon accumulated and unquestionable evidence, that, in not one of those conflicts was this army opposed by fewer than three-and-a-half times its numbers—in several of them, by a yet greater excess.

I recapitulate our losses since we arrived in the basin of Mexico.

August 19, 20.—Killed, 137, including 14 officers.—Wounded, 877, including 62 officers. Missing, (probably killed,) 38 rank and file. Total, 1,052.

September 8.—Killed, 116, including 9 officers.—Wounded, 665, including 49 officers. Missing, 18 rank and file. Total, 789.

September 12, 13, 14.—Killed, 130, including 10 officers. Wounded, 703, including 68 officers. Missing, 29 rank and file. Total, 862.

Grand total of losses, 2,703, including 383 officers.

On the other hand, this small force has beaten on the same occasions in view of their capital, the whole Mexican army, of (at the beginning) thirty-odd thousand men—posted, always, in chosen positions, behind intrenchments, or more formidable defences of nature and art; killed or wounded, of that number, more than 7,000 officers and men; taken 3,730 prisoners, one-seventh officers, including 13 generals, of whom 3 had been presidents of this republic; captured more than 20 colors and standards, 75 pieces of ordnance, besides 57 wall pieces, 20,000 small-arms, an immense quantity of shots, shells, powder, &c., &c.

Of that enemy, once so formidable in numbers, appointments, artillery, &c., twenty-odd thousand have disbanded themselves in despair, leaving, as is known, not more than three fragments—the largest about 2,500—now wandering in different directions, without magazines or a military chest, and living at free quarters upon their own people.

General Santa Anna, himself a fugitive, is believed to be on the point of resigning the chief-magistracy, and escaping to neutral Guatemala. A new President, no doubt, will soon be declared, and the federal Congress is expected to reassemble at Queretaro, 125 miles north of this, on the Zacatecas road, some time in October. I have seen and given safeconduct through this city to several of its members. The government will find itself without resources; no army, no arsenals, no magazines, and but little revenue, internal or external. Still, such is the obstinacy, or rather infatuation, of this people, that it is very doubtful whether the new authorities will dare to sue for peace on the terms which in the recent negotiations, were made known by our minister.

* * * * * * * *

In conclusion, I beg to enumerate, once more, with due commendation and thanks, the distinguished staff officers, general and personal, who, in our last operations in front of the enemy, accompanied me, and communicated orders to every point and through every danger. Lieutenant-colonel Hitchcock, acting inspector-general; Major Turnbull and Lieutenant Hardcastle, topographical engineers; Major Kirby, chief paymaster; Captain Irwin, chief quartermaster; Captain Grayson, chief commissary; Captain H. L. Scott, chief in the adjutant-general's department; Lieutenant Williams, aid-de-camp; Lieutenant Lay, military secretary; and Major J. P. Gaines, Kentucky cavalry, volunteer aid-de-camp; Captain Lee, engineer, so constantly distinguished, also bore important orders from me, (September 13,) until he fainted from a wound and the loss of two nights' sleep at the batteries. Lieutenants Beauregard, Stevens, and Tower, all wounded, were employed with the divisions, and Lieutenants G. W. Smith and G. B. McClellan, with the company of sappers and miners. Those five lieutenants of engineers, like their captain, won the admiration of all about them. The ordnance officers, Captain Huger, Lieutenants Hagner, Stone, and Reno, were highly effective, and distinguished at the several batteries; and I must add that Captain McKinstry, assistant quartermaster, at the close of the operations, executed several important commissions for me as a special volunteer.

Surgeon-general Lawson, and the medical staff generally, were skilful and untiring, in and out of fire, in ministering to the numerous wounded.

To illustrate the operations in this basin, I enclose two beautiful drawings, prepared under the directions of Major Turnbull, mostly from actual survey.

I have the honor to be, sir, with high respect, your most obedient servant,

WINFIELD SCOTT.

The Hon. Wm. L. Marcy, Secretary of War.

On the morning of the 18th of September all was quiet. MEXICO, the capital of the ancient Aztecs—the seat of the Spanish-American empire in America—had passed from Aztec and from Spaniard, to the Anglo-American—the Northman of the Goths, the Saxon of Germany, the Englishman of America—the same bold, hardy, energetic, ingenious, invincible, ambitious, and adventurous being, whose genius the forms of civilization cannot confine, and to whose dominion continents are inadequate! In what hour of time, or limit of space, shall this man of the moderns—this conqueror over land and seas, nations and governments—find rest, in the completion of his mighty progress? Commencing his march in the cold regions of Scandinavia, no ice chilled his blood—no wilderness delayed his steps—no labor wearied his industry—no arms arrested his march—no empire subdued his power. Over armies and over empires—over lands and over seas—in heat and cold, and wilderness and flood—amidst the desolations of death and the decays of disease—this Northman has moved on in might and majesty, steady as the footsteps of Time, and fixed as the decrees of Fate!

How singular—how romantically strange is this—his wild adventure and marvellous conquest in the valley of valleys! How came the Northman and the Moorish Celt here to meet, and here to battle, in this North-American valley? Look at it! Inquire! Ask yourself how they came here? Are they the citizens, by nature, of this continent? Are they the aborigines of these wild and wonderful forests? Never! How came they then to be contending for the lands and groves of those whose children they are not?

In the beginning of the 16th century, Hernando Cortez

landed on the coast of Mexico, and, at the head of Spanish troops, marched on to the conquest of Mexico, over whose effeminate inhabitants the Spaniard has, for three hundred years, held undivided dominion. Not many years after, the Anglo-Saxon landed on the coasts of the northern Atlantic. He, too, marched on to conquest. The native citizens of the forest disappeared before him. Forests, mountains, and Indians, were ineffectual to oppose him. From the banks of the St. Lawrence to the Sabine of Texas, he is a conqueror over nature. In the south, the natives die, or become slaves to the Spaniard. In the north, they fade and perish before the Anglo-American. The one spreads his empire from the Gulf of Mexico to the far shores of California; the other, from the hills of St. Francis to the mountains of Oregon. Both extend over breadths of land, and power of resources, unknown to the widest empire of antiquity. Egypt, and her millions, with the famed valley of the Nile, fade before the broad magnificence, the mighty growth, of these American empires! Even the terrible and far-seeing eagles of Rome grow dizzy and dim in their sight, as they look down from the summits of history upon these continental nations—these colossal giants of the modern world! And now, this Spaniard and this Northman meet, in battle-panoply, in this valley of volcanoes, by the ancient graves of unknown nations, on the lava-covered soil where nature once poured forth her awe-inspiring flames, and the brave Tlascalan once sung of glory and of greatness! Three centuries since, these warrior nations had left their homes beyond the wide Atlantic. Two thousand miles from each other, they had planted the seats of their empire; and now, as if time in the moral world had completed another of its grand revolutions, they have met in mortal conflict. Like the EAGLE and the VULTURE, who had long pursued different circles in the heavens, and long made prey of the weak tenants of the air, their circles have been enlarged till they cross each other. They shriek! They fight! The victorious eagle bears the vulture to the earth, and screams forth through the clouds his triumphant song! Has the bold bird received no wound? Has no blood tinged the feathers of his wing? Is there no secret flow of life from the portals of his heart? Will he continue to look, with unblenched eye, on the blazing glories of the sun? Hid in the eternal decrees of God, is the life of nations; and not till He has drawn away the curtains of time, will mortals know the secrets of His will in the government of nations.

CHAPTER XIV.

Siege of Puebla.—March of Santa Anna.—Desertion of his troops.—March of Rea.—Battle of Huamantla.—Santa Anna's resignation.—Peña y Peña President.—Negotiations for peace.—Treaty signed.—Ratifications. —The Treaty.—Territory acquired.—Losses of the army.—Names of officers killed.—Conclusion.

The military events which closed on the 18th of September, with the capture of the city of Mexico, closed also, with the exception of some incidental and minor engagements, the war with Mexico. To all practical intents, Mexico was conquered. From Santa Fé in the north to Tampico in the south,—from the Rio Grande to the shores of the Pacific,—from the heights of the Sierra Madre to those of the Sierra Nevada,—the troops and navy of the United States held every position which, either in a military or commercial view, was valuable or accessible to the channels of business and population. Henceforward, the chief movement of our troops was the advance of reinforcements, which, had they been earlier, had been useful, but were now too late to aid the victorious army, or share in the glory of its achievements. Collateral movements were made, and two or three small skirmishes took place which were honorable to our arms. But the burden and battle of the war was past. The victory was won, and the question of the day was, "When and how shall peace be made?"

Santa Anna, who had been driven out of Mexico by

the American troops, escaped with a body of two or three thousand men, and for some days was unheard of. On the 25th of September, however, he appeared in the city of Puebla, the surrounding heights of which were garrisoned and defended by Col. Childs. The American gar rison was weak, and had under its care the hospitals, which contained many sick. The object of the Mexican commander was the surprise and capture of this post, which had been left isolated by the advance of the American army on Mexico, and was now besieged by Rea. The movement was a good one, had the Mexican strength been sufficient for the purpose. On his appearance Santa Anna immediately summoned the American commander to surrender, to which Col. Childs returned a prompt refusal, couched in firm and dignified terms.[1] On the 28th, the positions around Puebla were occupied by Santa Anna with batteries, and a bombardment commenced on the American intrenchments. In return, the batteries of Col. Childs bombarded the city. On the 29th, the troops of Santa Anna occupied the convent of Santa Theresa, and began to cover themselves with cotton-bales. On the 30th, General Rea, who was joined by Santa Anna, commenced erecting batteries, and cannonading the Americans.

In the mean time, however, the Mexican troops were almost wholly destitute of provisions, and in a most suffering condition. Having heard of the advance of an American convoy on the National Road, Santa Anna, on the 1st of October, sallied out of Puebla with the view to intercept it. Before his arrival at the point of destination, he

---

[1] Correspondence in the *Washington Union*.

was deserted by all his troops, except about 130 hussars. They alleged that he was incapable of accomplishing any further service, and that certain destruction awaited them should they any longer follow a leader whose fortunes were so desperate. Thus after many bold enterprises, signal defeats, and sanguinary adventures, this celebrated Mexican chief found himself again a wanderer, alike deserted by fortune and by friends. He was soon after denounced by the new Mexican government, and became an exile from the shores of that country, where, for thirty years, he had been the star of its destiny, alternately rising and setting on its political horizon, attended by all the hues of a checkered fate, and by all the incidents of a various romance. Like other unfortunate warriors, he

"——— leaves his broken bands,
And shows his miseries in distant lands."

In the mean time, General Lane had left Vera Cruz about the 1st of October, with a corps of 3000 men, arrived at Perote on the 4th, and on the 8th nearly surprised Santa Anna, who barely escaped the village of Huamantla. On the 12th of October, General Rea raised the siege of Puebla, and marched, as it was supposed, to surprise General Lane and his convoy at Tinal. This was, however, not done, and Lane, hearing that he was at Huamantla, forthwith marched to attack him. A brilliant action took place, in which the usual success attended the American arms, and the Mexicans were driven out with considerable loss. In this action, Captain Walker, one of the most distinguished of the noted Texan Rangers, was killed. He was more distinguished for a barbarous desperation of adventure, than for true chivalry or magnanimous war

On the 19th of October, the Americans entered Atlisco with 1,500 men; and soon after, they captured Orizaba, with several other considerable places. The young officers of the army, searching with keen ambition for the novelties of romantic enterprise, planted the American flag in succession on the loftiest peaks of the Cordilleras, —on summits which looked down on the region of clouds, and are clothed with eternal ice. There, on rocks visited only in the waste of ages by the lone eagle in his sunward flight, the flag of the conqueror waves in the wind which bathes the silent volcanoes of Orizaba and Popocatepetl!

But the word which is now on the lips of conquered and conqueror is—PEACE. The United States desired not to govern the mixed races of Mexico, and Mexico felt that she had no longer opposition to offer. A new government and a new destiny was about to arise for Mexico.

On the 18th of October, Santa Anna resigned the supreme power into the hands of Peña y Peña, President of the Supreme Court of Justice. On the 22d, he issued his proclamation to the Mexican people, vindicating his conduct throughout the turbulent scenes and unfortunate events of the war, and from that time he has disappeared from the stage of Mexican affairs.

Previous to this resignation of Santa Anna, however, Peña y Peña had assumed the reins of government. The executive chair was declared vacant, and on the 27th of September, Peña took the vacant place, by virtue of being President of the Supreme Court of Justice. He immediately addressed circulars to the States, calling upon them to send deputies to Queretaro, to pay their expenses, and provide funds for their support. The President, in urging attention to this important business, says, "This is probably the last experiment of government which will be made in our unfortunate country."

Under these urgent solicitations, the Congress assembled at Queretaro in November, and on the 11th General Anaya was elected President. Peña y Peña was elected Secretary of State. One of the first acts of the new government was to appoint a commission to proceed to Mexico, and negotiate with Mr. Trist the terms of peace, on the basis of his former scheme. This commission consisted of Messrs. Couto, Atristain, Cuevas, and Rincon, who immediately proceeded to execute the duties of their office.

On the 1st of January the old Congress was dissolved, but a new one had in the mean time been elected; and on the 8th of January, the new administration was organized by the meeting of Congress at Queretaro, and the return of Peña y Peña to the executive chair. The period for which Anaya was elected President expired with the old Congress, and Peña returned to power in virtue of being President of the Supreme Court of Justice.

On the 2d of February the Treaty of Peace was signed at Guadaloupe by Nicholas P. Trist, on the part of the United States, and Messrs. Couto, Atristain, and Cuevas, commissioners, on the part of Mexico. The powers of Mr. Trist, as commissioner, had been withdrawn by the American executive; but he assumed to continue his authority on the very natural ground, it may be supposed, that the *necessities* for peace were so great, and felt so strongly by the government of the United States, that any treaty, not degrading to our government in its terms, would be ratified, without a very serious and special inquiry into the authority by which it was made. In this judgment he was justified by the event.

On the 6th of February, the Treaty was officially announced to the Mexican States by a circular from Secretary Rosas. Dispatches were immediately forwarded to Secretary Buchanan at Washington; and the sole inquiry now before the public mind was, whether the Treaty would be ratified by the Senate of the United States on one hand, or the Congress of Mexico on the other,—in whom was vested by the constitutions of the respective countries, the power of ratification. By some means the contents of the Treaty became known to the public, and it was perceived that the United States had agreed to pay a larger sum of money than was originally contemplated, while the land received in exchange was substantially no more valuable. This fact, taken in connection with another—that the Treaty was negotiated without authority—made it doubtful whether it would be ratified by the constitutional majority.

On the 22d of February, only twenty days after it was signed at Guadaloupe, President Polk formally submitted it to the Senate. On the 28th he transmitted another message, recommending its ratification.

The Hon. Daniel Webster proposed in a resolution, that a new commission should be appointed to negotiate a new treaty. This proposition was laid on the table.[1] The Senate then proceeded to consider the treaty in detail.

March 2d.—Part of the 10th Article, confirming former contracts for lands, was unanimously struck out.

---

[1] Journals of the Senate.

March 3d.—The secret article, extending the time for ratification to eight months, was stricken out, by 48 to 2.

March 7th.—The HON. J. J. CRITTENDEN introduced a resolution, that we should be confined in the Treaty to a "satisfactory settlement of the boundary of Texas, and the acquisition of the Bay of San Francisco." This resolution was rejected by the following vote,[1] viz.:

Yeas.—Badger, Baldwin, Bell, Berrien, Clarke, Clay ton, Corwin, Crittenden, Davis of Mass., Dayton, Greene, Hale, Johnson of Md., Miller, Spruance, Underwood, Upham.

Nays.—Allen, Ashley, Atchison, Atherton, Bradbury, Breese, Bright, Butler, Calhoun, Cameron, Cass, Dix, Dickinson, Davis of Miss., Douglas, Downs, Felch, Foote, Hannegan, Houston, Johnson of La., Johnson of Ga., Lewis, Mason, Moore, Niles, Rusk, Sevier, Sturgeon, Turney, Yulee.—17 yeas to 31 nays.

March 8th.—MR. BALDWIN moved to insert at the end of the 5th Article—"Provided, that there shall be neither slavery nor involuntary servitude in the territories hereby ceded, otherwise than in the punishment of crimes, whereof the party shall have been duly convicted." This also was negatived by the following vote:

Yeas.—Atherton, Baldwin, Clarke, Clayton, Corwin, Davis of Mass., Dayton, Dix, Greene, Hale, Miller, Niles, Phelps, Spruance, Upham.—15.

Nays.—Allen, Ashley, Atchison, Badger, Bagby, Bell, Benton, Berrien, Bradbury, Breese, Bright, Butler, Calhoun, Cameron, Cass, Crittenden, Davis of Miss., Dickinson, Douglas, Downs, Felch, Foote, Hannegan, Hunter,

---

[1] Journals of the Senate.

Johnson of La., Johnson of Md., Johnson of Ga., Lewis, Mangum, Mason, Moore, Pearce, Rusk, Sevier, Sturgeon, Turney, Underwood, Yulee.—38.

March 10th.—After several important amendments to the original form of the Treaty, that instrument was finally ratified, by two-thirds of the Senate advising and con senting thereto, by the following vote:

Yeas.—Ashley, Atherton, Bagby, Bell, Bradbury, Bright, Butler, Calhoun, Cameron, Cass, Clarke, Crittenden, Davis, Dayton, Dickinson, Dix, Felch, Foote, Greene, Hale, Hannegan, Hunter, Johnson of Md., Johnson of La., Johnson of Ga., Mangum, Mason, Miller, Moore, Niles, Rusk, Sevier, Sturgeon, Turney, Downs, Clayton, Yulee, Underwood.—38.

Nays.—Allen, Atchison, Badger, Baldwin, Benton, Berrien, Breese, Corwin, Douglas, Lewis, Spruance, Upham, Webster, Westcott.—14.

The Senate having thus ratified the Treaty, with several important amendments, it became necessary that the Treaty should be also ratified by the Mexican Congress. The President accordingly appointed NATHAN CLIFFORD, Attorney-general, and AMBROSE SEVIER, Chairman of the Committee of Foreign Relations in the Senate, as Commissioners on the part of the United States, to lay the Treaty, thus modified, before the Mexican Congress. These gentlemen hastened to Mexico, but some weeks elapsed before a quorum of the Mexican Congress could be assembled at Queretaro. At length the Congress met, and the ratification of the Treaty was urged upon the Congress ably and eloquently by President Peña. He succeeded. The Treaty was ratified by a large majority in the Congress, and by 33 to 5 in the Senate

The American Commissioners officially notified the Secretary of State that the Treaty was complete, and on the 19th of June, 1848,—being two years and two months from the commencement of the war,—the people of the United States were formally notified, that there was PEACE BETWEEN MEXICO AND THE UNITED STATES!

By the President of the United States of America.

A PROCLAMATION.

Whereas a treaty of peace, friendship, limits, and settlement between the United States of America and the Mexican republic, was concluded and signed at the city of Guadaloupe Hidalgo, on the second day of February, one thousand eight hundred and forty-eight, which treaty, as amended by the Senate of the United States, and being in the English and Spanish languages, is word for word as follows:

In the name of Almighty God:

The United States of America and the United Mexican States, animated by a sincere desire to put an end to the calamities of the war which unhappily exists between the two republics, and to establish upon a solid basis relations of peace and friendship, which shall confer reciprocal benefits upon the citizens of both, and assure the concord, harmony, and mutual confidence wherein the two people should live, as good neighbors, have for that purpose appointed their respective plenipotentiaries—that is to say, the President of the United States has appointed Nicholas P. Trist, a citizen of the United States, and the President of the Mexican republic has appointed Don Luis Gonzaga Cuevas, Don Bernardo Couto, and Don Miguel Atristain, citizens of the said republic, who, after a reciprocal communication of their respective full powers, have, under the protection of Almighty God, the author of peace, arranged, agreed upon, and signed the following

Treaty of peace, friendship, limits, and settlement, between the United States of America and the Mexican republic.

ARTICLE I.

There shall be firm and universal peace between the United States of America and the Mexican republic, and between their respective countries, territories, cities, towns, and people, without exception of places or persons.

Article II.

Immediately upon the signature of this treaty, a convention shall be entered into between a commissioner or commissioners appointed by the General-in-chief of the forces of the United States, and such as may be appointed by the Mexican government, to the end that a provisional suspension of hostilities shall take place, and that, in the places occupied by the said forces, constitutional order may be re-established, as regards the political, administrative, and judicial branches, so far as this shall be permitted by the circumstances of military occupation.

Article III.

Immediately upon the ratification of the present treaty by the government of the United States, orders shall be transmitted to the commanders of their land and naval forces, requiring the latter (provided this treaty shall then have been ratified by the government of the Mexican republic, and the ratifications exchanged) immediately to desist from blockading any Mexican ports; and requiring the former (under the same condition) to commence, at the earliest moment practicable, withdrawing all troops of the United States then in the interior of the Mexican republic, to points that shall be selected by common agreement, at a distance from the seaports not exceeding thirty leagues; and such evacuation of the interior of the republic shall be completed with the least possible delay; the Mexican government hereby binding itself to afford every facility in its power for rendering the same convenient to the troops on their march and in their new positions, and for promoting a good understanding between them and the inhabitants. In like manner, orders shall be dispatched to the persons in charge of the custom-houses at all ports occupied by the forces of the United States, requiring them (under the same conditions) immediately to deliver possession of the same to the persons authorized by the Mexican government to receive it, together with all bonds and evidences of debt for duties on importations and on exportations not yet fallen due. Moreover, a faithful and exact account shall be made out, showing the entire amount of all duties on imports and on exports collected at such custom-houses or elsewhere in Mexico by authority of the United States, from and after the day of ratification of this treaty by the government of the Mexican republic; and also an account of the cost of collection; and such entire amount, deducting only the cost of collection, shall be delivered to the Mexican government, at the city of Mexico, within three months after the exchange of ratifications.

The evacuation of the capital of the Mexican republic by the troops of the United States, in virtue of the above stipulation, shall be completed in one month after the orders there stipulated for shall have been received by the commander of said troops, or sooner if possible.

Article IV.

Immediately after the exchange of ratifications of the present treaty, all castles, forts, territories, places, and possessions, which have been taken or occupied by the forces of the United States during the present war, within the limits of the Mexican republic, as about to be established by the following article, shall be definitively restored to the said republic, together with all the artillery, arms, apparatus of war, munitions, and other public property, which were in the said castles and forts when captured, and which shall remain there at the time when this treaty shall be duly ratified by the government of the Mexican republic. To this end, immediately upon the signature of this treaty, orders shall be dispatched to the American officers commanding such castles and forts, securing against the removal or destruction of any such artillery, arms, apparatus of war, munitions, or other public property. The city of Mexico, within the inner line of intrenchments surrounding the said city, is comprehended in the above stipulations, as regards the restoration of artillery, apparatus of war, &c.

The final evacuation of the territory of the Mexican republic, by the forces of the United States, shall be completed in three months from the said exchange of ratifications, or sooner if possible; the Mexican government hereby engaging, as in the foregoing article, to use all means in its power for facilitating such evacuation, and rendering it convenient to the troops, and for promoting a good understanding between them and the inhabitants.

If, however, the ratification of this treaty by both parties should not take place in time to allow the embarkation of the troops of the United States to be completed before the commencement of the sickly season at the Mexican ports on the gulf of Mexico, in such case a friendly arrangement shall be entered into between the general-in-chief of the said troops and the Mexican government, whereby healthy and otherwise suitable places at a distance from the ports not exceeding thirty leagues shall be designated for the residence of such troops as may not yet have embarked, until the return of the healthy season. And the space of time here referred to as comprehending the sickly season shall be understood to extend from the first day of May to the first day of November.

All prisoners of war taken on either side, on land or on sea, shall be restored as soon as practicable after the exchange of ratifications of this treaty. It is also agreed that if any Mexicans should now be held as captives by any savage tribe within the limits of the United States, as about to be established by the following article, the government of the said United States will exact the release of such captives, and cause them to be restored to their country.

Article V.

The boundary line between the two republics shall commence in the gulf of Mexico, three leagues from land, opposite the mouth of the Rio Grande, otherwise called Rio Bravo del Norte, or opposite the mouth of its deepest branch, if it should have more than one branch emptying directly into the sea; from thence up the middle of that river, following the deepest channel, where it has more than one, to the point where it strikes the southern boundary of New Mexico; thence, westwardly, along the whole southern boundary of New Mexico (which runs north of the town called *Paso*) to its western termination; thence, northward, along the western line of New Mexico, until it intersects the first branch of the river Gila; (or if it should not intersect any branch of that river, then to the point on the said line nearest to such branch, and thence in a direct line to the same;) thence down the middle of the said branch and of the said river, until it empties into the Rio Colorado; thence across the Rio Colorado, following the division line between Upper and Lower California, to the Pacific ocean.

The southern and western limits of New Mexico, mentioned in this article, are those laid down in the map entitled "*Map of the United Mexican States, as organized and defined by various acts of the Congress of said republic, and constructed according to the best authorities. Revised edition. Published at New York in* 1847, *by J. Disturnell.*" Of which map a copy is added to this treaty, bearing the signatures and seals of the undersigned plenipotentiaries. And, in order to preclude all difficulty in tracing upon the ground the limit separating Upper from Lower California, it is agreed that the said limit shall consist of a straight line drawn from the middle of the Rio Gila, where it unites with the Colorado, to a point on the coast of the Pacific ocean distant one marine league due south of the southernmost point of the port of San Diego, according to the plan of said port made in the year 1782 by Don Juan Pantoja, second sailing-master of the Spanish fleet, and published at Madrid in the year 1802, in the Atlas to the voyage of the schooners *Sutil* and *Mexicana*, of which plan a copy is hereunto added, signed and sealed by the respective plenipotentiaries.

In order to designate the boundary line with due precision, upon authoritative maps, and to establish upon the ground landmarks which shall show the limits of both republics, as described in the present article, the two governments shall each appoint a commissioner and a surveyor, who, before the expiration of one year from the date of the exchange of ratifications of this treaty, shall meet at the port of San Diego, and proceed to run and mark the said boundary in its whole course to the mouth of the Rio Bravo del Norte. They shall keep journals and mark out plans of their operations; and the result agreed upon by them shall be deemed a part of this treaty, and shall have the same force as if it were inserted therein. The two governments will amicably agree regarding what may be necessary to these persons, and also as to their respective escorts, should such be necessary.

The boundary line established by this article shall be religiously respected by each of the two republics, and no change shall ever be made therein, except by the express and free consent of both nations, lawfully given by the general government of each, in conformity with its own constitution.

Article VI.

The vessels and citizens of the United States shall, in all time, have a free and uninterrupted passage by the gulf of California, and by the river Colorado below its confluence with the Gila, to and from their possessions situated north of the boundary line defined in the preceding article; it being understood that this passage is to be by navigating the gulf of California and the river Colorado, and not by land, without the express consent of the Mexican government.

If, by the examinations which may be made, it should be ascertained to be practicable and advantageous to construct a road, canal, or railway, which should in whole or in part run upon the river Gila, or upon its right or its left bank, within the space of one marine league from either margin of the river, the governments of both republics will form an agreement regarding its construction, in order that it may serve equally for the use and advantage of both countries.

Article VII.

The river Gila, and the part of the Rio Bravo del Norte lying below the southern boundary of New Mexico, being, agreeably to the fifth article, divided in the middle, between the two republics, the navigation of the Gila and of the Bravo below said boundary shall be free and common to the vessels and citizens of both countries; and neither shall, without the consent of the other, construct any work that may impede or interrupt, in whole or in part, the exercise of this right; not even for the purpose of favoring new methods of navigation. Nor shall any tax or contribution, under any denomination or title, be levied upon vessels or persons navigating the same, or upon merchandise or effects transported thereon, except in the case of landing upon one of their shores. If, for the purpose of making the said rivers navigable, or for maintaining them in such state, it should be necessary or advantageous to establish any tax or contribution, this shall not be done without the consent of both governments.

The stipulations contained in the present article shall not impair the territorial rights of either republic within its established limits.

Article VIII.

Mexicans now established in territories previously belonging to Mexico, and which remain for the future within the limits of the United States, as defined by the present treaty, shall be free to continue where they now reside, or to remove at any time to the Mexican republic, retaining the property which they possess in the said territories, or disposing thereof, and removing the proceeds wherever they please, without their being subjected, on this account, to any contribution, tax, or charge whatever.

Those who shall prefer to remain in the said territories, may either retain the title and rights of Mexican citizens, or acquire those of citizens of the United States. But they shall be under the obligation to make their election within one year from the date of the exchange of ratifications of this treaty; and those who shall remain in the said territories after the expiration of that year, without having declared their intention to retain the character of Mexicans, shall be considered to have elected to become citizens of the United States.

In the said territories, property of every kind, now belonging to Mexicans not established there, shall be inviolably respected. The present owners, the heirs of these, and all Mexicans who may hereafter acquire said property by contract, shall enjoy with respect to it guarantees equally ample, as if the same belonged to citizens of the United States.

Article IX.

Mexicans who, in the territories aforesaid, shall not preserve the character of citizens of the Mexican republic, conformably with what is stipulated in the preceding article, shall be incorporated into the union of the United States, and be admitted at the proper time (to be judged of by the Congress of the United States) to the enjoyment of all the rights of citizens of the United States, according to the principles of the constitution; and in the mean time shall be maintained and protected in the enjoyment of their liberty and property, and secured in the free exercise of their religion without restriction.

Article X.

[Stricken out.]

Article XI.

Considering that a great part of the territories which, by the present treaty, are to be comprehended for the future within the limits of the United States, is now occupied by savage tribes, who will hereafter be under the exclusive control of the government of the United States, and whose incursions within the territory of Mexico would be prejudicial in the extreme, it is solemnly agreed that all such incursions shall be forcibly restrained by the government of the United States whensoever this may be necessary; and that when they cannot be prevented, they shall be punished by the said government, and satisfaction for the same shall be exacted —all in the same way, and with equal diligence and energy, as if the same incursions were meditated or committed within its own territory against its own citizens.

It shall not be lawful, under any pretext whatever, for any inhabitant of the United States to purchase or acquire any Mexican, or any foreigner residing in Mexico, who may have been captured by Indians inhabiting the territory of either of the two republics, nor to purchase or acquire horses, mules, cattle, or property of any kind, stolen within Mexican territory by such Indians.

And in the event of any person or persons, captured within Mexican territory by Indians, being carried into the territory of the United States, the government of the latter engages and binds itself, in the most solemn manner, so soon as it shall know of such captives being within its territory, and shall be able so to do, through the faithful exercise of its influence and power, to rescue them and return them to their country, oı deliver them to the agent or representative of the Mexican government. The Mexican authorities will, as far as practicable, give to the government of the United States notice of such captures; and its agent shall pay the expenses incurred in the maintenance and transmission of the rescued captives; who, in the mean time, shall be treated with the utmost hospitality by the American authorities at the place where they may be. But if the government of the United States, before receiving such notice from Mexico, should obtain intelligence, through any other channel, of the existence of Mexican captives within its territory, it will proceed forthwith to effect their release and delivery to the Mexican agent as above stipulated.

For the purpose of giving to these stipulations the fullest possible efficacy, thereby affording the security and redress demanded by their true spirit and intent, the government of the United States will now and hereafter pass, without unnecessary delay, and always vigilantly enforce, such laws as the nature of the subject may require. And finally, the sacredness of this obligation shall never be lost sight of by the said government when providing for the removal of the Indians from any portion of the said territories, or for its being settled by citizens of the United States; but, on the contrary, special care shall then be taken not to place its Indian occupants under the necessity of seeking new homes, by committing those invasions which the United States have solemnly obliged themselves to restrain.

Article XII.

In consideration of the extension acquired by the boundaries of the United States, as defined in the fifth article of the present treaty, the government of the United States engages to pay to that of the Mexican republic the sum of fifteen millions of dollars.

Immediately after this treaty shall have been duly ratified by the government of the Mexican republic, the sum of three millions of dollars shall be paid to the said government by that of the United States, at the city of Mexico, in the gold or silver coin of Mexico. The remaining twelve millions of dollars shall be paid at the same place, and in the same coin, in annual instalments of three millions of dollars each, together with interest on the same at the rate of six per centum per annum. This interest shall begin to run upon the whole sum of twelve millions from the day of the ratification of the present treaty by the Mexican government, and the first of the instalments shall be paid at the expiration of one year from the same day. Together with each annual instalment, as it falls due, the whole interest accruing on such instalment from the beginning shall also be paid.

Article XIII.

The United States engage, moreover, to assume and pay to the claimants all the amounts now due them, and those hereafter to become due, by reason of the claims already liquidated and decided against the Mexican republic, under the conventions between the two republics severally concluded on the eleventh day of April, eighteen hundred and thirty-nine, and on the thirtieth day of January, eighteen hundred and forty-three: so that the Mexican republic shall be absolutely exempt, for the future, from all expense whatever on account of the said claims.

Article XIV.

The United States do furthermore discharge the Mexican republic from all claims of citizens of the United States not heretofore decided against the Mexican government, which may have arisen previously to the date of the signature of this treaty; which discharge shall be final and perpetual, whether the said claims be rejected or be allowed by the board of commissioners provided for in the following article, and whatever shall be the total amount of those allowed.

Article XV.

The United States, exonerating Mexico from all demands on account of the claims of their citizens mentioned in the preceding article, and considering them entirely and forever cancelled, whatever their amount may be, undertake to make satisfaction for the same, to an amount not exceeding three and one quarter millions of dollars. To ascertain the validity and amount of those claims, a board of commissioners shall be established by the government of the United States, whose awards shall be final and conclusive; provided, that in deciding upon the validity of each claim, the board shall be guided and governed by the principles and rules of decision prescribed by the first and fifth articles of the unratified convention, concluded at the city of Mexico on the twentieth day of November, one thousand eight hundred and forty-three; and in no case shall an award be made in favor of any claim not embraced by these principles and rules.

If, in the opinion of the said board of commissioners, or of the claimants, any books, records, or documents in the possession or power of the government of the Mexican republic, shall be deemed necessary to the just decision of any claim, the commissioners, or the claimants through them, shall, within such period as Congress may designate, make an application in writing for the same, addressed to the Mexican Minister for Foreign Affairs, to be transmitted by the Secretary of State of the United States; and the Mexican government engages, at the earliest possible moment after the receipt of such demand, to cause any of the books, records, or documents, so specified, which shall be in their possession or power, (or authenticated copies or extracts of the same,) to be transmitted to the said Secretary of State, who shall immediately deliver them over to the said board of commissioners: ***Provided,*** That no such application shall be made by, or at the instance of, any claimant, until the facts which it is expected to prove by such books, records, or documents, shall have been stated under oath or affirmation.

Article XVI.

Each of the contracting parties reserves to itself the entire right to fortify whatever point within its territory it may judge proper so to fortify for its security.

Article XVII.

The treaty of amity, commerce, and navigation, concluded at the city of Mexico on the fifth day of April, A. D. 1831, between the United States of America and the United Mexican States, except the additional article, and except so far as the stipulations of the said treaty may be incompatible with any stipulation contained in the present treaty, is hereby revived for the period of eight years from the day of the exchange of ratifications of this treaty, with the same force and virtue as if incorporated therein, it being understood that each of the contracting parties reserves to itself the right, at any time after the said period of eight years shall have expired, to terminate the same by giving one year's notice of such intention to the other party.

Article XVIII.

All supplies whatever for troops of the United States in Mexico, arriving at ports in the occupation of such troops previous to the final evacuation thereof, although subsequently to the restoration of the custom-houses at such ports, shall be entirely exempt from duties and charges of any kind; the government of the United States hereby engaging and pledging its faith to establish, and vigilantly to enforce, all possible guards for securing the revenue of Mexico, by preventing the importation, under cover of this stipulation, of any articles other than such, both in kind and in quantity, as shall really be wanted for the use and consumption of the forces of the United States during the time they may remain in Mexico. To this end it shall be the duty of all officers and agents of the United States to denounce to the Mexican authorities at the respective ports any attempts at a fraudulent abuse of this stipulation which they may know of, or may have reason to suspect, and to give to such authorities all the aid in their power with regard thereto; and every such attempt, when duly proved and established by sentence of a competent tribunal, shall be punished by the confiscation of the property so attempted to be fraudulently introduced

Article XIX.

With respect to all merchandise, effects, and property whatsoever, imported into ports of Mexico whilst in the occupation of the forces of the United States, whether by citizens of either republic, or by citizens or subjects of any neutral nation, the following rules shall be observed:

1. All such merchandise, effects, and property, if imported previously to the restoration of the custom-houses to the Mexican authorities, as stipulated for in the third article of this treaty, shall be exempt from confiscation, although the importation of the same be prohibited by the Mexican tariff.

2. The same perfect exemption shall be enjoyed by all such merchandise, effects, and property, imported subsequently to the restoration of the custom-houses, and previously to the sixty days fixed in the following article for the coming into force of the Mexican tariff at such ports respectively; the said merchandise, effects, and property being, however, at the time of their importation, subject to the payment of duties, as provided for in the said following article.

3. All merchandise, effects, and property described in the two rules foregoing, shall, during their continuance at the place of importation, and upon their leaving such place for the interior, be exempt from all duty, tax, or impost of every kind, under whatsoever title or denomination.

Nor shall they be there subjected to any charge whatsoever upon the sale thereof.

4. All merchandise, effects, and property described in the first and second rules, which shall have been removed to any place in the interior whilst such place was in the occupation of the forces of the United States, shall, during their continuance therein, be exempt from all tax upon the sale or consumption thereof, and from every kind of impost or contribution, under whatsoever title or denomination.

5. But if any merchandise, effects, or property, described in the first and second rules, shall be removed to any place not occupied at the time by the forces of the United States, they shall, upon their introduction into such place, or upon their sale or consumption there, be subject to the same duties which, under the Mexican laws, they would be required to pay in such cases if they had been imported in time of peace, through the maritime custom-houses, and had there paid the duties conformably with the Mexican tariff.

6. The owners of all merchandise, effects, or property, described in the first and second rules, and existing in any port of Mexico, shall have the right to reship the same, exempt from all tax, impost, or contribution whatever.

With respect to the metals, or other property, exported from any Mexican port whilst in the occupation of the forces of the United States, and previously to the restoration of the custom-house at such port, no person shall be required by the Mexican authorities, whether general or state, to pay any tax, duty, or contribution upon any such exportation, or in any manner to account for the same to the said authorities.

Article XX.

Through consideration for the interests of commerce generally, it is agreed, that if less than sixty days should elapse between the date of the signature of this treaty and the restoration of the custom-houses, conformably with the stipulation in the third article, in such case all merchandise, effects, and property whatsoever, arriving at the Mexican ports after the restoration of the said custom-houses, and previously to the expiration of sixty days after the day of the signature of this treaty, shall be admitted to entry; and no other duties shall be levied thereon than the duties established by the tariff found in force at such custom-houses at the time of the restoration of the same. And to all such merchandise, effects, and property, the rules established by the preceding article shall apply.

Article XXI.

If unhappily any disagreement should hereafter arise between the governments of the two republics, whether with respect to the interpretation of any stipulation in this treaty, or with respect to any other particular concerning the political or commercial relations of the two nations, the said governments, in the name of those nations, do promise to each other that they will endeavor, in the most sincere and earnest manner, to settle the differences so arising, and to preserve the state of peace and friendship in which the two countries are now placing themselves; using, for this end, mutual representations and pacific negotiations. And if, by these means, they should not be enabled to come to an agreement, a resort shall not, on this account, be had to reprisals, aggression, or hostility of any kind, by the one republic against the other, until the government of that which deems itself aggrieved shall have maturely considered, in the spirit of peace and good neighborship, whether it would not be better that such difference should be settled by the arbitration of commissioners appointed on each side, or by that of a friendly nation. And should such course be proposed by either party, it shall be acceded to by the other, unless deemed by it altogether incompatible with the nature of the difference, or the circumstances of the case.

Article XXII.

If (which is not to be expected, and which God forbid!) war shall unhappily break out between the two republics, they do now, with a view to such calamity, solemnly pledge themselves to each other and to the world, to observe the following rules: absolutely, where the nature of the subject permits, and as closely as possible in all cases where such absolute observance shall be impossible.

1. The merchants of either republic then residing in the other, shall be allowed to remain twelve months, (for those dwelling in the interior,) and six months (for those dwelling at the seaports) to collect their debts and settle their affairs; during which periods they shall enjoy the same protection, and be on the same footing, in all respects, as the citizens or subjects of the most friendly nations; and, at the expiration thereof, or at any time before, they shall have full liberty to depart, carrying off all their effects without molestation or hinderance: conforming therein to the same laws which the citizens or subjects of the most friendly nations are required to conform to. Upon the entrance of the armies of either nation into the territories of the other, women and children, ecclesiastics, scholars of every faculty, cultivators of the earth, merchants, artisans, manufacturers, and fishermen, unarmed and inhabiting the unfortified towns, villages, or places, and in general all persons whose occupations are for the common subsistence and benefit of mankind, shall be allowed to continue their respective employments unmolested in their persons. Nor shall their houses or goods be burnt or otherwise destroyed, nor their cattle taken, nor their fields wasted, by the armed force into whose power, by the events of

war, they may happen to fall; but if the necessity arise to take any thing from them for the use of such armed force, the same shall be paid for at an equitable price. All churches, hospitals, schools, colleges, libraries, and other establishments, for charitable and beneficent purposes, shall be respected, and all persons connected with the same protected in the discharge of their duties, and the pursuit of their vocations.

2. In order that the fate of prisoners of war may be alleviated, all such practices as those of sending them into distant, inclement, or unwholesome districts, or crowding them into close and noxious places, shall be studiously avoided. They shall not be confined in dungeons, prison-ships, or prisons; nor be put in irons, or bound, or otherwise restrained in the use of their limbs. The officers shall enjoy liberty on their paroles, within convenient districts, and have comfortable quarters; and the common soldiers shall be disposed in cantonments, open and extensive enough for air and exercise, and lodged in barracks as roomy and good as are provided by the party in whose power they are, for its own troops. But if any officer shall break his parole by leaving the district so assigned him, or any other prisoner shall escape from the limits of his cantonment, after they shall have been designated to him, such individual, officer, or other prisoner, shall forfeit so much of the benefit of this article as provides for his liberty on parole or in cantonment. And if any officer so breaking his parole, or any common soldier so escaping from the limits assigned him, shall afterwards be found in arms, previously to his being regularly exchanged, the person so offending shall be dealt with according to the established laws of war. The officers shall be daily furnished by the party in whose power they are, with as many rations, and of the same articles, as are allowed, either in kind or by commutation, to officers of equal rank in its own army; and all others shall be daily furnished with such ration as is allowed to a common soldier in its own service: the value of all which supplies shall, at the close of the war, or at periods to be agreed upon between the respective commanders, be paid by the other party, on a mutual adjustment of accounts for the subsistence of prisoners; and such accounts shall not be mingled with or set off against any others, nor the balance due on them be withheld as a compensation or reprisal for any cause whatever, real or pretended. Each party shall be allowed to keep a commissary of prisoners, appointed by itself, with every cantonment of prisoners in possession of the other; which commissary shall see the prisoners as often as he pleases; shall be allowed to receive, exempt from all duties or taxes, and to distribute whatever comforts may be sent to them by their friends; and shall be free to transmit his reports in open letters to the party by whom he is employed.

And it is declared that neither the pretence that war dissolves all treaties, nor any other whatever, shall be considered as annulling or sus pending the solemn covenant contained in this article. On the contrary, the state of war is precisely that for which it is provided, and during which its stipulations are to be as sacredly observed as the most acknowledged obligations under the law of nature or nations.

ARTICLE XXIII.

This treaty shall be ratified by the President of the United States of America, by and with the advice and consent of the Senate thereof; and by the President of the Mexican republic, with the previous approbation of its general Congress; and the ratification shall be exchanged in the city of Washington, or at the seat of government of Mexico, in four months from the date of the signature hereof, or sooner if practicable.

In faith whereof, we, the respective plenipotentiaries have signed this treaty of peace, friendship, limits, and settlement; and have hereunto affixed our seals respectively. Done in quintuplicate, at the city of Guadaloupe Hidalgo, on the second day of February, in the year of our Lord one thousand eight hundred and forty-eight.

N. P. TRIST, [L. S.]
LUIS G. CUEVAS, [L. S.]
BERNARDO COUTO, [L. S.]
MIGL. ATRISTAIN, [L. S.]

And whereas the said treaty, as amended, has been duly ratified on both parts, and the respective ratifications of the same were exchanged at Queretaro, on the thirtieth day of May last, by Ambrose H. Sevier and Nathan Clifford, commissioners on the part of the government of the United States, and by Señor Don Luis de la Rosa, Minister of Relations of the Mexican republic on the part of that government:

Now, therefore, be it known, that I, JAMES K. POLK, President of the United States of America, have caused the said treaty to be made public, to the end that the same, and every clause and article thereof, may be observed and fulfilled with good faith by the United States and the citizens thereof.

In witness whereof, I have hereunto set my hand and caused the seal of the United States to be affixed.

Done at the city of Washington, this fourth day of July, one thousand eight hundred and forty-eight, and of the Independence of the United States the seventy-third.

[L. S.]

By the President: JAMES K. POLK.

JAMES BUCHANAN, Secretary of State.

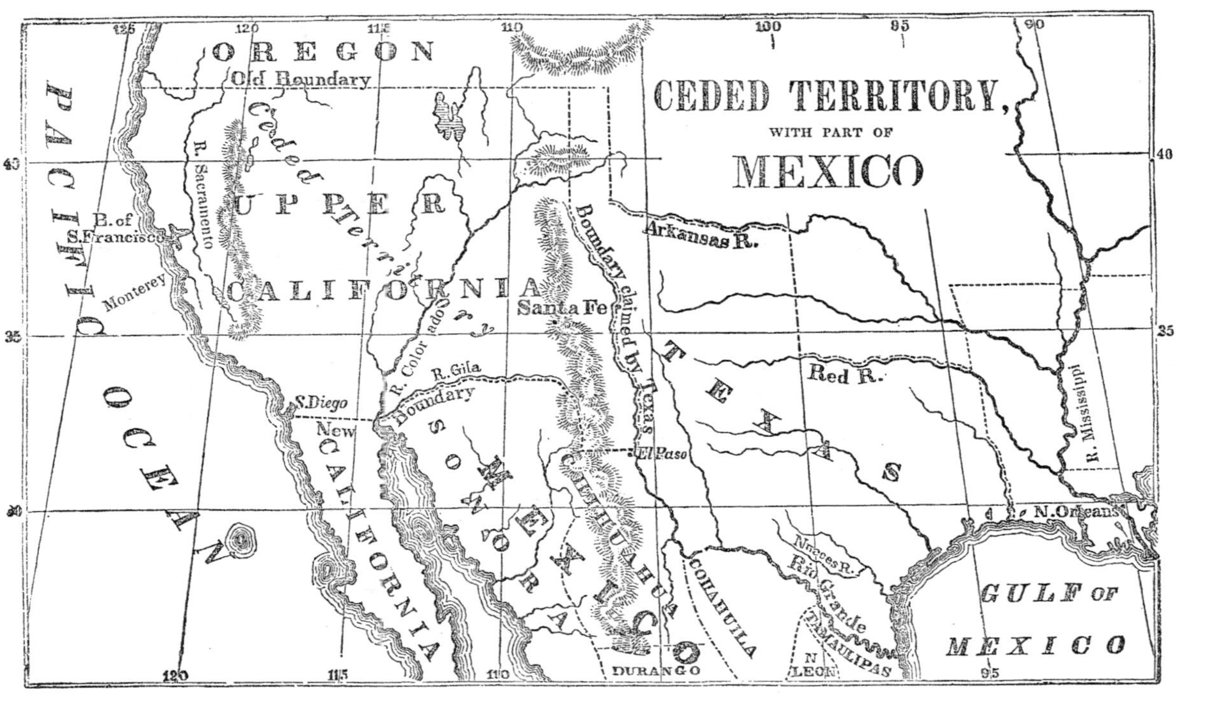
CEDED TERRITORY,
WITH PART OF
MEXICO
OREGON
Old Boundary
Ceded Territory
UPPER
CALIFORNIA
PACIFIC OCEAN
B. of S.Francisco
Monterey
R. Sacramento
S.Diego
New
CALIFORNIA
R. Colorado
R. Gila
Boundary
SONORA
MEXICO
CHIHUAHUA
DURANGO
COHAHUILA
N LEON
TAMAULIPAS
Santa Fe
Boundary claimed by Texas
El Paso
Arkansas R.
Red R.
TEXAS
Nueces R.
Rio Grande
R. Mississippi
N.Orleans
GULF OF MEXICO
125
120
115
110
100
95
90
40
35
30

Let us turn, for a moment, to the RESULTS OF THE MEXICAN WAR. The results may be summed up in three particulars, viz.:—the loss of lives, the loss of money, and the gain of territory. Each of these may be estimated with sufficient accuracy, for all the purposes of history.

1. OF THE LOSS OF LIFE. The official returns of our government show an actual loss, *in the field*—by battle and sickness—of fifteen thousand men. But this is by no means all. There were large numbers of men mustered into service in the interior of the United States, whose regiments were in Mexico, and who of course must take some time, and meet with much exposure, before they were entered on the rolls of the active force. Many of these were taken sick and died, without ever appearing on the rolls of the actual force. Again, thousands of men were discharged in Mexico, as their time expired. Of these, many died. These facts are known and admitted by the officers of the army. It may be said then, with truth, that the real and entire loss of life, from the invasion of Mexico, was not less than TWENTY-FIVE THOUSAND MEN.

2. LOSS OF MONEY. The treasury reports, the terms of the treaty, and some allowance for arrears, will enable us to come very near the true cost of the war. The war commenced, in respect to the action of our government for preparation and provisions, in May, 1846; and the army was not withdrawn from Mexico till June, 1848. The actual war, then, occupies a little more than two years. The appropriations by law we know, the balance in the treasury we know, and the payments under the treaty we know. There is nothing left to conjecture, then, but the amount which may be supposed necessary to cover ar

rears. There is, however, yet another expenditure, which is equivalent to money, although not paid in money. This is the bounty-lands. By the act of Congress passed February, 1847, each regular soldier and each volunteer, who dies, or is discharged by wounds, or is regularly discharged, is entitled to a warrant of 160 acres each of the public lands. The number of volunteers actually in Mexico was about 56,000 and the number of soldiers enlisted since the war about 29,000. About 85,000 men, or, if dead, their heirs and representatives, are entitled to land-warrants. Nearly the whole of them, we may assume, will be taken out, and entered in the land-offices, generally by those who have speculated in them. Nearly thirteen millions of acres will be required to meet the land-warrants issued to the soldiers of the Mexican war! If sold by the United States, the value, at the minimum price, is more than sixteen millions of dollars. The government has, however, fixed a commutation price of $100 in scrip for each 160 acres. Taking that as the standard of value for land-warrants, we have eight and a half millions of dollars for that account. The arrearages of expense attending the return and disbanding of the army, cannot be very closely estimated; but we may safely assume this item at not less than ten millions of dollars. The balance in the treasury, as reported by the Secretary of the Treasury, in May, 1846, was eight millions. The cost of the war, then, stands thus:—

Balance in the Treasury, May, 1846 - - - - - -	$8,000,000
Appropriated by Congress for the fiscal years 1846 and 1847 - - - - - - - - - - - - - - - - - -	120,000,000
Appropriated for the Arrearages of 1847 - - - -	16,000,000
To be paid under the Mexican Treaty - - - - -	20,000,000

Value of Land Warrants issued - - - - - - - -	8,500,000
Add probable Arrearages - - - - - - - - - - -	10,000,000
	$182,500,000
Deduct from this Civil Expenses - - - - - - - -	16,000,000
Total Expense of the Mexican War - - - - - - -	$166,500,000

To find the DEBT, which must ultimately appear on the books of the Treasury Department, the following deductions from the gross sum must be made.

Balance in the Treasury - - - - - - - - - - - -	$8,000,000
Value of Land Warrants - - - - - - - - - - -	8,500,000
Ordinary Revenue of two years - - - - - - - -	65,000,000
	$81,500,000
Deduct from the aggregate above, and there remains debt - - - - - - - - - - - - - - - - - - -	$85,000,000

At least this sum must remain, as a permanent debt against the United States, as a consequence of the war with Mexico.

3. THE GAIN IN TERRITORY. The gain may be stated, in general terms, as the provinces of New Mexico and New California. But what are these? Who knows them? Who can estimate them? Taken as so much surface of the earth, this is a vast space; but a space absolutely hid from the eyes of civilization—an untrodden, untenanted wilderness! The southern boundary of New Mexico is near the 32° of latitude, and San Diego on the Pacific is but a little north of it. The northern boundary of New California is in latitude 42°, being formerly the southern boundary of the United States. The eastern boundary of New Mexico is on the average longitude of 29° west of Washington, and the Pacific coast of Califor-

nia is on the average longitude of 44°, varying in fact from 40° to 47°. We have an immense space of country, then, —about ten degrees north and south, and fifteen degrees east and west. This makes 700 miles north and south, and 900 miles east and west. This surface makes 630,000 square miles, equal in space to FIFTEEN LARGE STATES! But will the greater part of this vast space ever be inhabited by any but the restless hunter and the wandering trapper? Two hundred thousand square miles of this territory, in New California, has been trod by the feet of no civilized being. No spy, or pioneer, or vagrant trapper has ever returned to report the character and scenery of that waste and lonely wilderness. Two hundred thousand square miles more are occupied with broken mountains and dreary wilds. But little remains, then, for civilization. Of that little, however, there is a future value which may not now be counted, in the fine ports and broad coast which look out on the noble Pacific. Beyond that live four hundred millions of the human race. Soon their minds, as well as their commerce and their kingdoms, will be open to the purer and brighter light of Christianity. We shall hurry the men and the produce of our land, in mighty railroads to the Pacific! Great cities we shall have there! Nations will come to us, and we shall go to them! And this continent will be the highway for the multitudes of the world, and the glorious light of Christian Progress!

STATISTICS

OF THE U. S. ARMY ENGAGED IN THE MEXICAN WAR.

The following tables show the number of regulars and volunteers, with the list of the commanding officers; the number furnished by each State; the total strength and losses of the army; the number of killed and mortally wounded in each engagement; and the names of the officers killed.

To exhibit the Mexican War in its completeness, we must look at the resources employed to carry it on, as well as the origin and results of the controversy. Below will be found tables of the strength of the army (both regulars and volunteers) employed in Mexico, with the losses it sustained.

TABLE I.

REGULAR ARMY EMPLOYED IN MEXICO FROM MAY, 1846, TO DECEMBER 31ST, 1847.

Descriptions.	General Staff.	Engineers.	Ordnance.	Artillery.	Riflemen.	Dragoons.	Voltigeurs.	Infantry.	Marines.	Aggregate.
Original army in Texas, May, 1846	20	—	—	976	—	388	—	2,170	—	3,554
Number of recruits sent to Mexico from May, 1846, to December, 1847	...	...	...	...	...	...	...	...	...	23,556
Total	...	...	...	...	...	...	...	...	...	27,110

Note. To the above aggregate must be added, by the report of the Adjutant-general, 2,493 recruits sent to the army in Mexico, (regulars,) from January 1st, 1848, to April 1st, 1848. These, added to the above, make **29,603** regular soldiers sent into Mexico from May, 1846, to April, 1848.

TABLE II.

VOLUNTEERS EMPLOYED IN MEXICO FROM MAY, 1846, TO DECEMBER, 1847.

States.	Regim'ts.	Commanding Officer.	Foot.	Horse.	Art.	Total.
Mass.	1	Col. Caleb Cushing	1,047	—	–	1,047
New York	1st	Col. J. D. Stevenson	1,179	—	–	1,179
"	2d	Col. W. B. Burnett	1,486	—	–	1,486
N. Jersey	½	Lt. Col. J. Woodruff	424	—	–	424
Pennsylv.	1st	Col. F. M. Wynkoop	1,125	—	–	1,125
"	2d	Col. W. B. Roberts	1,055	—	–	1,055
"	½	—	284	—	–	284
Maryl. & Dist. Col.	½	Lt. Col. W. H. Watson	528	—	–	528
"	1	Col. S. W. Hughes	666	—	–	666
"	1 Comp.	"	—	—	136	136
Virginia	1	Col. F. Hamtrenck	1,303	—	–	1,303
N. Carolina	1	Col. R. T. Paine	936	—	–	936
S. Carolina	1	Col. P. M. Butler	1,054	—	–	1,054
Georgia	1	Col. H. R. Jackson	924	—	–	924
"	½	Lt. Col. J. G. Seymour	466	—	–	466
"	½	Lt. Col. J. H. Calhoun	—	657	–	657
Alabama	1	Col. J. M. Withers	931	—	–	931
"	½	Lt. Col. P. H. Raiford	295	—	–	295
"	½	Capt. W. H. Pratt	278	—	–	278
"	1	Col. J. F. Coffee	945	—	–	945
"	½	Major J. J. Siebles	469	—	–	469
"	Comp.	Capt. J. M'Gee	—	93	–	93
Mississippi	1st	Col. J. Davis	942	—	–	942
"	2d	Col. B. Davis	947	—	–	947
"	½	—	431	—	–	431
Louisiana	½	Major L. Golley	—	—	286	286
"	1st	Col. J. B. Walters	698	—	–	698
"	2d	Col. T. F. Marks	912	—	–	912
"	3d	Col. J. H. Dokin	759	—	–	759
"	4th	Col. H. Davis	791	—	–	791
"	5th	Col. B. Peyton	864	—	–	864
"	6th	Col. E. Featherston	829	—	–	829
"	½	Lt. Col. W. F. Biscoe	—	494	–	494
"	1	Col. L. G. de Russey	1,094	—	–	1,094
"	½	Col. C. Pierce	656	—	–	656
"	Comp.	Capt. Blanchard	95	—	–	95
Tennessee	1	Col. J. E. Thomas	—	944	–	944
"	1st	Col. W. B. Campbell	1,054	—	–	1,054
"	2d	Col. W. T. Karcell	695	—	–	695
"	3d	Col. B. F. Cheetham	945	—	–	945
"	4th	Col. R. Waterhouse	800	—	–	800
"	5th	Col. C. R. M'Clelland	972	—	–	972

Table II. continued.

States.	Regim'ts.	Commanding Officer.	Foot.	Horse.	Art.	Total.
Kentucky	1st	Col. H. Marshal	—	838	-	838
"	1st	Col. S. Ormsby	877	—	-	877
"	2d	Col. W. R. M'Kee	919	—	-	919
"	3d	Col. M. V. Thompson	1,054	—	-	1,054
"	4th	Col. J. S. Williams	1,112	—	-	1,112
Ohio	1st	Col. A. M. Mitchel	838	—	-	838
"	2d	Col. S. R. Curtis	810	—	-	810
"	3d	Col. S. W. Morgan	738	—	-	738
"	4th	Col. C. H. Brough	1,011	—	-	1,011
"	5th	Col. W. Irwin	942	—	-	942
Michigan	1	Col. T. B. W. Stockton	888	—	-	888
"	1 Comp.	Capt. M. L. Gage	84	—	-	84
Indiana	1st	Col. J. P. Drole	856	—	-	856
"	2d	Col. J. Lane	853	—	-	853
"	3d	Col. J. H. Lane	869	—	-	869
"	4th	Col. W. A. Gorman	919	—	-	919
"	5th	Col. J. H. Lane	973	—	-	973
Illinois	1st	Col. J. J. Hardin	927	—	-	927
"	2d	Col. W. H. Bissell	902	—	-	902
"	3d	Col. F. Freeman	910	—	-	910
"	4th	Col. E. D. Baker	819	—	-	819
"	5th	Col. E. W. B. Newby	1,021	—	-	1,021
"	6th	Col. J. Collins	969	—	-	969
"	1	Capt. A. Dunlap	—	425	-	425
Wisconsin	2 Comp.	Capt. W. Knowlton	146	—	-	146
Iowa	Comp.	Capt. J. M. Morgan	73	—	-	73
"	2 Comp.	Capt. J. Porter	—	156	-	156
Missouri	1st	Col. A. R. Easton	687	—	-	687
"	2d	Capt. F. H. Holt	933	—	-	933
"	1st	Col. A. W. Doniphan	—	986	-	986
"	2d	Col. L. Price	—	845	-	845
"	Battal.	Lt. Col. D. Willoch	—	407	-	407
"	2 Comp.	Major M. L. Clark	—	—	239	239
"	"	"	141	—	-	141
"	Battal.	Lt. Col. A. Easton	507	—	-	507
"	1	Lt. Col. J. Balls	—	1,107	-	1,107
"	Battal.	Lt. Col. L. E. Powell	—	437	-	437
"	2 Comp.	Lt. Col. W. Gilpin	—	179	-	179
"	"	"	161	—	-	161
"	Comp.	"	—	—	104	104
Arkansas	1	Col. A. Yell	—	800	-	800
"	2 Comp.	Lt. Col. W. Gray	—	158	-	158
"	3 Comp.	"	265	—	-	265
"	1 Comp.	Capt. J. B. Eugart	—	100	-	100
Florida	4 Comp.	Capt. A. J. Johnson	323	—	-	323
Texas	1st	Gen. J. P. Henderson	—	1,045	-	1,045
"	2d	Col. J. C. Hays	—	524	-	524

Table II. continued.

States.	Regim'ts.	Commanding Officer.	Foot.	Horse.	Art.	Total.
Texas	3d	Col. S. T. Wood	—	718	-	718
"	4th	Major C. C. Cooper	—	802	-	802
"	5th	Col. J. C. Hays	—	870	-	870
"	6th	Lt. Col. Bell	—	711	-	711
"	2 Comp.	Henderson	95	—	-	95
"	1	Col. A. S. Johnson	615	—	-	615
"	Battal.	—	393	—	-	393
"	4 Comp.	—	—	209	-	209
"	2 Comp.	Capt. M'Cullough	—	168	-	168
"	Indians.	Black Beaver	—	35	-	35
"	Battal.	Major Chevallie	—	487	-	487
Mormons	"	Lt. Col. J. Alten	503	—	-	503
"	1 Comp.	Capt. D. C. Davis	82	—	-	82
California	Battal.	Major J. C. Fremont	—	470	-	470
"	1 Comp.	"	—	—	41	41
"	"	Capt. W. A. T. Maddox	47	—	-	47
Remust'd Volunt.	Battal.	Major R. Walker	—	257	-	257
"	3 Comp.	—	—	342	-	342
"	1 Comp.	Capt. Meers	—	109	-	109
Totals	76 Regiments and 3 Companies.		51,726	15,373	806	67,905

Note.—This excludes a large number of volunteers who were mustered for payment, but never in service; but includes the Texans called out in 1845.

TABLE III.

VOLUNTEERS FURNISHED BY EACH STATE, FROM THE MARCH TO CORPUS CHRISTI TO THE END OF THE WAR.

States.	Foot.	Horse.	Artil'y.	Total.
Massachusetts	1,047	—	—	1,047
New York	2,665	—	—	2,665
Pennsylvania	2,464	—	—	2,464
New Jersey	424	—	—	424
Maryland and Dist. of Columbia	1,194	—	136	1,330
Virginia	1,303	—	—	1,303
North Carolina	936	—	—	936
South Carolina	1,054	—	—	1,054
Alabama	2,918	93	—	3,011
Mississippi	2,319	—	—	2,319

Table III. continued.

States.	Foot.	Horse.	Artil'y.	Total.
Georgia	1,390	657	—	2,047
Louisiana	6,698	494	286	7,448
Tennessee	4,466	944	—	5,410
Kentucky	3,962	838	—	4,800
Ohio	4,694	—	—	4,694
Michigan	972	—	—	972
Indiana	4,470	—	—	4,470
Illinois	5,548	425	—	5,973
Wisconsin	146	—	—	146
Iowa	73	156	—	229
Missouri	2,429	3,967	343	6,739
Arkansas	265	1,158	—	1,423
Florida	323	—	—	323
Texas	1,103	5,569	—	6,672
Mormons	585	—	—	585
Californians	47	470	41	558
Aggregates	51,726	15,373	806	67,905

TABLE IV.

TOTAL STRENGTH OF THE ARMY EMPLOYED IN MEXICO, FROM APRIL, 1846, TO APRIL, 1848.

Description of Force.	Foot.	Horse.	Artil'y.	Total.	Remarks.
Army in Mexico, (regulars,) May, 1846	2,170	408	976	3,554	The general staff is under the head of "Horse."
Recruits for the old regiments	—	—	—	12,551	
Recruits for the new regiments	—	—	—	10,145	The 'new regiments' were the 3d Dragoons, the Voltigeurs, and the 9th, 10th, 11th, 12th, 13th, 14th, 15th, and 16th regiments of Infantry.
Recruits sent to Mexico after December, 1847	—	—	—	2,493	
Volunteers	51,726	15,373	806	67,905	
Marines	347	—	—	347	
Aggregates	54,243	15,781	1,782	96,995	

Note.—From the above table are *excluded* 12 companies called out in Ohio, and mustered in "Camp Washington," but not in actual service · so also, a portion of Louisiana volunteers called out in 1845; and so also of a few other companies. If these were included, the total number called out by government during the war would exceed ONE HUNDRED THOUSAND.

The actual number in service in Mexico exceeds eighty thousand. This number was not called out at one time, but in successive periods. At the time the war closed, the Adjutant-general reports, that there were actually more than forty thousand men in the field.

TABLE V.

TOTAL LOSS OF THE ARMY, BY REGULARS AND STATES, FROM MAY, 1846, TO JANUARY, 1848.

Description of Force.	Disch'd from disab'ty.	Killed in battle.	Died of wounds.	Died of disease.	Deserted.	Totals.
General staff	—	1	—	13	—	14
Engineers	—	1	1	12	6	20
Ordnance	—	6	4	14	5	29
1st Dragoons	—	25	5	56	108	194
2d "	—	33	8	91	112	244
Mounted riflemen	—	27	18	120	64	229
1st Artillery	—	32	10	154	123	319
2d "	—	24	29	126	145	324
3d "	—	19	24	121	148	312
4th "	—	20	15	108	99	242
1st Infantry	—	13	7	133	74	227
2d "	—	28	2	91	147	268
3d "	—	40	14	145	91	280
4th "	—	37	31	123	86	277
5th "	—	50	40	149	74	313
6th "	—	34	60	152	112	368
7th "	—	21	21	95	81	218
8th "	—	47	56	119	123	345
Total of the old army,	—	458	345	1,822	1,598	4,223
3d Dragoons	—	7	4	85	54	150
9th Infantry	—	9	5	83	64	161
10th "	—	3	—	88	25	116
11th "	—	10	12	102	47	171
12th "	—	7	13	50	19	89
13th "	—	—	—	100	30	130
14th "	—	8	9	85	45	147
15th "	—	21	24	222	37	302
16th "	—	—	2	98	30	130
Voltigeurs	—	9	10	92	94	205
Total of the new regiments,	—	74	79	1,005	445	1,601

Table V. continued.

Description of Force.	Disch'd from disab'ty.	Killed in battle.	Died of wounds.	Died of disease.	Desert-ed.	Totals.
United States Marines......	—	7	—	5	9	21
Volunt. from Massachusetts	33	—	—	30	105	168
" New York....	117	29	19	77	362	604
" New Jersey...	3	—	—	11	51	65
" Pennsylvania	212	28	10	199	182	631
" Md. & Dist. Columbia	148	8	3	54	176	389
" Virginia.......	135	—	—	66	38	239
" N. Carolina...	62	—	—	172	19	253
" S. Carolina ...	104	30	26	234	41	435
" Georgia.......	246	2	—	117	60	425
" Alabama......	220	—	—	103	27	350
" Mississippi....	513	54	4	258	42	871
" Louisiana	215	5	1	201	703	1,125
" Tennessee....	982	45	6	199	48	1,278
" Kentucky	533	78	4	176	132	923
" Ohio	424	18	—	218	435	1,095
" Michigan	4	—	—	3	77	84
" Indiana	550	47	—	218	105	920
" Illinois.........	489	89	11	362	68	1,019
" Wisconsin....	2	—	—	9	1	12
" Iowa..........	2	—	—	3	—	5
" Missouri	114	19	4	229	53	419
" Arkansas	68	19	2	153	27	269
" Florida	4	1	—	8	3	16
" Texas.........	243	39	2	118	115	517
" Mormons......	—	—	—	7	1	8
" Californians..	—	—	—	—	—	—
Remustered volunteers......	9	7	—	35	11	62
Total of volunteers..........	5,432	508	92	3,160	2,882	12,082
Total of new regiments....	—	74	79	1,005	445	1,601
Total of old regiments......	—	458	345	1,822	1,598	4,223
Aggregates......	5,432	1,040	516	5,987	4,925	17,906

Note.—It will be observed this return of loss includes only that between the 1st of June, 1846, and the 1st of January, 1848. Fifty thousand men remained in service, chiefly in Mexico, from the 1st of January, 1848, till the 1st of July, 1848. In this time, the hospitals were full of the sick, many of whom died. It is entirely within bounds to say, that one-fourth as many were lost in that period as had been previously. This, added to the above, would make twenty-two thousand five hundred. Of those discharged for *disability*, three-fourths died before they reached home. Many of these died in hospitals. Of the deserters many died, and many were found in the Mexican service. The official muster-rolls, as returned by the Adjutant-general, show also another fact, viz.: that the difference between the number of volunteers mustered *into* service and those mustered *out*, or on the rolls at the last return, was more than *sixteen thousand*. But the number accounted for above is only twelve thousand. Four thousand others must have disappeared in some way. About twelve hundred are accounted for, as discharged *by order;* but three thousand have gone without being heard of. The greatest number of them have unquestionably died in unknown ways.

The summary of these statements, then, may thus be made:—

Killed in battle, or died of wounds prior to January 1st, 1848	1,556
Died of disease	5,987
Disabled and discharged	5,432
Deserted	4,925
Disappeared, unaccounted for	3,000
Died, discharged, deserted, &c., from January to July, 1848	4,500
	25,400
Of this number, supposed to be dead	20,000

It is presumed that this is less than the real number; but it is the only result to which we can arrive by the official returns.

The *proportion* of loss among the different arms of service—the old and new regulars and volunteers—is an interesting object of inquiry. The reader, by running his eye over the columns, will readily ascertain any fact of this sort he may wish to know. The general result is, that much the heaviest proportional loss fell on the regulars of the old regiments. One great reason of this is, that they were more continually and actively employed, in the whole series of engagements in Mexico, than any other class of troops.

TABLE VI.

THE NUMBER OF KILLED AND MORTALLY WOUNDED IN EACH ENGAGEMENT DURING THE WAR, IN THE REGIMENTS OF REGULARS.

Engagements.	Killed.		Died of wounds.		Total.
	Officers.	Men.	Officers.	Men.	
Affair of Captain Thornton, on the left bank of the Rio Grande—April 25, 1846	1	10	—	—	11
Battle of Palo Alto—May 8, 1846	—	5	2	8	15
Battle of Resaca de la Palma, Texas—May 9, 1846	3	30	—	11	44
Battle of Monterey, Mexico—September 21–23, 1846	8	47	1	8	64
Siege of Fort Brown, opposite Matamoras—from May 4 to 9, 1846	—	1	1	—	2
Affair of San Pasqual, California—December 6, 1846	3	14	—	—	17
Affair of General Kearny, at San Gabriel, California—January 8–9, 1847	—	1	—	—	1
Affair of Col. Price at Puebla de Taos, New Mexico—February 4, 1847	—	5	—	—	5
Affair of Col. M'Intosh—June 6, 1847	—	6	—	—	6
Battle of Buena Vista—February 22–23, 1847	1	5	—	2	8
Siege of Vera Cruz—March 9–28, 1847	2	5	—	3	10
Battle of Cerro Gordo—April 18–19, 1847	1	39	2	19	61
Battles of Contreras and Churubusco—August 19–20, 1847	10	96	3	28	137
Battle of Molino del Rey, September 8, 1847	9	115	5	62	191
Battles of Chapultepec and city of Mexico—Sept. 12–14, 1847	7	97	1	39	144

Table VI continued.

Engagements.	Killed.		Died of wounds.		Total.
	Officers.	Men.	Officers.	Men.	
Major Lally's command—August, 1847	—	9	1	—	10
Siege of Puebla—Sept. and Oct., 1847	—	3	—	—	3
Battle of Huamantla—October 19, 1847	1	12	—	—	13
Galama, Mexico	1	—	—	—	1
Incidental	3	—	—	—	3
Totals	50	500	16	180	746

Note on the preceding Tables.—The above tables are deduced and compiled from more detailed and extended tables, prepared by the Adjutant-general. They are liable to one objection,—a defect which it is impossible wholly to correct,—viz.: that they are not *complete* to the end of the war, and do not correspond entirely to the actual condition of the several regiments on their return to the United States. There is one description of loss which will never appear in the returns of the army, viz.: the loss of men to and from their regiments, either before they had joined, or after they had been mustered out of service. This loss is a very large one. Subject, however, to this correction, the tables here given present a very fair view of the loss of the several corps while actually in Mexico.

It will be seen that Table VI. does not altogether correspond with the results in Table V. The discrepancy is chiefly found under the head of "Died of wounds." The reason is very obvious. The table of loss in each battle is taken by the Adjutant-general from the reports of that battle; but the aggregate results are taken from the muster-rolls subsequently. In the interval, many of those who were wounded died of their wounds, so that the last return is much increased.

TABLE VII.

LIST OF THE OFFICERS, KILLED OR DIED OF WOUNDS, IN THE WAR WITH MEXICO, WITH THEIR CORPS AND RANK.

Names.	Battle.	Corps.	Rank.	Remarks.
Trueman Cross,	Murdered, April 10, 1846.	Assis. Quartermaster-general.	Colonel.	Murdered by a Mexican party commanded by Falcon.
G. T. Mason,	Thornton's affair.	2d Dragoons.	Lieut.	At a Mexican rancho.
Jacob Brown,	Fort Brown, May 6th.	7th Infantry.	Major.	Killed by a bomb-shell at Fort Brown.
Samuel Ringgold,	Palo Alto, 8th May, 1846.	1st Artillery.	"	Commander of the Flying Artillery.
John Page,	"	4th Infantry.	Captain.	
J. E. Blake,	9th May, 1846.	Top. Engin.	Lieut.	Accid. killed.
Z. M. P. Inge,	Resaca de la Palma.	2d Dragoons.	"	In May's charge.
R. E. Cochrane,	"	4th Infantry.	"	
T. L. Chadbourne,	"	"	"	
W. H. Watson,	Monterey, 21-23 Sept.	Maryland Volunteers.	Lt. Col.	
Lewis N. Morris,	Monterey.	3d Infantry.	Captain.	
P. N. Barbour,	"	"	Major.	
G. P. Field,	"	"	Captain.	
D. S. Irwin,	"	"	Lieut.	
R. Hazlitt,	"	"	"	
C. Hoskins,	"	4th "	"	
H. M'Kavett,	"	8th "	Captain.	
J. S. Woods,	"	2d "	Lieut.	
W. G. Williams,	"	Top. Engin.	Captain.	
J. C. Terrett,	"	1st Infantry.	Lieut.	
R. Dilworth,	"	"	"	
W. B. Allen,	"	Tenn. Volun.	Captain.	
S. M. Putnam,	"	"	Lieut.	
M. Hett,	"	Ohio Volun.	"	
A. R. Johnston,	San Pasqual, Dec. 6th, 1846.	1st Dragoons.	Captain.	In California.
B. D. Moore,	"	"	"	"
T. C. Hammond,	"	"	Lieut.	"
J. H. K. Burgwin,	Pueblo de Taos, 7th Feb. 1846	"	Captain.	New Mexico
Von Valkenburg,	"	Mo. Volun.	Lieut.	"

Table VII. continued.

Names.	Battle.	Corps.	Rank.	Remarks.
George Lincoln,	Buena Vista.	Staff.	Captain.	A. Adjutant-general.
J. J. Hardin,	Buena Vista, 22d Feb. 1847.	1st Illinois Volunteers.	Colonel.	
J. W. Zabriskie,	"	"	Captain.	
B. R. Houghton,	"	"	1st Lieut.	
— Woodward,	"	2d Ill. Volun.	Captain.	
A. B. Roundtree,	"	"	Lieut.	
— Fletcher,	"	"	"	
— Ferguson,	"	"	"	
— Robbins,	"	"	"	
T. Kelley,	"	"	"	
— Steel,	"	"	"	
— Bartleson,	"	"	"	
— Atherton,	"	"	"	
— Price,	"	"	"	
W. R. M'Kee,	"	2d Ky. Volun.	Colonel.	
Henry Clay, jr.,	"	"	Lt. Col.	
W. T. Willes,	"	"	Captain.	
Archibald Yell,	"	Ark. Volun.	Colonel.	
A. R. Porter,	"	"	Captain.	
E. M. Vaughn,	"	1st Ky. Volun.	Adjutant.	
Francis M'Nulty,	"	Miss. Rifles.	2d Lieut.	
R. L. Moore,	"	"	1st Lieut.	
— Campbell,	"	Texas Volun.	"	
— Leonard,	"	"	2d Lieut.	
T. B. Kinder,	"	2d Reg. Ia. Volun.	Captain.	
W. Walker,	"	"	"	
Thos. C. Parr,	"	"	2d Lieut.	
J. Taggart,	"	3d Ia. Volun.	Captain.	
John R. Vinton,	Siege of Vera Cruz Mar. 22, 1847.	3d Artillery.	"	City of Vera Cruz, Mexico.
William Alburtis,	do. March 11.	2d Infantry.	"	
G. M. Coworden,	Cerro Gordo 18th April, 1847.	4th Illinois Volunteers.	Lieut.	
F. B. Nelson,	"	2d Tenn. Vol.	"	
C. C. Gill,	"	"	"	
Thomas Ewell,	"	Rifles.	"	
Wm. Yearwood,	"	1st Tenn. Vol.	"	
Richard Murphy,	"	4th Ill. Vol.	"	
Thomas Davis,	"	Rifles.	"	

Table VII. continued.

Names.	Battle.	Corps.	Rank.	Remarks.
E. A. Capron,	Churubus. Aug. 20, 1847.	1st Artillery.	Captain.	
M. J. Burke,	"	"	"	
S. Hoffman,	"	"	Lieut.	
Jas W. Anderson,	"	2d Infantry.	Captain.	
Thomas Easley,	"	"	Lieut.	
Chas. G. Henson,	Contreras 19th Aug.	7th "	Captain.	
Seth B. Thornton,	"	2d Dragoons.	"	
J. P. Johnstone,	"	1st Artillery.	Lieut.	
F. D. Mills.	City gate.	15th Infantry.	Major.	
John B. Goodman,	"	"	Lieut.	
August. Quarles,	Churubusco.	"	Captain.	
W. H. Goodloe,	"	"	Lieut.	Died at Vera Cruz.
J. F. Irons,	"	1st Artillery.	"	
Pierce M. Butler,	"	S. C. Volun.	Colonel.	
David Adams,	"	"	Lieut.	
W. R. Williams,	"	"	"	
J. P. Dickinson,	"	"	Lt. Col.	
E. Chandler,	"	N. Y. Volun.	Lieut.	
Martin Scott,	Mol. del Rey.	5th Infantry.	Lt. Col.	
Moses E. Merrill	"	"	Captain.	
W. T. Burwell,	"	"	Lieut.	
G. W. Ayres,	"	3d Artillery.	Captain.	
J. F. Farry,	"	"	Lieut.	
W. Armstrong,	"	2d Artillery.	"	
M. L. Shackelford	"	"	"	
J. S. M'Intosh,	"	Staff.	Colonel.	
W. Roberts,	"	"	Ass. Surg.	
E. Kirby Smith,	"	5th Infantry.	Captain.	
R. F. Ernst,	"	6th "	Lieut.	
J. G. Burbank,	"	8th "	"	
Charles F. Morris,	"	"	"	
Wm. M. Graham,	"	11th "	Lt. Col.	
R. H. L. Johnston,	"	"	Lieut.	
A. P. Rodgers,	Chapultepec, 13th Sept.	4th "	"	
J. P. Smith,	"	5th "	"	
S. Smith,	"	4th "	"	
Levi Gantt,	"	7th "	"	
S. H. Drum,	"	4th Artillery.	Captain.	
C. Benjamin,	"	"	Lieut.	
T. Ransom,	"	9th Infantry.	Colonel.	
L. Twiggs,	"	Marines.	Major.	

Table VII. continued.

Names.	Battle.	Corps.	Rank.	Remarks.
A. Van Olinda,	Chapultepec.	N. Y. Volun.	Captain.	
J. Willes,	City gate.	S. C. Volun.	Lieut.	
J. B. Moragne,	"	"	"	
Charles Baxter,	Chapultepec.	N. Y. Volun.	Lt. Col.	
E. H. Pearson,	"	"	Captain.	
S. H. Walker,	Huamantla, October, 1847.	Mounted Rifles.	"	
G. D. Twiggs,	National bridge, 12 Aug. 1847	Staff.	Lieut.	
R. Ridgely,	Monterey.	3d Artillery.	Captain.	Killed by a fall from his horse.
G. Stevens,	Fort Brown.	2d Dragoons.	Lieut.	Drowned in crossing the river from Dinan.
Alex. J. Swift,	New Orleans.	Engineers.	Captain.	Taken sick at Vera Cruz.
J. A. Richey,	Villa Garra.	5th Infantry.	Lieut.	Murdered.
Stevens T. Mason,	Cerro Gordo.	Mounted Rifles.	Captain.	Died of w'nds.
Theo'c H. Porter,	16 miles from Matamoras, Apr. 19, 1846.	4th Infantry.	Lieut.	Killed in action.
Chs. B. Daniels,	Mol. del Rey.	2d Artillery.	"	Died of w'nds.
Jno. D. Bacon,	Churubusco.	6th Infantry.	"	" "
Hender. Ridgely,	Pass Galaxra, 24 Nov. 1847	4th Infantry.	"	
Erastus B. Strong,	Mol. del Rey.	5th Infantry.	"	
Jas. H. Calwell,	Paso Ovejas, Aug. 10, 1847.	Voltigeurs.	Captain.	" "
Edwin Guthrie,	La Hoya, June 20, 1847.	15th Infantry.	"	" "
J. W. Winder,	National bridge, 12 Aug. 1847	Voltigeurs.	Lieut.	" "
Whit. B. Brooks,	Churubusco.	12th Infantry.	"	" "

125 officers killed; of whom there were

Regulars	79
Volunteers	46

The RANK and CORPS of the officers—thus killed in the Army of Mexico—may be thus stated:—

Colonels	7	Captains	37
Lieut. Colonels	6	Subalterns	65
Majors	5	Staff officers	5—125

Staff	5	9th Infantry	1	Marines	1
Engineers	3	10th "	0	Maryland Volunteers	1
1st Artillery	6	11th "	2	Tennessee "	5
2d "	3	12th "	1	Ohio "	1
3d "	4	13th "	0	Missouri "	1
4th "	2	14th "	0	Illinois "	1[illegible]
1st Infantry	2	15th "	5	Kentucky "	4
2d "	4	16th "	0	Arkansas "	[illegible]
3d "	5	1st Dragoons	4	Mississippi "	[illegible]
4th "	6	2d "	3	Texas "	[illegible]
5th "	7	3d "	0	Indiana "	[illegible]
6th "	2	Riflemen	4	S. Carolina "	6
7th "	3	Voltigeurs	2	New York "	4
8th "	3				

The total number of officers killed and wounded during the war, was about 450. Of this number, more than half were of the regular army, and more than half were graduates of the U. S. Military Academy at West Point. To this institution, more than to any state, or any arm of the service, or any mere exertion of valor, is the country indebted for the success and brilliant achievements of the war. The modern art of war is a science requiring the union of many arts to its perfection. It is the mind of an army, not its physical force only, which wins its victories and makes its conquests. This mind is developed in its officers. These must be accomplished men, equipped in the knowledge of many things, and disciplined by much study. This work of high education is performed at West Point; and no school of military science in the world, at the present period, is equal to it. We cannot close this brief history of the most brilliant career of the army, without pointing to the Military Academy as the great source of military instruction, and to the victories of the Mexican War as monuments to its glory and its excellence.

NATIONAL SERIES OF STANDARD SCHOOL-BOOKS.

HISTORY AND MYTHOLOGY.

MONTEITH'S CHILD'S HISTORY OF THE UNITED STATES. Price $0 50
(DESIGNED FOR PUBLIC SCHOOLS: COPIOUSLY ILLUSTRATED.)

WILLARD'S SCHOOL HISTORY OF THE UNITED STATES........ 0 75
(WITH MAPS AND ENGRAVINGS.)

WILLARD'S LARGE HISTORY OF THE UNITED STATES......... 1 50
(WITH MAPS AND ENGRAVINGS.)

WILLARD'S HISTORY OF THE UNITED STATES 2 00
(IN SPANISH LANGUAGE.)

WILLARD'S UNIVERSAL HISTORY IN PERSPECTIVE............ 1 50
(WITH MAPS AND ENGRAVINGS.)

RICORD'S ROMAN HISTORY 1 00
(WITH ENGRAVINGS.)

DWIGHT'S GRECIAN AND ROMAN MYTHOLOGY 0 75
(SCHOOL EDITION.)

DWIGHT'S GRECIAN AND ROMAN MYTHOLOGY 1 50
(UNIVERSITY EDITION.)

MILLS' HISTORY OF THE ANCIENT HEBREWS 0 75

Monteith's History of the United States is designed for young scholars, on the catechetical plan, with Maps and Engravings. It has also Biographical Sketches of the most prominent men in early history.

Willard's Histories are used in a large proportion of the High Schools, Academies, and Female Seminaries throughout the United States, and have been recommended by several State Superintendents. The History of the United States is so highly esteemed, as accurate, reliable, and complete, that it has been translated, and published in the German, Spanish, and French languages.

The large work is designed as a Text-book for ACADEMIES and FEMALE SEMINARIES; and also for DISTRICT SCHOOLS and FAMILY LIBRARIES. The small work being an *Abridgement* of the same, is designed as a *Text-book for Common Schools*. The originality of the plan consists in dividing the time into *periods*, of which the beginnings and terminations are marked by important events; and constructing *a series of maps illustrating the progress of the settlement of the country, and the regular advance of civilization*. A *full Chronological Table* will be found, in which all the events of the History are arranged in the order of time. There is appended to the work the *Constitution of the United States*, and a series of Questions adapted to each chapter, so that the work may be used in schools and for private instruction.

Dwight's Mythology is peculiarly adapted for use as a Class-book in High Schools, Academies, and Seminaries, and is indispensable to a thorough acquaintance with Ancient History, and to a proper appreciation of the classical allusions constantly occurring in the writings of the best authors. It is also very valuable for private reading and study.

Ricord's Roman History is also designed as a Text-book for Schools, and for private reading and reference. It is the most complete and condensed History of the Romans before the public, and will be found exceedingly interesting, and very valuable to all, especially to those wishing to be familiar with the classics.

A. S. BARNES & BURR, Publishers,
51 & 53 John Street, New York.

www.ingramcontent.com/pod-product-compliance
Lightning Source LLC
LaVergne TN
LVHW020119110826
845151LV00001B/207

* 9 7 8 1 4 2 5 5 4 2 1 2 2 *